# All About
# BICYCLING

Rand McNally & Company

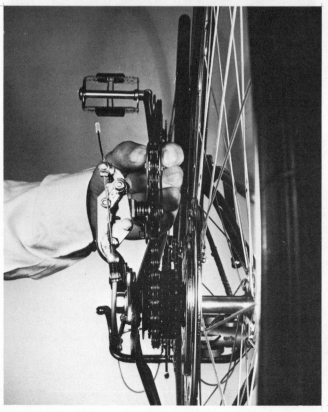

# Contents

Cover picture credits: Raleigh Industries of England, Schwinn Bicycle Co.

It is difficult to avoid cliches when describing the bicycle's renaissance in the United States. For a people who have been ridiculed as being too lazy to change channels on their television sets to embrace a machine that requires constant energy expenditure is something of a revolution. Since the advent of the automobile nearly 70 years ago, the bicycle had suffered a slow but steady decline as a serious mode of adult transportation and been relegated to the level of a toy. Of course, there were always some die hard aficionados of the genre that pedaled bicycles for the sheer freedom of movement and sense of well-being the machines provided, but they were in a large minority in the United States, where loyalty to the family car came right after Mom and apple pie.

By 1970, however, American attitudes were undergoing sweeping change. During the last years of the past decade, Americans had to face the fact that their lifestyle was poisoning the environment and their bodies. Air pollution, largely from automobiles was threatening health in urban and suburban areas. Untreated and unchecked industrial wastes were threatening to strip our water resources of life and make the water supply undrinkable. In addition, the sedentary yet tension-filled daily lives of most working Americans were shown to be responsible for the alarming death rate from heart and related circulatory diseases. Environmental and medical forecasters warned of dire consequences if our national lifestyle remained unchanged for another decade.

Fortunately, people can change. In the past five years, almost every aspect of life in America has been affected by new attitudes regarding the environment and its use. Though it has taken far too long, many Americans no longer take their natural environment for granted, but cherish it knowing that we depend on nature for our continued survival. This philosophy coupled, perhaps, with our new concern for physical health, may have been largely responsible for the zeal with which America rediscovered the bicycle.

It is refreshing and inspiring to note that bicycles are now outselling cars in the United States. The application of modern technology to bicycle design and construction has resulted in a machine that bears little resemblance to the heavy and

*The bicycle can exist anywhere without imposing itself. Totally clean and vital, it represents perhaps the best marriage of man's and nature's present needs—transportation without environmental harm.*

awkward behemoths of years ago that were an effort to pedal around the block and impossible to pedal up the slightest incline. Riding a modern high efficiency bicycle is exciting and fun. With a modern lightweight bicycle, today's rider, even a neophyte, can gauge his afternoon jaunts in terms of miles, not blocks.

As quickly as the bicycle has been assimilated into the mainstream of American life, new bicycle devotees have discovered additional sources of enjoyment to be derived from the bicycle, such as bicycle polo, or forms of bicycling once thought to be unique, like bicycle touring. Bicycle racing is gaining both new participants and spectators. American families are actually taking their vacations on bicycles; experiencing, rather than zooming through, their natural heritage.

In an age demanding environmental protection and the maximum efficient utilization of existing energy sources, most notably the petroleum derived from fossil fuels, the bicycle has a lot to recommend

# The Bicycle Renaissance
# 1

*There are few activities that offer the serenity and joy of bicycling—silent motion through nature, free and unhindered.*

With carefully chosen routes, bicyclists can range cross-country without ever having to worry about fuel availability or bumper-to-bumper traffic jams.

it. It requires no economist to realize that a bicycle costs you nothing in terms of fuel and is about the most reliable form of transportation beyond your own legs to use. Motorized forms of transportation may be an inescapable part of modern society, but bicycles certainly offer one of the most practical measures of keeping their pollution to a minimum.

Perhaps the most obiquitous advantage of bicycle riding is its effect on your health. Most people's schedule, if not their lack of discipline, prevent them from following a regular physical fitness program. Ride a bicycle regularly, though, and you will feel your body respond. Your muscles will firm almost overnight. Your lungs will clear, your circulation will improve, and you may see your body assuming a shape you left years behind.

Pleasure and practicality are not always found together, and yet this is what bicycling is all about. Whether you ride once a day or once a week, the bicycle will still offer you its own unique advantages. It is fun, it is healthy, it does not pollute or soil anything, it costs virtually nothing to operate, and for in-town travel, it can get you around as fast as your car.

## PROTECTING RIDER AND MACHINE

When a bicycle jousts with an auto for the same road space, the bicycle and its rider are invariably the losers. Bicycling demands that you know and practice certain safety rules and principles, whenever you mount up. While there is currently some disagreement as to whether the rate of bicycle-related accidents is increasing, there is no denying that more people are getting injured in such accidents each year. Safety education is crucial if people are to recognize potential traffic dangers and act to minimize risks. With so many new riders on the road, many of them adults who have not bicycled in years, there is increasing sentiment in many communities

*Bicycles can change even routine errands into enjoyable family outings that conserve fuel and exercise your body while you do things you would have to do anyway.*

for separating bicycle and automobile traffic through the creation of bikeways — roadways built exclusively for the use of bicycles. As the bike boom continues in America, new methods of protecting the cyclist will be developed.

Bicycles of course, are machines, and all machines must be maintained and repaired when necessary to operate properly. Every bicycle rider should know the fundamentals of bicycle maintenance. More complicated work can be left in the hands of a skilled professional bicycle mechanic. The modern multi-speed bicycle requires little effort to pedal when properly tuned, and anyone can keep a bike in prime condition with a few tools and a few basic instructions.

## BICYCLING'S MYSTIQUE

No book could do justice to every aspect of bicycling. Much of the pleasure in riding a bicycle is

a truly personal experience, sometimes likened to the profound satisfaction achieved in yoga. This book, though, will concentrate on giving you a frame of reference through which you can familiarize yourself with bicycling and your bicycle.

A chapter on touring tells you how to travel with a bicycle and the fascinating and beautiful places you can see in both North America and abroad. The sporting side of bicycles is highlighted in the chapter on racing. A section on health details the bodily benefits of bicycling, and you should never ride your bike further than your back door until you have thoroughly acquainted yourself with the chapter on bicycle safety. All the basic information you need to keep your bike in top running condition is contained in the maintenance section.

Riding a bicycle can open roads of discovery to you. The purpose of *All About Bicycling* is to give you the information you will need to insure that all your discoveries are good ones.

10

The bicycle appears well on its way to getting the last laugh. After nearly 75 years of residing in the automobile's shadow, the bicycle is emerging from obscurity and capturing the attention of those who want an alternative to increasingly unpalatable gasoline prices and pollution.

The relationship of bike and car is an old and interesting one. Many of the people whom we associate with the development of the automobile — Henry Ford, Glen Olds, and George N. Pierce — were bicycle mechanics before they manufactured the cars bearing their names. Their transition from bikes to cars was, of course, momentous for the history of transportation as well as for their personal careers. When these men turned their attention to motor vehicles, the bicycle — which appeared headed to replace the horse as the primary vehicle of personal transportation — was relegated to the background, and finally even to the realm of a child's toy.

Actually, the first bicycles resembled toys. In the late 1790's, a Frenchman named Comte de Sivrac constructed a crude wooden horse, mounted it on two wheels, and placed a padded saddle on top. Unfortunately, the Comte's wooden horse had no front fork so that it could not be steered, and no drive mechanism so that the rider had to push the "Celerifere" like a child's scooter.

Around 1816, Baron Karl Von Drais, the superintendent of forests in the city of Karlsruhe, Germany, developed a steerable two-wheeled vehicle. The Baron's "Draisine" (or "Hobby Horse") helped him move about on forest paths during his inspection tours, and contemporary accounts credit him with making a 20-mile trip in three hours. In 1818 Von Drais took his machine to Paris, and the first bicycle boom swept Europe. Nevertheless, poor road conditions, the machine's cost, and the effort required to move the Draisine doomed its popularity.

Not until 1840 was there a two-wheeled vehicle that could be ridden with both feet off the ground. Kirkpatrick Macmillan, a Scottish blacksmith, developed a treadle-operated machine, which marked the true beginning of self-propelled bicycles. Although Macmillan's machine promptly fell into obscurity, records indicate that the inventor proved the practicality of his device when he rode his bicycle on a 40-mile trip in 1842.

## PEDAL PROGRESS: THE BONESHAKER

The next two decades were relatively quiet insofar as bicycles were concerned. Sometime during the 1860's, however, a Frenchman named Ernest Michaux placed pedals on the front axle, and the world greeted the birth of the "boneshaker." The Michaux invention had wooden wheels, iron tires, and heavy iron frame. Riding a mechanism with this sort of construction, the cyclist had to be both strong and courageous. The boneshaker provided precisely the type of ride which its name implies. It is interesting to note that a disgruntled employee of Ernest Michaux, Pierre Lalloment, came to America and on November 20, 1866, took out the first U.S. bicycle patent.

Meanwhile, Michaux produced about 400 of his machines in 1865, and manufacturers throughout the world subsequently made hundreds of improvements to the basic boneshaker. Because of its extreme awkwardness, weight, and poor maneuverability, however, the boneshaker lapsed into obscurity just as the age of the bicycle was about to begin.

Around 1870, James Starley of Coventry, England, enlarged the size of the bicycle's front wheel, reduced the size of the back wheel, and offered the world what came to be known as the "ordinary." Since the rider was, for the first time, able to thrust his legs downward effectively, the ordinary must be considered the original truly practical bicycle.

During the 1876 Centennial Exposition in Philadelphia, English manufacturers exhibited the ordinary to incredulous Americans. When the Exposition closed, the unsold ordinaries were purchased by the Cunningham Company, the first bicycle importing firm in the United States. Shortly thereafter, the first bicycles to be manufactured in America went on the market under the "Columbia" trade name. The Columbia ordinary weighed over 70 pounds and cost $313.00, but bicycle fever was soon rampant throughout the nation.

Touring had become a popular sport in 1873 when four riders pedaled from London to the northern coast of Scotland, a distance of 800 miles in 14 days. Not to be outdone, a Bostonian named Thomas Stevens, riding for two years on an 1884

# Bicycle History
## 2

*The Columbia ordinary was heavy and expensive, but Americans bought them in record numbers.*

*The chain-driven safety bicycle (right) was a major step forward from the strange-looking ordinary (left). With the invention of pneumatic tires (1888) and coaster brake (1898), bicycles resembled modern two-wheelers.*

## RACING INTO OBLIVION

With the pneumatic tire, a whole new sport was created: racing! The first six-day bicycle race in America took place in New York's old Madison Square Garden in 1891. Champion ''Plugger Bill'' Martin pedaled over 1466 miles during the six-day event. Although few bicycle enthusiasts at the time realized the fact, however, a new invention was looming on the horizon that would push the bicycle aside as a vehicle for touring and racing. In fact, nearly every improvement designed for the bicycle soon was applied to the upstart automobile: pneumatic and cord tires, ball bearings, differential steering, seamless steel tubing, expansion brakes, and gearing systems. Yet, it was not only the car that drew upon bicycle technology; two bike specialists named Wilbur and Orville Wright soon turned the world upside down with their aviation adventures.

Columbia, became the first man to circumnavigate the globe on a two-wheeler. Stevens faced and surmounted incredible difficulties, among which were hostile Indians in his own country.

In 1885 John Kent Starley developed the ''Rover'' safety bicycle, a chain-driven rear-wheel vehicle. The Starley invention featured the familiar diamond-shaped frame with equal-sized wheels. In 1898 the New Departure Company added a coaster brake to make cycling safe for the entire family. Only details distinguish the modern bicycle of today from Starley's Rover.

The first Rover had wheels about 30 inches in diameter and solid rubber tires. Pneumatic tires did not come into widespread use until 1888 when John Boyd Dunlop patented a process he discovered while making more comfortable tires for his son's tricycle. By 1891, the pneumatic tire was being manufactured by many firms, and was accepted as a standard bicycle feature.

In 1902, when young Henry Ford was seeking publicity for his horseless carriage, he turned to Barney Oldfield, a colorful bicycle racing champion from Ohio. Oldfield thrived on speed, and he was eager to race the 80-horsepower ''Old 999.'' On October 25 at Grosse Pointe, Michigan, Oldfield won his first automobile race, and thereby symbolized the shift from bike to car that would dominate most of the following century.

THE MACMILLAN BICYCLE

*A casual break by the Sea Lion Pond in
Lincoln Park, Chicago, during 1889
illustrates the transition from the ordinary to
the diamond-shape bicycle.*

*Courtesy The Chicago Historical Society*

THE MICHAUX BICYCLE

## REVIVAL AND BOOM

It was not until the 1950's that adults once again thought about the bicycle as a means of pleasurable transportation. During the previous 50 years, bicycles were relegated to the ranks of children's toys, or — at best — tools of the trade for newspaper and delivery boys. When, however, Dr. Paul Dudley White (then President Eisenhower's coronary specialist) recommended cycling as the ideal light exercise, the first inroads into exclusive dependence on the automobile were underway.

Improvements in the machines themselves contributed tremendously to revived interest in bicycling. During the early 1960's, the public discovered decent, ridable — usually imported — bicycles at reasonable prices. Gone were the atrociously heavy mechanisms with fat tires that made pedaling a chore rather than a pleasure. Instead, there was the European three-speed lightweight that allowed riders to break out of riding just around the neighborhood, and permitted them to pedal out on 10- and 20-mile jaunts.

By the early 1970's — as problems of fuel and pollution began to seep into the awareness of auto-conscious Americans — the bike boom grew to enormous magnitude, with new bicycle sales even surpassing new car sales. By now both domestic and imported bicycles were incredibly efficient machines; equipped with 3, 5, or 10 speeds, the lightweight bicycles were designed to take a rider nearly any place he wanted to go. And the places riders wanted to go kept pace with the technological improvements in the machines themselves.

Commuting on a bicycle in good weather became a common sight in the nation's most congested urban areas, and the demand for bicycle pathways replaced the demand for new superhighways in many city council chambers. Family vacations often started as usual in the car, but the automobile served merely as a conveyance to the starting point for a healthy tour through some scenic section of America. As Americans moved into the middle 1970's, bicycles became much more entwined in their lifestyle than had been the case for nearly a century.

*When* Harper's Weekly *portrayed bicycle touring — April 11, 1896 — it indicated quite clearly that by this date the ordinary had been replaced by the modern two-wheeler with pneumatic tires.*

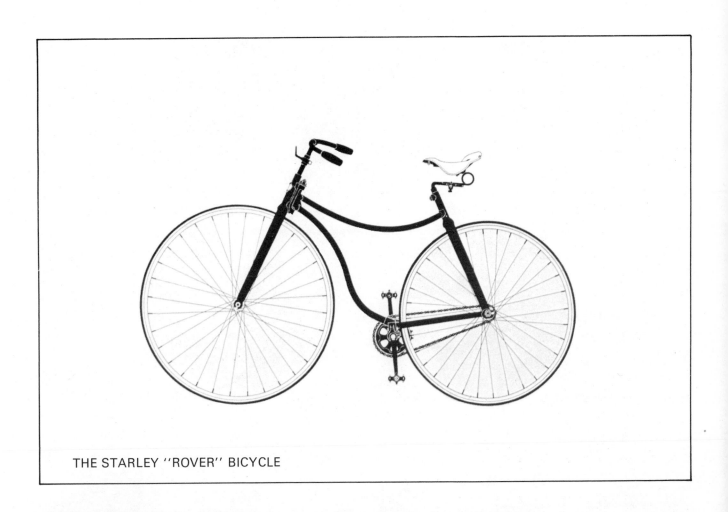

THE STARLEY "ROVER" BICYCLE

*Courtesy The Chicago Historical Society*

Since the sudden popularity explosion of bicycle riding, many adults are learning for the first time that bicycles are available to fit almost every need, temperament, and body size. There is the sturdy and reliable coaster-brake bicycle, like you had when you were a child; the English Racer that fascinated you in the fifties, with its mysterious three-speed gears and hand-operated brakes; or the ten-speed bicycle, with drop bars on which to ride cross country; there is even the customized imported bicycle, with its Old World craftsmanship and $800 price tag. No matter which bicycle you select, however, you must get one that fits you properly.

## SELECTING THE FRAME

Certainly the most basic difference between bicycles is the configuration of the frame. Bicycle frames are manufactured in men's style, ladies' style, and a combination style — the mixte frame.

The men's frame is probably the most common; manufacturers like to advertise and promote the diamond frame, which consists basically of two triangles. The men's style, with its triangular construction, is the strongest of the three; it presents the fewest problems in the fitting of cables and other accessories; and it is more aesthetically pleasing in design. Since it is stronger and more rigid, the diamond frame also provides better handling characteristics. Less prone to oscillations (or frame whip) when subjected to hard riding, the men's frame is tops for either sex.

The ladies' frame style survives only as an anachronism — a tradition that has outlived its purpose. The ladies' frame, with its angled top tube, was designed in deference to feminine modesty during the 1890's. The purpose behind such a design was to allow ladies to mount, ride, and dismount demurely without entangling their cumbersome long skirts and petticoats. Even until the 1930's and 1940's, ladies' bicycles were fitted with "skirt protectors," which consisted of a network of twine extending from the rear fender to the rear axle. The protectors were designed to prevent skirts from catching in the spokes of the rear wheel.

Unless women plan to undertake long rides in flowing skirts, they should not feel bashful about buying a men's style bicycle. The ladies' style frame is neither as strong as the men's style, nor does it provide as precise handling. Incidentally, racers of both sexes ride the men's diamond frame bicycle in competition. For women who simply do not want to pedal a men's bike, however, a compromise frame is available.

The mixte frame is an attempt to combine the best of both worlds in bicycle frame design. Actually a modified ladies' frame with the top tube higher than its traditional location, the mixte frame makes for easy mounting and dismounting, yet provides a somewhat better ride than the traditional ladies' style. If you plan to pedal with an accessory baby seat or other cumbersome baggage on your bike, then the mixte frame makes a great deal of sense. The availability of the mixte style can be a problem, however, as only a few European manufacturers offer mixte bicycles.

## SADDLE AND HANDLEBAR OPTIONS

Besides differences in frame configuration, there are basic options available in the types of saddle and handlebar fitted to your bicycle. Saddles come in two styles: the mattress (or tourist) saddle and the racing type. Handlebars also come in the two basic categories: the upright (or tourist) bars and the drop bar style. The tourist saddle and bar generally go hand in hand, and they do not mix well with racing equipment.

The tourist saddle is soft, blunt nosed, usually well padded and sprung, and generally manufactured from some plastic material. Many beginning riders purchase a tourist or mattress saddle because of its initial comfort. On longer rides, however, the synthetic base and padding can trap considerable heat, and the large blunt contours can chafe the inside of the legs and impede efficient pedaling. The springs of a tourist saddle may also develop an irritating squeak with each pedal stroke and shift in body weight.

The alternative to the tourist saddle is the so-called racing saddle, which actually has little to do with racing. More pointed in the nose and generally firmer, the racing saddle's padding and springs can vary from a little to none. Materials also vary widely,

*Cyclists (left) ride the traditional ladies' and men's frames. Her bike, with the angled top tube, also features the upright (or tourist) handlebars; his bike, with the triangular construction, has dropped handlebars.*

Bicycle Fitting
3

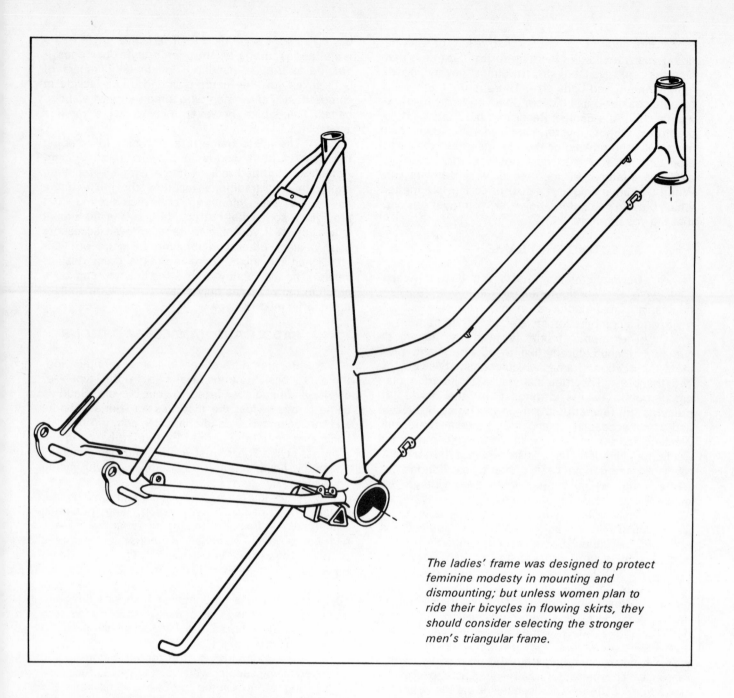

The ladies' frame was designed to protect feminine modesty in mounting and dismounting; but unless women plan to ride their bicycles in flowing skirts, they should consider selecting the stronger men's triangular frame.

from an all-leather construction to a plastic base with leather or buffalo-hide covering. The racing saddle sometimes elicits highly unfavorable comments from beginning riders who object to its stiffness and lack of comfort, but it grows on you or — more literally — around you.

An all-leather saddle gradually softens and eventually molds itself to your individual contours. Given enough time and tender loving care, a racing saddle becomes as comfortable as an old pair of slippers; some riders even transfer their old broken-in saddles to their new bicycles. Racing saddles of synthetic construction (with perhaps some padding and springs) do not require a break-in period, and are quite satisfactory for most riders. The racing saddle

minimizes leg chafing and allows for easy pedaling action.

On the debit side, however, racing saddles — especially the all-leather variety — require a great deal more attention and care than do the prosaic tourist saddles. Leather saddles usually have a tension nut at the nose which requires tightening from time to time to prevent the saddle from sagging. Periodically, these saddles also require a complete overhaul with some type of leather treatment. Moreover, an all-leather racing saddle is absolutely unforgiving of such cavalier treatment as being left in the rain, scratched or scuffed, or adulterated with oil and grease.

The complement of the tourist saddle is the

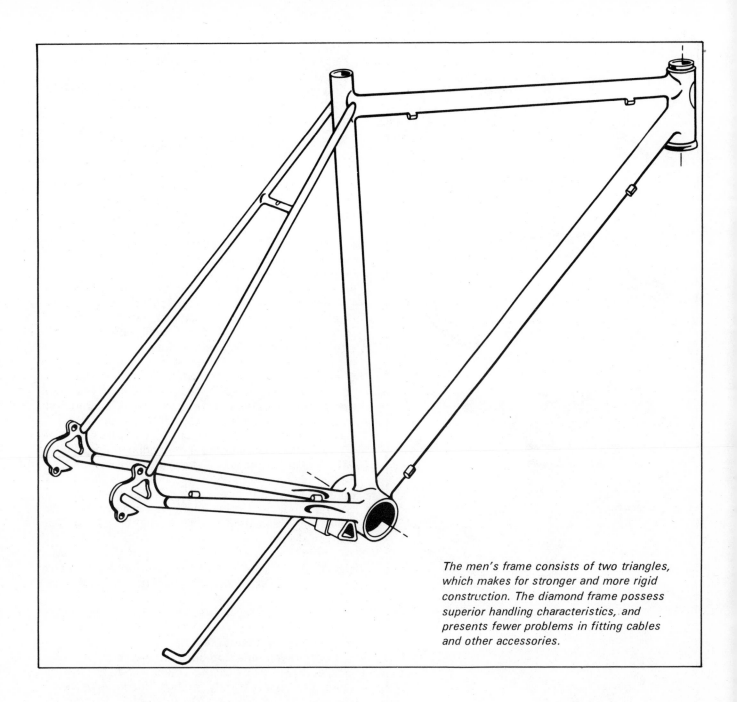

*The men's frame consists of two triangles, which makes for stronger and more rigid construction. The diamond frame possess superior handling characteristics, and presents fewer problems in fitting cables and other accessories.*

tourist or upright handlebar, which is the traditional style. While quite acceptable for short rides, an upright handlebar has no provision for allowing the rider to change the position of his hands. As a result, a tourist handlebar can cause some numbness and tingling on the palms, unless it is adjusted precisely to the rider's requirements. In addition, the upright sitting position which tourist equipment demands can create considerable aerodynamic drag, especially in the face of a stiff headwind; the upright sitting position also can prevent exertion of maximum leverage on the pedals.

The drop style handlebar eliminates all these unpleasant problems, and adds considerably to cycling enjoyment. Drop bars curve downward and to

the rear, providing several different positions for the hands. For easy riding, you can rest your hands on the straight top portion of the bar, cup them around the first curve of the bars, or straddle the brake levers between your thumb and forefinger. For hard riding (bucking a headwind or climbing uphill), you should position your hands directly behind the brake levers or on the straight bottom portion of the bar. Change hand positions as conditions require or merely to break the routine of using a single set of muscles.

The hunched-over riding position — which drop bars require — allows greater expansion of the chest and lungs and lowers the center of gravity, increasing overall stability. The hunched position

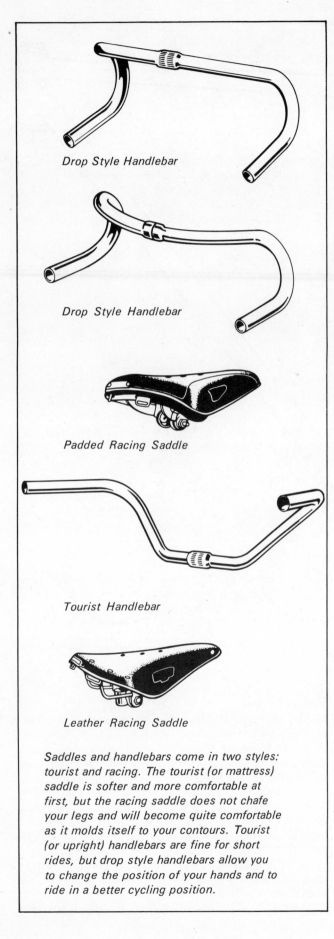

Drop Style Handlebar

Drop Style Handlebar

Padded Racing Saddle

Tourist Handlebar

Leather Racing Saddle

*Saddles and handlebars come in two styles: tourist and racing. The tourist (or mattress) saddle is softer and more comfortable at first, but the racing saddle does not chafe your legs and will become quite comfortable as it molds itself to your contours. Tourist (or upright) handlebars are fine for short rides, but drop style handlebars allow you to change the position of your hands and to ride in a better cycling position.*

also allows greater leverage on the pedals and better use of both calf and thigh muscles. To prove this to yourself, try sitting in a chair and standing up without using your hands. Stand up first from a bolt upright position, and then see how much easier it is from a hunched-over position.

## MEASURING FRAME SIZE

The choice of frame configuration and choice of handlebar and saddle eventually boil down to matters of personal preference. There is no right or wrong for making a certain choice once you are aware of the alternatives and their different applications. The question of frame size, however, does definitely have a right and a wrong answer; proper selection in this area is an absolute must.

Why not just have one size bicycle made to fit all people? The answer is that people come in a variety of shapes and sizes, while bicycles only stretch a little bit. Measurements of torsos, arms, legs, and other parts of the anatomy vary widely, and the bicycle must accommodate your individual requirements. The most noticeable difference between people is, of course, height, and that is the first measurement to consider when fitting a bicycle.

The range of standard bicycle sizes is from 17 to 26 inches, with the most common ones being 20 through 23 inches. Ladies' style frames tend to be available at the lower end and men's styles at the upper end of the size range. These bicycle sizes correlate not with your height, but rather with your inside leg measurement from the crotch to the bottom of your stocking feet. The rule of thumb for selecting a proper bicycle is that the frame size should equal your inside leg measurement minus nine inches. While not an absolute standard, this measuring technique usually proves correct.

To test the accuracy of the rule of thumb for your particular case, see if you can stand over the bicycle frame with both feet flat on the ground. If you cannot straddle the top tube comfortably, go to a smaller frame size. On the other hand, if there is more than approximately ½-inch clearance between you and the top tube, try the next larger frame size. Although it is possible to adjust for some fairly severe anatomical differences by raising or lowering the saddle, you should never buy a bicycle if the frame size is incorrect. Shop around if the dealer does not have the right frame size for you. A frame that is too small will either be uncomfortable and cramped with the seat at normal height or precarious and hazardous with the saddle raised to its maximum. A frame that is too large will present handling problems that make it unsafe to ride.

Besides height, there are other body dimensions which must be considered to obtain a properly fitted bicycle. For example, the distance from the saddle to the handlebar increases with the frame size to accommodate the longer arms and torsos of taller

*The first procedure in fitting a bicycle is to straddle the top bar with both feet flat on the ground. If you cannot do so comfortably, go to a smaller size frame; if there is more than ½-inch clearance, go to the next larger frame. The second procedure is to adjust the saddle and handlebars so that they are approximately level, and so that your knee is slightly bent when the pedal is in its bottom position.*

riders. For tall riders with short arms or short riders with long arms, the distance from saddle to bar can be altered by changing the original handlebar stem to a longer or shorter version.

## SADDLE ADJUSTMENTS

The first task in fitting the bike to you — once the proper frame size is determined — is the saddle height adjustment. The saddle is clamped onto a hollow piece of tubing, which in turn is clamped into the seat mast of the frame. The saddle tube can slide within the seat mast when the clamp

bolt is loosened. To adjust the saddle height, you can choose between a trial-and-error method and a mathematical method. Actually, the two methods complement each other, and both should be used to give you the right adjustment.

Using the scientific method, first set one pedal in its lowest position. Next, determine your inside leg measurement in stocking feet, and multiply it by 109 percent. Raise or lower the saddle until the distance between the pedal and the top of the saddle agrees with your leg calculation. This figure of 109 percent, incidentally, derives from a study of a number of champion bicycle riders.

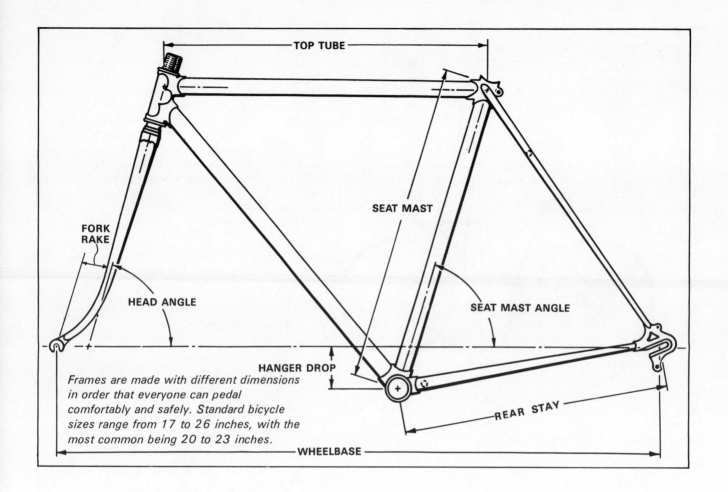

TOP TUBE

SEAT MAST

FORK RAKE

HEAD ANGLE

SEAT MAST ANGLE

HANGER DROP

*Frames are made with different dimensions in order that everyone can pedal comfortably and safely. Standard bicycle sizes range from 17 to 26 inches, with the most common being 20 to 23 inches.*

REAR STAY

WHEELBASE

To double check the saddle setting, keep one pedal in its lowest position and sit on the saddle. It helps if you put both feet on the pedals while a friend holds you upright. Place the ball of your foot on the low pedal; you should have only a slight bend at the knee. Next, place your heel (in stocking feet) on the pedal while keeping your foot horizontal; the bend in your knee should disappear. The final step is to test ride the initial saddle setting and to make adjustments if any are needed. Keep in mind, however, that the proper saddle height will probably feel too high at first; most riders, in fact, usually have their saddles set too low.

Always remember to leave at least two inches of the seat post within the seat mast of the frame. Any less than two inches is an invitation to disaster, because the seat post can snap if strained when it has so little support. Since most seat posts do not have a maximum height indication, mark the seat post at two inches above its end, and do not raise the saddle above that marking.

In addition to the height, the saddle's horizontal positioning must be set. On the less expensive saddles there is no adjustment possible; you can only make sure that the saddle clamp has not been rotated out of position. The closed portion of the saddle clamp should face the front of the bicycle. On the more expensive saddles there are two support

wires to secure the saddle to the seat post. Move the saddle backward or forward until the nose of the saddle is 2½ to 3 inches behind the center of the crank hanger (or front sprocket). The nose of the saddle should point slightly upward.

## HANDLEBAR AND STEM SETTINGS

For top efficiency, raise the handlebar stem until it is approximately level with the saddle. To raise the bar, loosen the stem bolt and tap it lightly with a mallet until the stem is freed. Raise or lower the handlebar stem as required, and then tighten the stem bolt fully. As with the saddle, be careful not to raise the handlebar stem too high. Handlebar stems are generally marked with a line or legend indicating the maximum extension. If there is no such marking, make sure that at least 2½ inches of the stem remain in the fork stem.

Next, check the distance from the saddle to the handlebar; it should be roughly equal to the length of your lower arm as measured from the fingertips to the elbow. If your arm measurement is much different than the distance between saddle and handlebar, purchase a different size stem. Stems are available at modest cost, and the proper one is well worth the investment. Changing the stem, however, requires considerable labor (the handlebar and at least one brake lever and one side of tape must be removed); for this reason, check the measurement carefully before your decide to change handlebar stems.

The handlebar position within the stem is also critical. If the bicycle is equipped with drop bars, check to see that the bottom straight portion of the bar is positioned at a 10- or 15-degree angle with the ground. If your bicycle is equipped with tourist style bars, make sure that the ends point to the rear and slightly down. To adjust the handlebar position, loosen the binder bolt in the handlebar stem, and position the handlebars as required.

## READY TO USE

A final word of caution before you ride: Check all the nuts and bolts to make sure they are fully tightened. See if you can twist the saddle, handlebar, and handlebar stem. If you can twist any of these parts, retighten the appropriate nut or bolt. If the saddle or handlebar still moves, the nut or bolt threads may be binding at some point, preventing full tightening. Place a drop of oil on the nut or bolt, and then tighten fully again.

Check to see that the handlebar is properly aligned in relation to the front fork. Sight down over the handlebar toward the front hub axle. The straight top portion of the handlebar should be parallel with the front hub axle.

With all the adjustments properly set, you will experience the thrill of riding a finely tuned machine. You will be able to use your leg muscles to full advantage without feeling cramped or strained. Your weight will be properly distributed among pedals, saddle, and handlebar without excessive pressure in any one area. Brake and shift levers will be within easy reach during both normal riding and emergency situations. Give these settings a fair chance before changing them, especially if you are new to this type of equipment. After pedaling several miles, change the settings if they still feel uncomfortable, but make only gradual alterations.

## CHILDREN'S BICYCLES

All of the rules for fitting an adult apply with equal force to fitting a bicycle to a child. The major problem most parents have in fitting their child's bike is in resisting the temptation to purchase a bicycle which is too large or too complex. Buying a bicycle which is too large for the child because you think he will eventually grow into it is foolhardy and dangerous. The learning process will be slowed, and no amount of adjustments or pedal blocks will correct the basic problem. Mounting and dismounting will be hazardous, and the whole experience may prove totally disheartening to a youngster.

Complicated equipment such as gearshifts and hand-operated brakes should be questioned. Can the child operate such equipment safely and efficiently? Why risk the spoiling of a lifetime of cycling fun by increasing the potential of a serious accident? The safety of children is so important that some reputable bicycle dealers refuse to sell a bicycle which exceeds the child's ability to control in all situations.

Make the same sort of adjustments on a child's bike as on an adults, but revise the settings as the child grows. Remember that children tend to be a little rougher on their bicycles than adults are; therefore, check all nuts and bolts periodically to see that they are still tight and that all equipment is still adjusted properly.

*Always make sure that the handlebar (above) is parallel with the front hub axle. The rider's knee (below) must be straight when his heel is on the pedal.*

If it is possible, buy your bicycle from a bicycle dealer. If you must buy from a mass-merchandizer, check that the particular outlet has parts and repair facilities on hand. For the most part, bicycle dealers have a better selection of vehicles and repair facilities and expertise are readily available. Bear in mind that bicycle dealerships are fairly unique among commercial enterprises, in that people who go into the business are often intimately connected with some aspect of "bicycle culture." Many dealers are former racers or tourers, or they worked for manufacturers or made frames, or were in some way connected with bicycles before they went into business. Unless you are fully prepared to maintain your equipment yourself, or are prepared to learn, a reputable dealer, who is himself or who employs a first-rate mechanic, is your best defense against problems with your bike.

Almost all new bicycles look good — from a distance. Most bicycle frames are made of special steel tubing. Regardless of the quality of the steel, it requires a protective coating to prevent rust. Paint, enamel, lacquer and chrome are the usual coatings, together or in single applications. Usually, good frame construction and good finish go together, but sometimes a flashy finish is used to obscure inferior frame construction. Look especially at the points where frame members join: neat junctures, with no lumps, cracks, or holes, are fair assurance that a frame is decent and will perform as designed without breaking.

Heavier, less expensive frames are often welded together. The more expensive and specialized frames are made from specialized tubing made expressly for bicycles. These steel-alloy tubes may contain varying amounts of chrome, molybdenum, manganese, carbon, or traces of other metals and minerals. More expensive bikes sometimes have a decal indicating the make of tubing used. The better-known brands of tubing are Reynolds 531 (English), Columbia (Italian), Vitus and Durifort (French), and Tange and Ishiwata (Japanese). Other makes are seldom labeled. Frankly, though each of these brands has slightly different characteristics of flexibility and tensile strength, each is about as good as the others.

A welded-frame bike may be perfectly adequate for general riding, especially in generally flat

Bicycles, even 10-speeds, intended for use by children, have heavier, usually welded frames to withstand the abuse and heavy handling given them by their owners.

areas. It may even be superior if it is going to suffer from weather, heavy handling, or minor abuse. Bikes made from the name-brand tubes are generally brazed (hard-soldered — sweated) together, usually with bronze alloys, sometimes with bronze-silver, nickle-bronze, or nickle-silver alloys. Brazing means that the tube joints, whether directly joined or lugged (a lug is a tight-fitting sleeve into which the tubes are inserted), are subjected to a lower temperature than welding; hence, they retain high strength at the joints (heating steel tubing lowers its tensile strength).

## FRAME DESIGN

Bicycle frame design is a function of the bicycle's intended use. The materials used are a function of use as well. Heavy, welded-frame, single-gear, coaster-brake bikes are designed to be sturdy and stable. They are difficult to damage and easy to

# How to Buy A Bicycle
4

*Since the bicycle boom has flooded America's bike shops with a multitude of two-wheel vehicles, you must be extremely careful and knowledgeable to purchase a quality bicycle.*

*No longer considered toys, bicycles are now recognized as an enjoyable and efficient mode of transportation.*

repair. They are not, however, fast. Bikes of this type receive undue ridicule by riders of lightweight bikes and some so-called experts.

Outside of the heavy-frame approach, there are a number of significant differences in frame design. Basically, frames are designed to be flexible or rigid. Virtually all lower-priced and medium-priced bicycles, and touring bikes — even the most expensive in this class — are designed to be relatively flexible, i.e., to absorb shock and ride comfortably. This is accomplished by building frames that have relatively "shallow" head- and seat-tube angles (nominally, 72 degrees or less), long fork rake, long rear, or chain stays, and a consequently long wheelbase. Bikes like this, whether they cost $65 or $800 track well in a straight line, steer widely, and absorb and distribute road shock in the frame members, thus saving the rider, to some extent, from absorbing these jolts.

Bike frames of this design may be welded or brazed, light or heavy, 3- or 10-speed, with straight or turned-down bars, and they account for most of the adult bike sales of recent years. Finally, bikes of this design should be preferred for average riding.

The other type of significant "solo" bicycle frame is one that is designed to be rigid. Rigid frames are best for racing. Road racing frames, criterium frames (a criterium is a short-length race over a close urban route), hill-climb racing frames, track, time-trial, and other racing frames are designed to be rigid — and fast — faster than the average, healthy rider can ride them without about a year of physical conditioning. Rigidity is achieved by building these frames with steeper head- and seat-tube angles (72 to 75 degrees), shorter fork rake and shorter rear chain stays (with a consequent short wheelbase).

Rigidity allows the racer to push the pedals without losing energy into the frame's flexibility. The shorter wheelbase allows the racer to turn and maneuver more quickly (an average rider would feel

that a racing frame is "unstable" the first time on one). As to holes and bumps, the racer either flies right over them or crashes. Racers have to ride to win, not to be comfortable.

The special features of racing frames do not preclude their use for pleasure riding. But racing frames, that is real racing frames — not bikes called "racers," are expensive. They are hand-made — none are made on assembly lines. The only true racing frame made by a major manufacturer in the United States is the Schwinn Paramount racing series, and it is hand-made. It takes a skilled craftsman the better part of a week to build a single frame from start to finish. The parts for a racing frame are scarce and costly. Racing frame prices start at about $200, and that is without wheels, gears, handlebars, or anything. A fully assembled bike with such a frame would be worth about $500 or $600 at 1975 retail prices.

If one can afford such a rig for pleasure, it is indeed a pleasure to ride one. Remember, though, that to a great extent they are impractical: they are only good for riding. It is silly to put racks, carriers, bags, or baskets on a racing bike, for these upset the balance and steering, weight distribution of the rider vis a vis the bicycle, and naturally, the overall weight of the machine. If one is not going to maintain the lightness of a lightweight bike, why pay extra for it? On the other hand, one might own two bikes.

The solo "man's" bicycle has for some time been the state-of-the-art in bicycle design, and will undoubtedly continue to be so for some time more. There is nothing wrong with ladies' frames for recreational riding, however. Women racers, however, use the man's or diamond design frame exclusively, and more and more women are buying men's bicycles for general use. "Ladies'" frames are for people who do not want to put their leg over the bike to get on it, but rather, through the frame, and for people who wear skirts or robes.

There are many other kinds of specialized vehicles: Tandems are for two or more riders, adult tricycles are for those who might have a balance problem with a bicycle, and folding bicycles may solve a storage problem. Obviously, each of these vehicles has a secondary function to solo riding; yet each is a relevant solution that will allow one to enjoy the movement and exercise of cycling. If one is not interested in moving, one should pedal a static exercise cycle indoors.

## BICYCLE COMPONENTS AND RUNNING GEAR

Wheels, ultimately, are the most important part of a bicycle. Without wheels, frames are just aesthetic and theoretical. Actually, to speak of bicycle wheels is to speak of wheel-tire, or better, rim-tire combinations. There are basically two types of rim-tire combinations in general use today: one is the tube-type tire, with separate inner tube, used with a "drop center"-type rim. This is commonly called a "clincher" wheel. The rim may be steel or aluminum alloy. Tires in this class are durable and readily available; they are the usual original equipment on low- and middle-priced bikes and in many cases are the tire of preference of riders of expensive rigs, especially for touring.

The other rim-tire combination is that of the "sew-up," or tubular tire, with a trapezoidal-section tubular rim that is quite different in construction than a clincher rim. These types of tires and rims are not interchangeable.

Sew-ups cost much more than clinchers, but balancing the cost is the fact that they roll faster. They are also much lighter than clinchers: a sew-up tire and rim, with a hub and spokes, may weigh half of what a clincher weighs. To illustrate what this means in practical terms, a high-grade lightweight frame with fine components and running gear may weigh, with sew-ups, 21 pounds, and the same set, except with clinchers, 26 pounds. Anyone who claims, dealer or rider, that a particular rig with clinchers weighs 22 pounds is, at best, exaggerating. An inescapable fact of sew-ups is that they are more prone to puncture-flats than clinchers.

For the average rider on a medium-price bike, the weight difference alone is not a great advantage and is offset further by the cost factor and maintenance problems involved with sew-ups. One is well-advised to choose clinchers for general riding, especially at first, and perhaps always. If you cannot resist a passion for sew-ups, then be prepared to handle their higher cost, to have several, not just one spare, and to learn to repair them yourself — often.

Brakes are the next most important item on a bicycle. Aside from foot brakes, there are two types of handbrakes in common use: side- and center-pull brakes. There is no fixed rule about which is better. Side-pull brakes feel "faster" or tighter, center-pulls "softer." But both stop effectively. The best-known makes of side-pull brakes (listed in rough order of cost) are Weinmann, Universal, Shimano, and Campagnolo. The main difference among these brakes is finish. They all stop bikes with almost equal efficiency, despite contrary claims.

Center-pull brakes widely available (in no particular order) are Weinmann, Universal, Mafac, Shimano, Dia-Compe, Balilla, and GB, to mention several. They are all roughly equal in quality and operation. Any of the above brakes might be found as original equipment, and they are all more or less available as replacement brakes. Do not be shocked, however, to find that Campagnolo brakes, if you can get them, will cost well over $100. Most of the others cost considerably less, some in the area of $20 or so.

There are two types of gear-changing devices: the planetary gear type, built into the rear hub (three-speed application), and the derailleur type, attached to the frame (front sprocket and rear sprocket — five- and 10-speed applications). Of the three-speed type, Sturmey-Archer, Bendix, and Shimano are the most common makes as original equipment. They are all about equally good. They are heavy in weight and heavy-duty.

Contemporary derailleurs (rear) are of two types: there are the horizontal type and vertical type. Makes of the vertical type (the older design) include Simplex, Huret, Zeus, and Campagnolo. Makes of the horizontal type (more recent an innovation) include SunTour (the patent holder on the design), Shimano, and the recent Campagnolo adaptation. Both types and all of these makes are quite good to excellent, and selection of one brand or another is a matter of cost or taste. All of them change gears effectively. Front derailleurs (by the same manufacturers as above) are all similar to one another in operation. Derailleur bodies may be made of steel or aluminum alloy (or plastic nylon in the case of the less-expensive Simplex "Criterium" and "Prestige" models).

Other components include cranksets — steel cottered, alloy cotterless, and integral crank-arm-axle units. Cotterless are the most expensive, integral the least. The better hubs are one-piece aluminum alloy. Steel hubs are usually pieced together, and again, are heavier.

Saddles are of leather, plastic, or leather-covered plastic. Contoured, slender saddles — properly adjusted, are the most comfortable of all three types. Seats with springs are often flat and, hence, less comfortable. Troxell makes a plastic-covered, sprung, padded, contoured, slender saddle that is one of the few "non-racing" saddles that is actually comfortable.

Recent studies have shown that turned-down bars afford better control of a bike, but if straight, or "tourist," bars make you feel more secure, then, by all means, use them. Tourist handlebars with tight-fitting handles of rubber or plastic are a must for adequate gripping; with turned-down bars, tape covering is similarly essential, preferably of cloth tape (plastic gets slippery). Obviously, handles or tape are of a different nature than the other parts of a bike, but they should not be considered mere decorative accessories; they are an integral part of the riding system of any bicycle.

A bike is made to be ridden and you should ride what you like. Remember that more expensive is not necessarily better, just more expensive. Let a dealer help analyze your riding needs, and above all, follow the dealer's advice on fitting the bike to your size and dimensions. It is unwise to make irrational choices about bike size and adjustment: if you are short, get a small frame. Do not adjust the seat too high, just because it looks "racy;" do not readjust the angle of handlebars for looks, either. Bicycles and their components are designed to be used a certain way, within a certain latitude, and the rider should learn to accept and utilize that design, or else change vehicles.

As a rule, the less one carries while riding, the better. Need, rather than whim, should dictate the addition of accessories to the bike — or the rider. Accessories add weight to the total package you pedal, and certain poorly designed or badly attached items may be a hazard by interfering with the balance, steering, or free wheel rotation of the bicycle. When buying accessories put as much care and thought into what you buy as you put into the bike itself: when a needed accessory fails, it can be as much a headache as if the bike itself was to fail.

## SECURITY DEVICES

In big cities, many riders riding through the parks, will actually take their bikes in with them when they go into public washrooms. This may seem a little extreme, but some riders have had their bikes literally stolen out from under them. This should prepare you for the reality that there is *no* security system for bicycles that is foolproof — if somebody wants your bike badly enough, he may get it, no matter what precautions you take.

In fact, then, locking devices only serve to *discourage* the less serious thief. A motorcycle chain is not better than a quarter-inch cable, only heavier and costlier. Under the right circumstances, the determined thief will defeat any locking system. If you must lock up outside of your home, one of two systems is best for bicycles: 1/4-to 3/8-inch plastic-coated cables, or U-shaped devices made from flat-stock steel. Simply put, chains are usually too heavy to warrant carrying them on a bike. Your best bet is to use a cable with a hardened-shackle key lock. When not in use, this is a light and compact arrangement. In use, assuming you bike is in an extremely visible place where many people pass, thieves know it will take a long time to defeat that combination.

## NOISE MAKERS

If you ride through parks and in quiet lanes, then a little, tinkly bell, of the tricycle variety, is a polite and adequate way to let others know you are approaching on your bicycle. Such a bell is, however, inadequate for street traffic. Horns with rubber bulbs

may be audible to automobile drivers, but a better solution is the gas-powered horn, whose volume rivals that of a car. Bear in mind, though, that it is too loud for parks and lanes.

One criticism of these devices is that you are required to remove one hand from the handlebars to use them. Some riders have relied instead on shouting, loud whistling, or whistles as signals. In a cycling environment, that is, where there are lots of other bikes, verbal signals, moderately profered, are sufficient to alert other cyclists: such phrases as ''excuse me'' often work well. In movement, a phrase such as ''on your left'' or ''on your right'' may be adequate to enable you to pass safely.

## BAGS AND CARRIERS

You may mount bags on the bicycle or on yourself. Waterproof nylon bags with aluminum interior frames, of the sort that instantly clip on and off the bike, are the lightest bags you can add to your bike. Many companies make these: they are relatively inexpensive. Waterproofed canvas — an older type of bag — may prove more durable if you plan to tour a lot. For everyday use, bags on the rear of the bike are superior to a handlebar bag, since these may, when loaded, upset steering. Even unloaded they clutter up handlebars. For serious touring, bolt-on bag holders are a good idea. If you carry a great deal, there is then little chance that the bags can interfere with wheels or pedaling.

Bags you wear should carry most of the weight as low as possible on your back. Bikers' day knapsacks, now widely available, are so designed and are to be preferred to objects on the bike for carrying small loads. Also, skiers' belt packs are nice for cycling. To carry a larger load, cross-country-ski packs, with or without internal frames, are best. Hikers' frame packs create problems for cyclists: they cause a lot of wind resistance, reduce your flexibility, and tend to be top-heavy. You should not carry as much on your back riding as walking anyway: 25 to 30 pounds is a typical maximum load before real steering and crosswind difficulties begin.

Racks and baskets may be useful for small loads. The lightweight aluminum rear carrier rack that attaches to the seat stays and axle ends, provides a

# Bicycle Accessories 5

*As more Americans use their bicycles as practical modes of transportation, specialized accessories are becoming available, helping the serious cyclist to make his riding safer, more enjoyable, and even more efficient.*

(A) Super Sound bike horn. (B) Sport West saddle pack. (C) Handlebar front bag support. (D) Cannondale "Bugger" trailer.

means for carrying books, a briefcase, small parcels, or attaching the newer rear bag models. Rear baskets are also excellent, but for some reason are not widely used. Most baskets in use attach to the handlebars.

A unique new device for cycling is the Bugger, put out by Cannondale. It is a trailer for bikes that comes in two models: one to carry luggage and the other with seats to carry at least two small children. In moderate riding this adds remarkably little more effort to pedaling and allows you to carry much more than you could on the bike or yourself in any other fashion.

## LIGHTS

Riding a bicycle at night can be pleasant, but not in automobile traffic. The function of bicycle lighting in traffic is not to see better, but to be seen. Nearly all bike lights are inferior for seeing under most circumstances. As a rule, if there is no available light, do not ride — your lights will not help.

Generator-driven lights work only when the bike is moving. A voltage-regulator / storage battery

system recently became available for use in conjunction with generators. This indeed provides a constant light, even when stopped, but only adds to an already complicated system.

Battery-driven lights that clamp on are less expensive and may throw a more effective light. If the sole object is to be seen, the flashlight-type light that straps to arm or leg is probably your best bet. Strapped to one's leg, it is in constant motion and so is readily seen by drivers and other cyclists.

## MISCELLANEOUS EQUIPMENT

There are many other accessories you can add to your bicycle, making it safer, more versatile, and pleasurable to ride:

**Mirrors:** Most rear-view mirrors are of doubtful use. The tiny kind that attach to glasses or to cap brims usually work best. Learn, as motorcyclists do, to look quickly over your shoulder in the direction you are turning.

**Distance meters:** Odometers, or more properly, cyclometers, are useful and fun for keeping track of distance on short exercise runs or on long tours. They are easily installed and can be extremely accurate. The Lucas Brand seem to be the sturdiest.

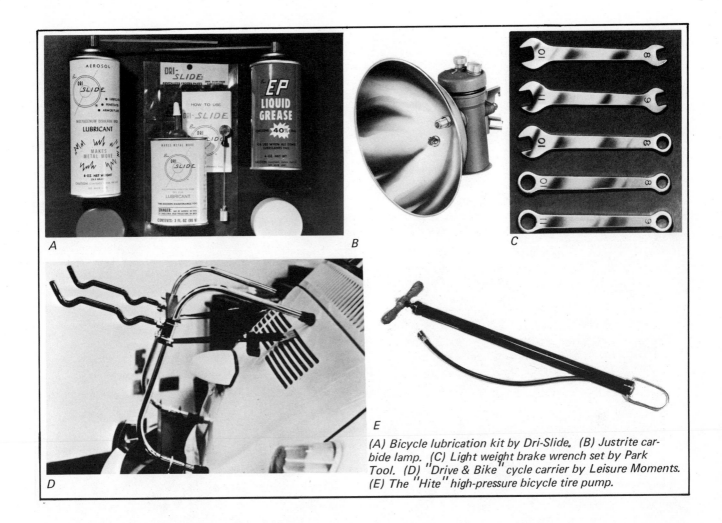

(A) Bicycle lubrication kit by Dri-Slide. (B) Justrite carbide lamp. (C) Light weight brake wrench set by Park Tool. (D) "Drive & Bike" cycle carrier by Leisure Moments. (E) The "Hite" high-pressure bicycle tire pump.

**Tools:** Make up your own kit of tools, of the best quality you can afford, rather than buying a pre-assembled kit; you will then have only what you need and have much better tools.

**Tape and grips:** Cloth tape is always the best material for wrapping your bars. Plastic is slippery. Racers use only cloth — take a tip from them. And plug bar ends: this makes the bar ends safer and prolongs the life of the tape. The best plugs are of rubber or soft plastic. As for grips, they should not twist. If they do, they should either be cemented in place or replaced.

**Flags and triangles:** There are mixed reactions to flags. They are indeed visible, but their whippy staff may be hazardous to other riders, and it is almost impossible to mount or dismount by throwing your leg over. You should resist having one only for decoration. The slow-moving vehicle triangle sign plate is an especially good idea when riding in rural areas.

**Speedometers:** These are a useless item for bicycles. Serious cyclists will calculate their speed from the gear they are riding in and their pedaling cadence or by timing a known distance. Anything that takes a cyclist's attention off the road can be dangerous.

**Kickstands:** Kickstands are only marginally useful in standing a bicycle. Laying a bike in grass or leaning it securely against something will usually provide better support for the bicycle.

**Radio holders:** A holding bracket can be mounted on the handlebar to hold a transistor radio. This is better than dangling the radio. (It is bad to carry or dangle anything — books, purse, bags, etc. — when riding.)

**Pumps:** Frame-mounted pumps are not effective for U.S.-style valves (Schroeder) unless the pump connection and the valve are modified. With a cutter, cut off the shaft of the valve core, leaving only the conical valve seat, and throw away the spring. Then, with a long-nose pliers, pull out the center piece of metal in the pump connector. You will then be able to pump 75 pounds or more into the tube with ease.

**Water bottles:** Racers use lightweight, plastic, half-liter (one-pint) bottles — one or two — to replenish the water they lose copiously when racing. Others use them, but they often stop and get off the bike to drink. In this case such bottles are not so useful. They do not keep liquids hot or cold, they make almost anything taste bad, and they do not hold much. You are better off with an army canteen, a hiker's one-liter bottle, or a small thermos carried in a bag or on the rack.

Your bicycle may require little or no attention at all, beyond keeping the tires filled with air. We know of bicyclists who have done nothing to their bikes for years! But as cycling becomes more popular, and as you spend more time with your bike, you may want to consider keeping your own machine in good repair. You can save money by doing so, and with a little patience, you can do as good a job on many repairs or maintenance jobs as a professional mechanic.

First of all, as a rule, if you think something is wrong with your bike, it probably is. Either you have the wrong bike for you — too big, too small — or part of the bike is adjusted improperly, has become bent or broken, or was improperly installed initially.

Second, be cautious in attacking your bike repairs until you think you know what you are doing. Some things are obvious, but others such as fixing a wheel that wobbles may get you into expensive trouble. Read this chapter, and then ask people — other cyclists and bike mechanics — how to approach difficult tasks; then come back to the chapter and use it as a guide.

The chapter is broken down into the following subject categories:

- Tools
- Lubricants, Solvents, and Cleaners
- Bearings
- Wheels, Tires, and Hubs
- Brakes
- Gears, Changers, Levers, and Chains
- Steering System
- Seat and Seat Post
- Crank and Pedal System
- Frame and Front Fork
- Finish and Appearance

By turning to the appropriate section, you can quickly evaluate what your bicycle needs in terms of maintenance and repairs, and then proceed to put your bike in top pedaling condition.

## TOOLS

The most common tool for bicycle repair is the six-inch adjustable wrench, often called a Cres-

cent wrench. Crescent is a manufacturer and not the only one that makes adjustable wrenches. Whatever brand or size wrench you purchase, make sure that the movable jaw does not wobble (at least not much); a wrench that wobbles could slip and damage the nut. In addition, the wrench that slips could damage the finish of your bike frame and, most importantly, could injure your hand.

You might find an eight-inch wrench more to your liking than a six. If you plan to do thorough maintenance yourself, then consider owning all of the following adjustable wrench sizes: four-, six-, eight-, and fifteen-inch models. There is a twelve-inch size, but since it does not fit bottom-bracket cups, its use is limited. The fifteen-inch wrench fits bottom brackets, headsets, and freewheel removers; and since it is longer than a twelve-inch, it provides better leverage anyway.

Frankly, nonadjustable wrenches — open-end, box, and specially designed bike wrenches — that fit specific nut and bolt-head sizes are better than any adjustable wrench. Nonadjustable wrenches are less likely to slip, and they wear the nut less. Remember that since most better bicycle equipment employs nuts with metric dimensions, you must obtain nonadjustable metric wrenches that are properly sized for the nut.

Finally, you can use socket wrenches with a ratchet handle. Fortunately, metric-size sockets are widely available with quarter-inch and three-eighth-inch insert slots. Therefore, if you already have a ratchet handle, you can simply get a few extra sockets for your bicycle needs.

Never use a pliers of any kind on bicycle nuts or bolt heads! Smooth-faced pliers cannot grasp a nut at all, and knurled-face pliers invariably chew up a nut and render it ungripable for a proper wrench.

In addition to wrenches, you also need at least one screwdriver. A forged, chrome-vanadium, four-inch blade screwdriver will do for most purposes. You should also have a long-nose pliers with knurled faces and with integral side cutter for pulling cables taut and trimming their ends. In addition, buy a set of three tire irons for removing tube-type tires from the rim.

With these four types of tools — an adjustable wrench, a screwdriver, a long-nose pliers, and

*Pleasurable cycling requires a machine in good working order. Most bicycle maintenance is not difficult, but all major assemblies should be disassembled, cleaned, and lubricated at least once every two years.*

# Bicycle Maintenance
# 6

*Servicing the crank assembly requires a cone wrench to remove the crank cone locknut.*

tire irons — you can do most of the everyday maintenance on your bicycle: tighten and loosen the nuts and bolts; adjust the brakes, gear changers, seat, and handlebar; and change flats or install new tires.

Multiple-gear bikes require that at least the rear wheel, and preferably both wheels, be off the ground for proper adjustment of the gear changers and for checking brake operation. Carbondale makes an inexpensive bike stand for this purpose, but you can simply hang the bike at two points (the seat and the handlebar) from a basement pipe or from ceiling hooks — using ropes, straps, or stretch cords. Or, if you have a convenient empty wall, you can mount two six-inch wall standards with two eight- to twelve-inch shelf brackets about fifteen inches apart.

Pad each bracket (a towel is sufficient), and lay the top tube of the bike over the brackets to catch the seat and the handlebar stem. If you are on the road or if you cannot hang your bike, turn it upside-down and rest it on the seat and handlebar.

For more involved work, you will need a spoke wrench to adjust or replace spokes, cone wrenches to overhaul hubs, and a freewheel remover — absolutely essential to remove a freewheel from the rear hub. If you plan to work on crank arms, chainwheels, and bottom bracket, you need crankset tools and a vise to hold dismounted components as you work on them.

## LUBRICANTS, SOLVENTS, AND CLEANERS

Your bicycle needs continual lubrication because the moving or bearing parts continuously pick up dirt and grit as you ride. The best lubricants to use are good-quality motor oil — such as SAE 20 or 30 — or oil made specifically for bikes, such as that by Sturmey-Archer. Use grease for all the ball bearing parts, for installation of threaded parts, and for installation of tight-fitting parts such as cotterless crank arms on the axle ends. The new spray lubricants such as WD-40 — with the skinny tube attached to the nozzle — are good for pin-point application.

Use oil only for off-bike overhaul of parts. Oil can deteriorate tires and can render brake pads ineffective. In contrast, spray lubricant not only does not do such things, but it also — through the force of the spray — helps remove the dirty residue from brake pivots, brake levers, front and rear derailleurs, and their levers and chains.

Grease is primarily used for overhauling components. Use only grease made for bicycles: Lubriplate, Phil Wood, and Campagnolo manufacture the best greases. Remember, oils and greases made for high-speed automotive applications are totally unnecessary for bicycles, since no moving part of a bike runs as fast as that of an automobile. Bike lubricants do not solidify from heat or break down from oxidation at high temperature. Buy grease in squeeze tubes; that way it stays clean and is easier to apply than from a can. If you get grease in cans, use a finger to apply it; no tool works as well. Have a cloth handy before you start to use grease.

For thorough off-bike overhaul or cleaning of components, you will need a good solvent to remove old grease, grime, and grit. Never use kerosene or gasoline! They will explode. The other solvents — lacquer thinner, oleum spirits, turpentine, or turp-based paint-thinner — are flammable, but they are not explosive. Of these, lacquer thinner is the most penetrating, and it evaporates quickly leaving no residue of its own. Nevertheless, be careful when using lacquer thinner around your frame if it is lacquer-finished or epoxy-enamel-finished.

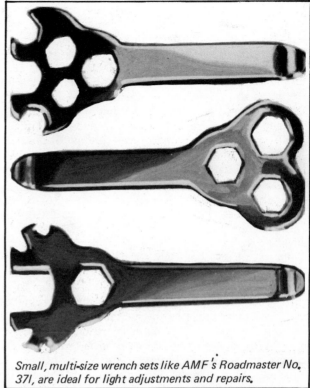

*Small, multi-size wrench sets like AMF's Roadmaster No. 371, are ideal for light adjustments and repairs.*

To clean a component, get a metal or glass pie plate and pour solvent into it. Take the component apart and put all the pieces in the dish. Clean each part first with your fingers, then with a toothbrush, and finally with a clean cloth. As each piece is cleaned, put it in another clean and empty container or on a clean piece of cloth. Do only one component at a time so as not to mix up pieces, and reassemble each component before starting another.

You should keep your bike clean as well as lubricated. Wash it with liquid detergent and water. If the bicycle is heavily coated with mud, hose it down. This is best done on a warm, sunny day. The waterless spray cleaners — Fantastik, Windex, and Formula 409 — are excellent for cleaning the whole bike at any time of the year. If you live in a northern city and ride in the winter, then these cleaners are especially effective as they help neutralize the salt you pick up. Use these cleaners on the tires as well as on the frame and components; then use a spray lubricant immediately after cleaning.

## BEARINGS

All of the moving parts of your bicycle run on bearings, usually ball bearings, and these require periodic overhaul. A very small number of components come equipped with needle or roller bearings, and some newer equipment comes with sealed bearings that require no maintenance. Since the needle bearing type is similar to the ball bearing type, if you understand one, you will understand the other.

The moving parts all have cup and cone ball bearing arrangements. This is true of wheel hubs, headset, bottom bracket, and pedals. In each case, a cone holds the balls in a cup, and a locknut holds the entire apparatus in a fixed position. Thus, a rotating axle is entirely supported by the balls. Bicycle grease is used to lubricate this system, preventing dirt and grit from interfering with the free running of the balls in the cup and cone. Each bearing assembly may have loose balls, or — on some more expensive components — there may be a set of balls held in a cage or clip.

When reinstalling balls, always install as many as the cup will hold. There will always be a little space left over, but this will be less than the diameter of one ball. With caged balls, the cage is always more closed on one side, more open on the other. The open side goes toward the cup, or larger part. To install balls or clips, pack the bearing cup with as much grease as you can, then put the balls in one at a time. The grease will more or less hold the balls in place until the cup or cone is tightened. For hubs and pedals, tighten the cone and lock it; for brackets and headsets, tighten the cup and lock it.

In either case, adjusting these bearings takes a little time. You must tighten the cup or cone involved, adjust it, and lock it. First, tighten the cup or cone a little, say from twelve o'clock to nine o'clock (one-quarter turn). Then, tighten the locknut. If the component still binds, it is too tight and you must start over. If the axle moves back and forth along its axis, it is too loose. Again, you must start over. Keep adjusting until the axle rotates firmly and smoothly in its bearing without binding and without wobbling. Make sure the locknut is on tightly, but not so tightly that you are forced to ruin it in order to remove it. Finally, if you want to practice bearing adjustment, get an old adjustable pedal and put it together a few times. The pedal mechanism is roughly the same as all the bearings on the bike.

## WHEELS, TIRES, AND HUBS

Many publications tell you that the frame is the most important part of your bicycle, but have you ever tried riding a frame without wheels? Wheels are definitely the most important bicycle components. Any bicycle racer or experienced rider will validate this point.

Wheel, and especially tire, problems are the most common. The best rider with the most expensive equipment can get a flat as easily as you can. To reduce the probability of getting flats, keep the following in mind: 1) tires should be properly inflated; 2) never ride over anything — such as curbs, storm sewer grates, pieces of glass — that can damage your tires; 3) when you get a flat, repair it properly so that it will not blow again, at least in the same spot.

Inflate your tires properly. A gas station pump delivers air too quickly and can blow the whole tire right off the rim. Most bicycle dealers have a slower pump at their store, and — if they are good dealers — they usually encourage you to use it. Hand pumps you carry on the bike may not be strong enough to inflate your tires, especially tube-type tires. It seems that to date only the Silca pump, made for sew-up tire inflation, is the single consistently adequate take-along pump. You could use this pump for tire and tube combinations if you replace your tubes — which have American or Schroeder valves — with tubes that have Presta or European valves. Silca pump connections only fit Presta or European valves.

Your best bet for ease of operation and accurate pumping is the old-fashioned, T-handled bicycle pump. Better models have built-in pressure gauges that are very accurate. Those sold by Schwinn and Raleigh dealers are excellent, and the

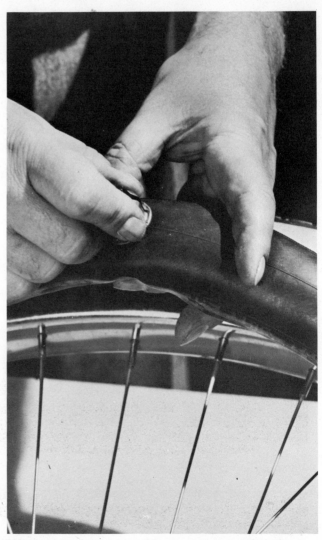

*Most tube patch kits provide a scraper to roughen the rubber for a better bond with the patch.*

Hite pump is quite popular.

Whatever kind of pump you use, never inflate your tire with the valve at six o'clock, as the tube may rupture opposite the valve. Keep the valve either at nine o'clock or three o'clock. In addition, keep the cores of Schroeder valves well tightened, and keep Presta valves locked tightly. A run of slow-leak flats, where no puncture can be found, is often caused by a loose valve core. Core-tightening valve caps are widely available, and should be used on either type of valve. If the valve gets ruined, you cannot inflate the tire.

To remove a tire and tube from the rim, use tire irons. Mechanics often use only one or two irons, but the three that come in sets are often necessary. Start the removal opposite the valve by inserting the spoon-end of the iron under the bead of the tire, being careful not to get the tube between the tire and the iron. Bend the iron all the way back until the other end touches a spoke; then hook the iron onto the spoke. Take another iron, insert the spoon next to the first one, and slide it along under the bead for several inches; then bend it back and hook it. Or, if you can keep on sliding, keep going with the second iron until the whole bead lifts out of the rim. If the second iron is insufficient, use the third one.

If you are only removing the tube and not the tire, pull the tube out, leaving the other bead in the rim. Otherwise, pull the tire off the rest of the way by hand. To put the tire and tube back on, first put some corn starch or talcum powder in the tire to prevent the tube from binding in the tire. Then, get one side of the tire on the rim. Take the tube, insert the valve in the hole in the rim, and stuff the tube — deflated, of course — into the tire and onto the rim. Then, working with your hands only — no tools! — start at the valve and push the bead onto the rim, working in both directions from the valve. The last foot or so opposite the valve is the hardest, but you can do it. You may get frustrated, but never use a tire

*Core-tightening valve caps are widely available and should be used with either Schroeder or Presta valves.*

iron or a screwdriver or anything else to pry it on. If you do, you will pinch the tube and ruin all your effort. Bicycle tire irons are used for removing bicycle tires, not for installing them.

To repair tires and tubes, get a patch kit from any bike or hardware store, Sears, or a gas station; there is no difference in patches. Follow all directions carefully. Put solution only on the tube, not the patch; let it dry first, apply the patch, and press firmly. Then, let it set before inflating. Tires can be repaired from the inside with treated canvas that comes with many patch kits. If your kit does not have any treated canvas, you can use a rubber patch.

To repair a sew-up tire, locate the puncture by partially inflating the tire and running it through a sink full of water until you see bubbles. This procedure works with a tube as well. Mark the bubbling spot with a crayon, and pull back the tape that covers the stitching for three inches or so in both directions from the puncture. Using a small scissors or an Exacto knife, cut the stitching for two inches in either direction from the puncture, being careful not to cut the tire or inner tube. Pull the tube partially out and locate the puncture. Patch as described above, and powder the patched area.

Return the tube to the casing, and push it around to distribute it evenly so that it does not bunch up. Then stitch the tire back up using the needle and linen thread that come in sew-up patch kits, stitching through the old holes. You can also use a darning needle that has been blunted with sandpaper or a file, and button thread or number eighteen nylon upholstery thread. Start stitching from an inch into the old stitching, and overlap the old stitching an inch at the other end of the opening.

An alternate method of stitching is to use two needles, one on either end of the cord; again starting in the old stitching, run one needle through both sides of the opening. Then, with the cord ends evened, do a criss-cross stitch, as if you were tying a shoe, again using the old holes. This method allows you to pull the stitches tight evenly. Stitch the opening closed, being careful not to pierce the tube near the end. Stretch the tire and, using rim cement, put the tape back in place over the stitching.

To mount either a repaired or a new sew-up on the rim, make sure that the rim is perfectly clean. On an old rim, eliminate the old cement with lacquer thinner. Apply new cement to the rim as thinly as possible, consistent with complete coverage. Apply cement to the inside of the tire as well, again thinly, and let the cement set completely. Then, insert the valve through its hole in the rim. Starting at the valve, and using no tools whatever, work the tire onto the rim as far as you can — all the way if possible. If you have difficulty with the last part, take your time and do a little at a time; it will go on the rim (keep telling yourself that). If the valve comes out cocked in its hole, take the whole tire off and start over. Otherwise, the tube can — and probably will — burst at the valve.

Spoke adjustment and wheel building are too important and complicated for full treatment in a general description of bicycle maintenance. In any case, wheel work cannot really be learned from books; experience is the best teacher. But we will give some general tips about bicycle wheels.

The best way to learn to adjust wheels is to watch someone doing it who knows how the job should be done. Ask your mechanic if you can watch him some time. But if you plan to plunge ahead with spoke adjustment, remember this: use a spoke wrench only. Never attempt to adjust a spoke with any other tool; otherwise, you will gouge or round the square portion of the nipple, necessitating its replacement. Remember, too, that spoke nipples are right-hand threaded; this means that when a nipple is at six o'clock on the rim, it tightens counter-clockwise; and when the nipple is at twelve o'clock, it tightens clockwise. Also, when tightening or loosening spokes for adjustment, make only small turns with the wrench; otherwise, you can strip the nipple, tear its threads, or over-torque the spoke.

The other part of the wheel is the hub — the part from which the spokes radiate. To maintain the bearing of the hub you need a cone wrench. On some hubs the dimensions of the front and rear cones are different. Cones usually are made in metric sizes: thirteen, fourteen, fifteen, or sixteen millimeters. The wrenches come in sets of two double-ended wrenches in the four sizes. To overhaul a hub bearing, follow the procedure given in the section on **BEARINGS**. Add to that procedure, however, the fact that there are washers between the locknut and the cones. Remember to include them in the reassembly. Moreover, there are dust caps that cover the bearings; make sure that they are firmly seated as far as they can go.

### BRAKES

About all that can really go wrong with foot brakes is that the hand that holds the torque arm to the left chainstay can loosen or fall off. If it does, tighten or replace it. For handbrakes, sidepull or centerpull, the areas that need maintenance are the brake pads, the cables, the cable casings, and the clearance adjustments.

The material of brake pads, even expensive ones, is — to put it mildly — not very good. Brake pads wear out quickly. Replace them when they wear out, not according to any schedule. You can replace the whole shoe or just the composition insert. In

*On centerpull caliper brakes, the main cable is attached and centered on the short cable via the cable carrier. When properly adjusted, squeezing the brake lever pulls the main cable which causes both pivot arms to press the brake shoes against the wheel rim. Though most enthusiasts prefer centerpulls, they require frequent adjustment.*

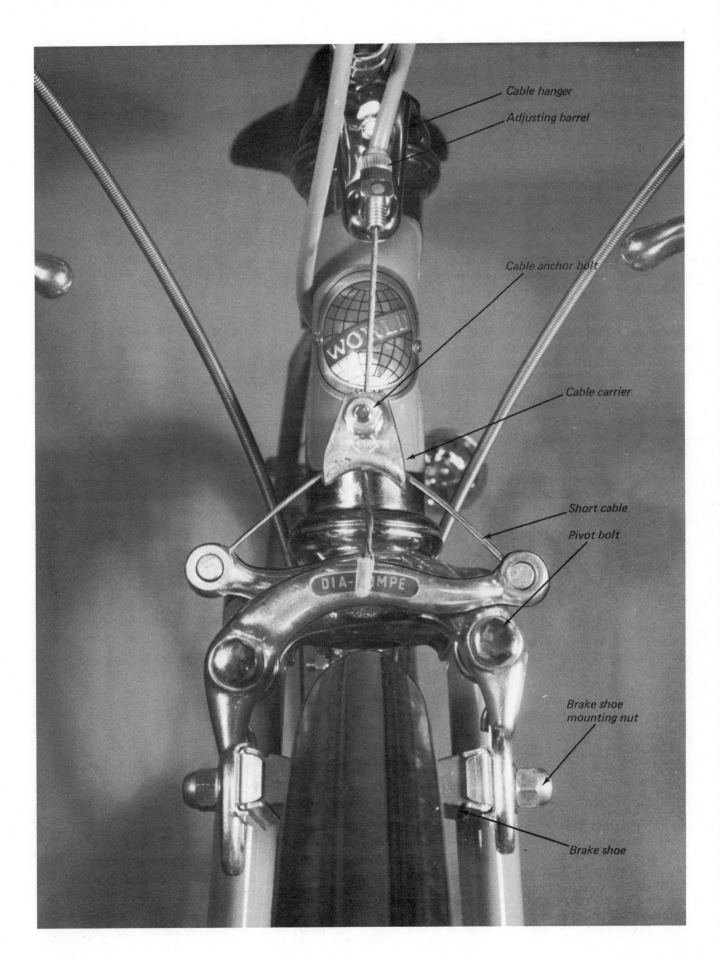

Cable hanger

Adjusting barrel

Cable anchor bolt

Cable carrier

Short cable

Pivot bolt

Brake shoe
mounting nut

Brake shoe

Mounting nuts

Adjusting barrel

Cable

Cable anchor bolt

Brake shoe

Brake shoe mounting nut

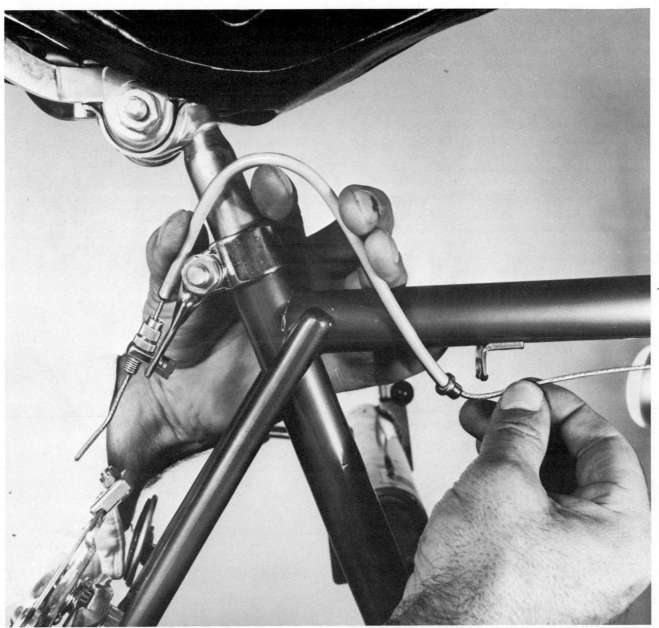

Opposite: On sidepull brakes, the brake cable pulls
one arm and the cable housing pushes the other arm
to bring the brake shoes in contact with wheel rims.

Above: When installing new brake cables, make certain
that they are correctly routed along the bicycle frame.
Cable housings should be firmly seated in their stays.

either case, you must remove the shoe from the
brake arm.

Replace the pad, if that is all that is
necessary. To replace the whole shoe, put it in the
brake arm slot and tighten the nut by hand, with the
shoe at the proper height to grip only the rim, not the
tire or the spokes. Tighten the nut on the shoe with a
wrench, without worrying that tightening swings the
shoe out of position with regard to the rim; get it
tight first. Then with an adjustable wrench adjusted
to the width of the shoe, crank the shoe into the right
angle.

Cables stretch and wear, and the ends fray.

When you replace cables, make sure that you get
brake cables with the proper ball-end size to fit your
levers; specify front or rear when you buy cables
(fronts are shorter than rears). Centerpull brakes also
use yoke cables which sometimes need replacement.
Make sure those ball-ends fit your brake arms.

To replace the long cables, use a wrench to
release the end from the cable clamp nut at the
brake. Note how the ball-end engages in the handle.
Then, pull the cable all the way out through the
casing. Grease the new cable by picking up a dollop
of grease on a piece of cloth, and then pulling the
cable through the grease. Reinsert the cable through

the lever, the casing, and the cable clamp to the brake. Carefully engage the ball-end in the handle fitting, and pull the cable taut. You may soon discover that you need a third hand because you must now squeeze the brake arms to the rim, pull the cable tauter, and tighten the cable clamp nut, all at the same time. If you do not have a friend to perform one of these operations, then get a device called a ''third hand'' that squeezes and holds the brake arms shut while you do the other two things.

Cable casings consist of a strong steel-wire coil, usually covered with cloth or plastic. Nothing is wrong with the casing if this cover is damaged. If the casing gets compressed or kinked, however, replace it. Be sure to replace casings with the same length you remove; too long a casing may cause the cable to bind. Also, when you trim a casing to length, use your side-cutter pliers, and make sure that the coil end does not project into the opening. Cable casings last longer with ferrules on the ends.

Remember, keep the cables well greased, and keep the arm pivots and the levers well lubricated with spray lubricant. Replace the brake pads when they show wear, but even if you do not ride often, change the pads once a season; they get brittle when not used.

## GEARS, GEAR CHANGERS, LEVERS, AND CHAINS

The multiple freewheel clusters on derailleur-equipped bikes always wobble when the wheel is turning and the freewheel does not; this is normal. There is little you can do to your freewheel cluster, except to keep it clean. If a tooth breaks on one of the sprocket wheels, have your dealer replace that sprocket wheel, not the whole cluster. Never use grease on a freewheel, as it may prevent the pawls (the things that make the clicking noise) from engaging. Use solvent to clean, and oil or spray to lubricate.

Three-speed hub-type gear changers, such as those made by Sturmey-Archer and Shimano, have around forty moving and stationary parts. We suggest that you do not try to overhaul one without an instruction manual. You can, however, lubricate the gear-changer hub often with oil through the oil fitting on the barrel.

A ten-speed derailleur system consists of levers (either handlebar, stem, or down-tube type), cables (which have different ball-ends than brake cables), front derailleur (steel or aluminum body, but almost always with a steel chain guide), and rear derailleur (steel or aluminum body with fittings made of steel).

Tighten the pivot bolt of the levers enough so that the cable tension does not pull the lever out of position; conversely, if your bike often slips out of gear, the lever may be loose. Lubricate levers with a spray.

*The shift lever pivot bolts should be kept tightened so that cable tension does not pull the lever out of position. If the derailleur shifts by itself, the lever is too loose.*

Derailleur cables are of a lighter gauge than brake cables and the ball-ends are smaller and shaped differently. The cables must be pulled taut, with no slack, for the derailleurs to function. For most derailleurs, you must know the normal position of the component to make the proper adjustment. For most rear derailleurs, the normal position in which one should pull the cable taut is with the chain on the smallest rear sprocket (high gear).

To adjust cable tautness on front derailleurs, you must determine if the cage rests low and is pulled up (from smaller to larger chainwheel) or vice versa; Campagnolo front derailleurs rest low — Suntour Compe-V rests high. At any rate, pull the cable taut with the device in its resting position. The levers must be in the right position when you pull the cables taut. Handlebar levers must be all the way down; stem and down-tube levers must be all the way forward.

The main adjustments which derailleurs need are setting the limit screws. These limit the side travel of both front and rear chain guides so that the chain cannot be thrown off the gear sprockets. Determine which screw sets the limit for which direction, and set it so that the chain will not come off the gears, even if you pull the lever a little too

*Cables must be kept taut for derailleurs to function. For most rear derailleurs, pull the cable taut with the chain on the smallest rear sprocket (high gear).*

hard. The only other adjustment you may want to make is to the front derailleur chain-guide cage; sometimes the guide takes a long time to move the chain from the small front chainwheel up to the large. You can bend the nose or leading edge of the inside portion of cage toward the chain — that is, toward the right of the bike so that it pushes the chain better. Do the bending with an adjustable wrench, and do it slowly.

If parts of the derailleurs get bent, especially aluminum parts, replace them. A bent part can sometimes be unbent, but unbending can break or put internal stresses on the piece that will cause it to break later. Otherwise, derailleurs need little care except cleaning and lubrication. Again, we prefer the use of spray lubricant for the whole derailleur system. Spray the lever pivots, the cable guides, the pivoting parts of the derailleurs themselves, and the jockey wheels of the rear device.

The chief maintenance of the chain also lies in cleaning and lubricating. Chains rust very easily, even if they are plated. Since a chain picks up more grime than any other part of your bike, clean it more often than you might other parts. Remove the major accumulation of dirt first — using a waterless detergent if need be — then wipe the chain clean, oil

with bicycle oil, and wipe as clean as possible again. You must oil each link; otherwise, you are wasting your time. You could use the spray lubricant here also; it is good for dislodging grit in the links, but you must use the spray more often than you would oil. Oil is a fine lubricant; the trouble with using it for bicycles, however, is that it picks up and holds dirt. Nevertheless, chains seem to function better and more smoothly with the heavier oil than with the lighter spray.

To remove or replace a chain, remember the following: one-speed and three-speed bikes have chains with a master link that can be popped off with a screwdriver. Derailleur chains use no master link, and require a special chain-link tool for assembly and disassembly. All chain tools have a pin that pushes out one of the chain's rivets, thus releasing one link. Be careful with any chain tool not to push the rivet all the way out, because it is difficult to get back in. And never force the issue; if a rivet does not want to come out smoothly or go in smoothly, you are wrong — not the chain. Start over.

The last word here is about derailleur cable ends (though it can apply to brake cable ends as well). The best way to keep them from fraying is to solder them. Clean the cable end thoroughly with

Low gear limit screw

High gear limit screw

Chain guide

Top, facing page: Setting the limit screws is the main derailleur adjustment. Proper adjustment of the low gear
limit screw prevents the chain from being thrown off the
low gear sprockets.

Left, facing page: Setting the high gear limit screw is a
simple operation. The limit screw (usually the top one on
Japanese derailleurs), is adjusted when the chain stays on
its sprocket even if the lever is pulled too far.

Above: The front derailleur's body is usually made of aluminum or steel with a steel chain guide. It has two shift
limit screws (one for each chainwheel) which are adjusted
in the same manner as the rear derailleur limit screws.

Right: Five and 10-speed bicycle chains require a chain
rivet remover for servicing because of their narrow width.
Other chains can be removed by prying off the master link
with a screwdriver.

solvent (lacquer thinner or alcohol) to remove all oil. Twist any loose ends back into a compact bundle. Heat the end with a soldering iron, and apply solder to form a small ball on the end of the cable. Let it cool before you touch it. You can also use a match to heat the cable end sufficiently to receive solder. The match makes the cable look black, but this is only soot and can be wiped off. The solder keeps the cable from raveling. You can purchase the little cable-end caps that look like tiny ballpoint pen caps, but we feel these are useless; either they fall off or fail to prevent a strand of cable from raveling.

## STEERING SYSTEM

The steering system includes the handlebar, the stem, and the headset. A tourist handlebar with grips on the ends should have grips which fit tightly. If the grips are loose, then replace them. You can try coating the bar end with rubber cement or contact cement and replacing the grip while the cement is wet. If — after the cement sets overnight — the grip is still loose, however, then definitely buy new grips.

Drop or racing bars come in a great variety of shapes, some for road racing, track racing, or touring. These bars normally are taped. We recommend the use of cotton adhesive-backed handlebar tape to obtain a sure grip on the bar. You can also use 3/4-inch cotton twill tape (without adhesive), available at most dime stores. Actually, you can use almost any flat, fairly flexible, and fairly substantial material to wrap the handlebar; some people use the

*The handlebar stem requires no maintenance, but it should be replaced at the first sign of cracking.*

leather designed for wrapping the handle of a tennis racket. Rubber and plastic, however, do not provide as good a grip as cloth, especially when wet or greasy.

A double layer of tape makes for a thicker, more comfortable grip. Many riders agree that adding this second layer eliminates hand discomfort. When the tape needs changing, of course, you need only change the top layer. Some riders with large hands might even prefer three layers of tape, but more than

*Tourist style handlebar grips must fit tightly. If the grips are loose, they should be cemented or replaced.*

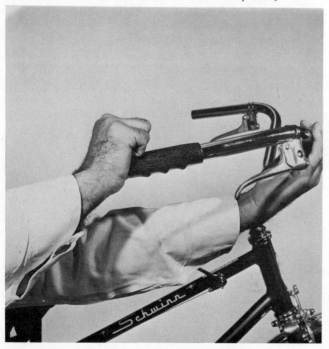

*When replacing or raising the stem, unscrew the stem bolt, tapping it down occasionally with a soft-faced hammer.*

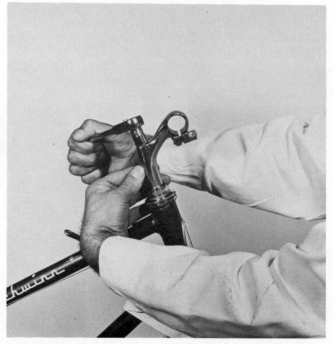

three is not practical; it looks bad and shifts around in warm weather.

Drop bars should be angled properly. Even newly delivered bikes may have the bar set improperly. Most bars on touring and pleasure bikes should be set with the lower hand-grip portion at an angle of ten degrees below horizontal. Change the bar angle by loosening the stem binder bolt, moving the handlebar and tightening the bolt again. Work from one side, and use the bicycle's top tube as a horizontal reference when setting the bar.

Handlebars and stems obviously require no maintenance in themselves, but remember that when a handlebar or stem shows signs of cracking, replace it immediately, especially if it is made of aluminum alloy. An aluminum bar that has been bent in an accident should be unbent very carefully or it may crack. If it cracks, replace it. Never use a handlebar with an outside width greater than the outside width of your shoulders, as this may cause fatigue. If your bar width is presently the same as your shoulder width and you experience fatigue, try a narrower bar.

The stem bolt — which holds the stem in the steering tube of the fork — may have a hex-head top or an Allen wrench slot. In either case, when removing the stem, unscrew the bolt slowly; it will seem to rise out of its hole. Tap it down gently with a soft-faced hammer well before it is all the way out; this releases the truncated cone-shaped nut that wedges itself into the stem's slotted end and expands the stem. Then, remove the stem by rocking it back and forth.

To replace the stem, put the bolt in its hole and screw the wedge nut to hand tightness, but not so tight that it spreads the slotted portion of the stem. Then insert the stem into the steering tube, rock it down into place — at least two inches down into the tube — and tighten slowly and not too much. If your stem bolt has an Allen slot, use nothing but an Allen wrench; do not substitute.

The headset and its bearings require the least attention of all the bearings on the bicycle. To overhaul the headset bearings, follow the procedure given in the section on **BEARINGS**; use grease when overhauling, and do not attempt to lubricate between overhauls or you will get lubricant on your front tire and brake pads. Do an overhaul every second season, whether you think it is needed or not.

If the fork loosens — that is, if it travels up and down in the head tube — then mark the stem with a soft pencil so you know how deep it was in the steering tube. Loosen the stem bolt, loosen the top locknut with a wrench (but do not remove the nut), and adjust the top cup so that there is no longer any fork play. Then tighten the top locknut of the headset slightly. Return the stem to its proper position, and finish tightening the locknut. If there is still play — and there should be none — start over.

## SEAT AND SEAT POST

The seat of a bicycle supports most of the rider's weight. The remarkable thing is that people can sit on a badly adjusted seat for years and blame

*The headset consists of the fork, bearings, top cup, spacing washer, and locknut. Tighten it to stop vertical fork play.*

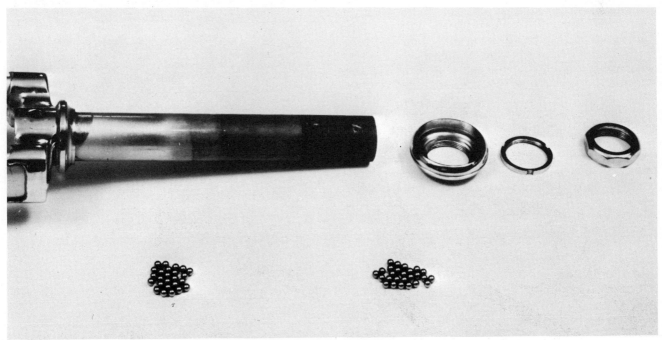

The stresses imposed on the seat post during cycling are enormous. The seat post should be the exact size required by the seat tube, and there should be as much seat post in the tube as sticks out.

the seat for being uncomfortable. In general, the flat portion of the seat, regardless of type, should be level. The usual reason for discomfort is that the nose of the saddle is aimed too far up or down.

The seat post should be the exact size required for your particular seat tube. When reinserting a seat post in the tube, grease it very slightly and wipe away the excess. The seat post should go in the tube as far as it sticks out. If the post is positioned properly, it cannot work its way out, perhaps damaging the seat tube in the process.

If you have a leather saddle, treat it the way you would any other fine leather article; you can clean it periodically with saddle soap and a good shoe polish, or you can use the expensive but excellent Proofide. If you use shoe polish, use the neutral color, and rub it into the underside of the saddle as well as the top. Use Neat's-foot oil if you want to make the saddle more pliable, and a matching analine spirit dye to hide scratches. Light coats of mineral oil or petroleum jelly are also good for the leather. To give the surface of the leather a shiny coat you can use a spray lacquer or Neat-Lac, a lacquer and wax compound specially formulated for leather.

With leather or nylon racing-type saddles keep the tension bolt fairly tight; the saddle should give a little, not be as hard as a rail. A good racing-type saddle should actually be more comfortable than a spring-type saddle; since the racing type is narrower, it should make less contact with the inside of

your thighs. The chief cause of racing-saddle discomfort is overly tight tension and the nose of the saddle pointed upward at too great an angle. Adjust your saddle, and you will sigh with relief.

## CRANK AND PEDAL SYSTEM

The crank system consists of the crank arms, chainwheels, pedals, and bottom bracket. Separate crank arms are either cottered — that is, a solid cotter pin holds the arm on the spindle ends — or cotterless, wherein the crank arms bolt directly to the axle ends. Most cotterless cranks are of high-grade aluminum, and most cottered cranks are of steel.

To remove cottered crank arms, remove the nut on the threaded end of the pin with an adjustable wrench. Then place the hole in the handle end of the wrench over the unthreaded end of the pin. Take a C-clamp with a four-inch jaw, place the movable side over the wrench hole and the immovable side on the threaded end, and twist the clamp closed, squeezing the pin out. Hammering only deforms the pin.

To remove the cotterless cranks, you need a special crank remover; it is a bolt in a threaded bushing that threads into the dust-cap threads in the crank arm. First, loosen the bolt and washer that

The crank system consists of the crank arms, chainwheels, and pedals. The system mounts through the bottom bracket.

push the arm onto the spindle, but do not remove them. Carefully thread in the remover bushing, and then slowly turn the remover counterclockwise. The remover bolt will bear against the concave head of the spindle-end bolt and push the arm right off. A long adjustable wrench makes this job easier.

To replace the arms, make sure that the spindle ends and the corresponding crank-arm slots are clean, rub a film of grease on the spindle arm, and bolt the arms back on. For this you will need a crank installing tool or an appropriate socket wrench. To replace cottered cranks, insert the pin in the crank arm, engaging the slot in the spindle. You may tap it lightly with a soft-faced hammer if it does not go in readily. Put the nut on the threaded end, and make it very tight.

The main things to check on the chainwheels are that the wheels are not bent, that the teeth are not broken or badly worn, and that the bushings or bolts that hold them to the crank arms are tight. The chainwheel should be flat when dismounted from the assembly. It can be straightened in a vise off the bike. On the bike, a minor bend or misalignment can be straightened with an adjustable wrench closed to the thickness of the chainwheel. Grasp the wheel with the wrench and pull it straight, but be careful of the teeth. If teeth are

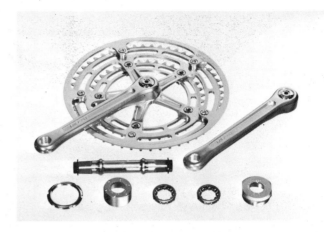

*Better quality bikes have aluminum alloy cotterless cranks and chainwheels. Crank axle bearings are caged.*

broken or badly worn, replace that chainwheel. If your chainset is of an obscure brand, consider upgrading to a reputable brand that has open stock on replacement parts.

To overhaul pedals, follow the general procedures in the section on **BEARINGS**. To tighten or adjust pedal cones, use a long-nose pliers for grasping the flat sides of the cone. Pedals usually require several adjustments because it is hard to hold the cone in place while locking the locknut; hence, the cone often gets tightened with the locknut. Be patient. You will find it easier to tighten the locknut with an inexpensive open-end or box wrench of the appropriate size than with an adjustable wrench.

Pedals are designed to go on one side only. The right pedal is right-hand threaded and is marked with an ''R'' at the threaded end of the spindle. The left pedal is marked ''L,'' and is left-hand threaded; turn it counterclockwise to tighten.

To overhaul bottom brackets, refer once again to the section on **BEARINGS**. The cup on the right side is called the stationary cup. It is left-hand threaded and loosens clockwise. It is tightened securely counterclockwise, and all the adjustments are made from the left side of the bike. There you will find the other cup, with right-handed external threads and the lockring. You need a hook wrench for the lockring. The least expensive model around is part of the multislotted bike wrench available at Raleigh dealers.

Most left-hand cups are adjusted by means of holes engaged by a pin wrench. These wrenches are not always easy to get, and the pins often break. You can adjust these cups using the points of a divider, or you can use the tips of a long-nose pliers if the jaws spread open enough. If the tips of the pliers do not quite fit, they can be ground or filed until they do. In any event, the left cup should be held in place while the lockring is tightened down so that the cup does not tighten more.

*Integral crank arms are found on most inexpensive bicycles and are usually directly joined to the crank axle.*

Low gear limit screw

High gear limit screw

Chain roller

*The rear derailleur is usually made of aluminum or steel with steel fittings. It has two shift limit screws.*

## FRAME AND FRONT FORK

The frame and front fork constitute the foundation of your bicycle. In normal riding, assuming you avoid collisions and riding over high curbs, almost nothing can go wrong with your frame. Even if you have minor spills or drive over short curbs occasionally, not much is likely to happen to the frame. Some mechanics can straighten a frame that has been bent in a collision; but if the tubes crack in bending, the frame should be replaced. On more expensive frames, a tube can often be replaced, but this is not a home remedy.

You can, however, straighten fork ends should they get bent out of parallel. This can be done with a vise or with a long-handled wrench, both to the rear and front fork ends. Fork ends, even the best ones, are fairly malleable; you can bend them without fearing that they will break easily. Bent fork blades or steering columns can also often be straightened, but it is best to leave these frame and fork fixing tasks to skilled hands.

## FINISH AND APPEARANCE

You should not let the paint and chrome on your bike deteriorate. Paint scratches and chips should be covered with touch-up paint, and the

---

### Derailleur Troubleshooting Chart

| PROBLEMS | CAUSES | REPAIRS |
| --- | --- | --- |
| 1. Chain slips off low gear when shifting. | 1. Derailleur low gear adjusting stop is out of adjustment. | 1. Adjust the low gear stop screw so the derailleur cannot force the chain to override the low (big) gear. Since all derailleurs have two adjusting stops, one for the big and one for the small gear, you can determine which screw controls override on which gear by simply screwing one in and determining which override is affected. |
| 2. Chain slips off high (small) gear when shifting. | 2. Derailleur high gear adjusting stop is out of adjustment. | 2. Readjust the high gear stop screw on the derailleur to prevent this chain override. Location of the adjustment screw depends on the make of the derailleur. |
| 3. Chain grinds when shifting gears. | 3. Gear shift lever requires adjustment. | 3. Readjust the gear shift lever so that the chain is moved directly on the gear you selected and is not grinding. |
| 4. Chain slips off gear. | 4. Gear shift lever has loose tension adjustment nut. | 4. The tension adjustment nut is, on most levers, equipped with a "wing" to permit you to tighten it by hand. Rarely, some levers have nuts which must be tightened with a screwdriver. These nuts need frequent tightening, as they tend to work loose as gear shift levers are used. |
| 5. Derailleur cannot shift to low gear. | 5. If the derailleur low gear adjusting stop nut does not need readjusting, then cable has stretched too much to pull the derailleur enough to move the chain onto the low gear. | 5. Loosen the cable clamp nut on the derailleur, and pull the slack cable taut; then retighten the cable locknut. But, first be sure that the chain has been shifted to the high (small) gear. |

## Caliper Brake Troubleshooting Chart

| PROBLEMS | CAUSES | REPAIRS |
|---|---|---|
| **1. Brakes do not stop bicycle.** | 1. a. Worn brake shoes. | 1. a. Replace worn brake shoes. |
| | b. Brake cable has stretched. | b. If bicycle cable has stretched, take up slack by turning the adjusting barrel on the brake yoke counterclockwise about five turns and re-tighten barrel locknut. Brakes should grab when the brake levers are depressed about one-half inch. |
| **2. Brakes squeal when applied.** | 2. Hard foreign object embedded in brake shoe. | 2. Pry out foreign particles with small screwdriver or ice pick. |
| **3. Brakes rub on wheel rim when not applied.** | 3. a. Brake adjusting barrel not set properly. | 3. a. Turn adjusting barrel clockwise to permit brake yolks to open wide enough to move brake shoes away from rim. |
| | b. Brake yokes are unevenly spaced. | b. Even up spacing so brake shoes on both sides of rim are the same distance from the rim, by loosening brake bolt nut behind front fork, or behind rear seat stay center bar. When nut is loose, re-position brake yokes so brake shoes are equidistant from rim, and tighten nut. |
| | c. Wheel rim is out of line. | c. Spin the wheel, put finger near rim and check to see if rim is out of line. No amount of brake yoke adjustment can compensate for badly misaligned rim. Rim must either be straightened professionally or replaced. |

chrome should be polished occasionally with chrome polish, or with toothpaste (yes, toothpaste). Many dealers of well-known bicycles sell factory touch-up paint. If you cannot match colors exactly, it is still better to put on a fair match than to leave the scratches.

Since lacquer will lift an epoxy refinishing coat — even if it has dried and set — never use lacquer over epoxy. Actually, you should test any overcoat on the finish of your bike in an obscure place to make sure the finish will not lift. Whether the bike is lacquered or not, give it a wax coating with a clear liquid wax. Do not use the automobile waxes that dry to a cloudy appearance before you wipe them off; they only accumulate in the crevices and catch dirt.

You might want to refinish the whole frame and fork. Use a good paint stripper and follow directions (be sure to wear rubber gloves). Go down to bare metal; then sand and polish with 120-grit aluminum oxide cloth torn in half-inch strips and used shoe-shine fashion. Give a final wash with alcohol or vinegar; then, roll up newspaper and put a roll through the head tube and one through the bracket. These rolls should fit tightly to keep paint out. At this point you can do one of two things: either prime and paint the frame yourself, or take it to a car painting place and have them prime and paint it for you. Most automobile painting shops have a broad selection of colors, and they do an excellent job.

To do it yourself, prime the surface with

zinc chromate primer, titanium dioxide, or aluminum primer, and let it dry completely. Use spray cans in a well-ventilated, well-lighted area. If your bike has chromed parts, mask them with masking tape and paper. Then use a spray enamel or epoxy enamel, applying two coats and letting the first coat dry overnight. Rub out bumps and runs after the first coat dries with #400 wet-dry sandpaper, and wash the dust away with alcohol before doing the next coat. If you can bear waiting, let it dry a week .

When you put new decals on the bike, it should look as good as new. There is no law, by the way, that says you must put on the same stickers that came with the bike. For the price of the decal, you can convert your bike from a Peugeot to a Schwinn Paramount. Or get some rub-on transfer letters from an art-supply store. Then you can put your own name on the frame. Whatever you do to your frame, refinishing it is certainly cheaper than buying a new frame or a whole new bike, and the frame's new appearance may give you a whole new outlook toward your bike.

## DEVELOPING YOUR EXPERTISE

There are several publications, books, and catalogs that can assist you in becoming an expert in bicycle maintenance. The best all-round magazine — covering riding, new equipment, maintenance, and general cycling news — is "Bicycling!." Bicycle dealers often carry it in their shops. The catalogs from Cyclopedia (in Cadillac, Michigan) and from Wheel Goods (in Minneapolis, Minnesota) list many replacement components, parts of components, and tools that are hard to find.

Of the available books on maintenance, the large (two-volume) and expensive *Schwinn Manual* is far and away the most thorough and comprehensive guide around. *Anybody's Bike Book* by Tom Cuthbertson, is cheaper, a little less thorough, yet very engaging. There are many more books, catalogs, and magazines on the market that will appeal to you and aid you in discovering the pleasures and satisfaction of biking and of fixing bikes.

An even better source of information is other people. Ask experienced riders for advice, and they will usually give it. Ask dealers and mechanics their advice, especially during slow periods, and they will often give it. Seek out bike clubs and organizations. Talk to other riders on the bikeways. The more you ride, the more you will want to try your own maintenance; and the further from home you ride, the more you will need to do your own maintenance. Bicycle riding is great for your health and for the sense of freedom it gives you. And maintenance ability provides you with the sense of satisfaction that you can take care of your bicycle the way it deserves.

## Freewheel Troubleshooting Chart

| PROBLEMS | CAUSES | REPAIRS |
|---|---|---|
| **1. Chain "leaps" or "jumps" off gear.** | 1. Worn gears. | 1. The problem is due to worn gears, which have an "edge" or fish hook at the top of the gear tooth. This edged fish hook picks up the chain and literally throws the chain off the gear. Solution is to replace the freewheel entirely. Freewheel gears are hard steel; much too tough to grind down with home equipment. |
| **2. Pedals turn, but bicycle does not move.** | 2. Freewheel pawls are not closing. | 2. Squirt kerosene or naphtha into the freewheel while spinning the rear wheel to wash away any dirt which may be holding a pawl open. If this does not wash out the dirt particle, remove the freewheel and immerse in kerosene, spinning vigorously to wash out dirt. If freewheel is still malfunctioning, it will have to be discarded and a new one installed. |

Early last spring, someone said, "Let's go ride up a mountain," and 179 bicyclists showed up for the climb. Well, it may not have happened quite that casually, but that is precisely the number of starters who arrived, beginning at 4:00 A.M., at the Fremont Community Center in the Bay area of Northern California for the fourth annual running of the Pedalera Wheelmen's Mt. Hamilton Century Challenge Ride. These riders were not highly trained, superbly conditioned competitive bicycle riders. They were men, women, and children from all walks of life, ranging from grade-school age to senior citizens.

With banks of ominous dark clouds cloaking the upper reaches of the peak, the cyclists set off for a climb of 4600 feet to the Lick Observatory, on the first leg of a tough, 120-mile circuit. Aided by cool weather, most of the riders reached the summit in good shape, mopping a mixture of perspiration and fog from their brows. Then, putting the mountain behind them, they rode into the rolling hills of the back country to find pleasantly mild 50-degree temperatures and wildflowers in bloom. Perhaps it was the flowers that settled the riders into a moderate touring pace; after all, this was not a race but a century run — an intriguing 100-miles-in-one-day test of endurance that is popular with bicycling enthusiasts across the United States. Each year there are some 7000 century runs, plus 2500 half-centuries, and a goodly number of 200-milers.

Apart from the mountainous course, the Pedalera Wheelmen's century is fairly typical. The 90 percent of the starters who completed the course included Ed Delano, age 68 and well known in bicycling circles as "Foxy Grandpa," and Charlie Burns, age 13. Ryan Levy, age 11, completed 90 miles before an accident forced him to retire.

## MENTAL AND PHYSICAL SATISFACTION

As is usual with these events, the consensus was that the ride provided a challenge that was both mentally and physically satisfying. And these are the two big pluses of recreational bicycling that, along with the camaraderie of group outings, motivate the many thousands of Americans who

meet each weekend to ride in club-sponsored century runs, leisurely scenic tours, and picnic outings. The same kind of mental and physical satisfaction motivates those who ride in family groups or even as lone pedalers. For these avid bike riders, the appeal of a two-wheel trip was perhaps best summed up by former Secretary of the Interior Stewart L. Udall, himself a dedicated bicyclist, when he observed: "The bicycle is certainly unique when you recall how it is possible to combine so much health in pursuit of pleasure."

For many, bicycling not only helps keep them physically fit and mentally alert, but also provides therapy for a number of specific ailments,

*Pedaling a bicycle (left) not only takes a rider closer to nature; it also provides a great deal of mental and physical satisfaction.*

*Riders (above, right) skim the shore of Lake Michigan as they traverse Chicago's lakeshore bike path. Cycling is a fine way to lose weight, firm muscles, and have fun.*

# Bicycling And Health
# 7

*Tandem riders enjoy great relaxation and find interesting scenery, making bike riding more fun than other forms of exercise.*

ranging from bad backs to respiratory and cardiovascular problems. A surprisingly large number of those who ride their bicycles regularly — rain or shine, summer or winter — also attribute to regular pedal-pushing such palliative effects as remissions from emphysema, lowered blood pressure, and recoveries from heart attacks. And legions of bicyclists wax enthusiastically about firm, well-toned muscles and the miracle of pounds shed and waistlines trimmed.

Endless is the list of those who endorse the health benefits of bicycling. Claire Cobb, M.D., a 38-year-old Washington, D.C., psychiatrist, turned to bicycling upon the suggestion of her neurologist after she had slipped two cervical discs in an automobile accident. The therapy proved effective. "As long as I do about 60 miles a week," she said, "I don't have pain. If I miss, because of the weather, I suffer."

William Buchele, age 77, completed last year's 12th running of the Tour of the Scioto River Valley, Ohio, a 200-mile, two-day event that is one of the most popular in all of bicycling. This septuagenarian's performance was made all the more remarkable by the fact that he had been so seriously injured the year before that he was in intensive care and given last rites.

Clyde Nitz, who owns a Baltimore printing business, underwent nine hours of open-heart sur-

gery and had a plastic valve implanted to keep him alive. To assist his recovery, he too turned to regular bike riding; he also devoted much of his time to promoting recreational bicycling as a commissioner of physical fitness for the state of Maryland.

Eugene Sloan, author of the definitive book for pedalers, *The Complete Book of Bicycling,* was 43 years old, working at an office job and wondering how best to tone up sagging muscles and melt off some fat, when he consulted a U.S. Olympic bicycle team coach. From then on, bicycling became first an absorbing avocation and then an enjoyable full-time job, as Sloan became internationally known as a bicycling authority and devoted himself to writing and consulting on the subject. Now in his late 50's, he looks at least 10 years younger and remains trim, erect, and vigorous.

Taking his cue from Sloan is Morgan Groves, appointed this year as executive director of the League of American Wheelmen. Writing in the LAW Bulletin, Grove notes; "I realized that my middle age was beginning to spread . . . . My six-year-old son got a bike: and I got a copy of Sloan's book. I was incurably hooked. I joined the Richardson Bicycle Touring Club and plunged headlong into cycling activities, dragging my family with me. The yard went untended, the house unpainted, and other hobbies were ignored."

It seems, then, that it is with some justification that so many bike enthusiasts recommend their favorite sport as a magical panacea for physical and mental ills. Dr. Paul Dudley White, the eminent cardiologist who pulled President Eisenhower through a critical heart attack, was a life-long bicyclist who continued to ride right up to his recent death at 87. He probably would have welcomed the nation's enforced cutback on auto travel, because he believed that automobiles were crippling American hearts. "I'd like to put everybody on bicycles," he said, "not once in a while, but regularly as a routine. It's a good way to prevent heart disease."

Dr. White pointed out that by promoting good circulation, bicycling assists the heart in its work of keeping the blood moving. He noted that it also aids the lungs by improving the tone of the diaphragm and thus permitting the lungs to bring oxygen into the body more easily and to pump carbon dioxide out.

Bicycling aids nerves, Dr. White noted, by improving sleep "and maintaining equanimity and sanity." He also observed that it helps digestion, may protect against peptic ulcer, and can — along with sensible diet — be an adjunct to weight control.

## VALUE OF REGULAR EXERCISE

Dr. White suggested that bicycling (as does any other healthful exercise) "probably contributes to longevity by reducing the amount of high blood pressure, coronary thrombosis, and diabetes that have engulfed us, although the certainty of this," he added, "must be determined by further research."

Hippocrates expressed it succinctly: "That which is used develops, and that which is not used wastes away." The heart is a pump built of muscle, and just like the muscles of the arms and legs, when it is not worked hard enough it gets soft and becomes inefficient. When the heart is strengthened through exercise, the entire body benefits — circulation of blood improves, and lungs, heart, and other organs and muscles also work together more efficiently.

In addition to becoming an important factor in reducing the risk of heart attack, and in giving those who have heart attacks a better chance of survival, regular exercise can produce these additional benefits:

1. Enables people to accomplish more and not tire as easily.
2. Gives an increased zest for living and greater resistance to stress and strain (physical activity produces a good outlet for built-up tensions and helps relax the body).
3. Helps keep weight close to the normal level for height and size (excess weight increases the risk of heart attack).
4. Markedly improves appearance through

Bicycle riding promotes good circulation, and many doctors recommend cycling to strengthen the heart.

better posture and slimmer figure.
5. May help lower high blood cholesterol levels, another risk factor in heart disease.

To be of true and lasting benefit, however, the exercise should be steady and continuous — the infrequent jogger may do more harm than good to his heart. A major reason for recreational bicycling's popularity is that it is more pleasant than many other forms of exercise. Bicycling is fun, and it can provide a change of scenery and can open new vistas for the exercise-seeker, whereas the monotony of jogging or programs involving calisthenics and routine exercises can quickly collapse the best of intentions.

Before you embark upon a program of regular bicycling or other daily physical exercise, however, it is important that you get a checkup and secure your doctor's approval. Only he can tell how much and what type of exercise will be safe and beneficial for you. Usually, he will counsel you to proceed slowly, building gradually to a more strenuous level of exercise.

As we have already noted, for bicycling or any other form of exercise to be a beneficial part of a personal get-fit and stay-fit program, it must be carried out regularly. The awards of the President's Council on Physical Fitness are strong and popular

incentives for regular pedaling. They are designed to recognize individuals over 18 years of age who regularly pursue the sport of their choice. To receive an award in the bicycling division, one must pedal during a period of four months a minimum of 650 miles if five gears or fewer are used, or a minimum of 1000 miles if more than five gears are used. To ensure that this pedaling is carried out regularly, however, the award requirements stipulate that no more than 20 miles in any one day may be credited to the total mileage in the five-plus gear category, and that no more than 13 miles a day may be credited to the cumulative total for those who pedal with five or fewer gears.

A personal log, application form, and other pertinent information are available from: Presidential Sports Award, P.O. Box 129, Radio City Station, New York, New York 10019. Upon completion of the required distance, the bicyclist can send in the log and $3 and receive a certificate, pin, and jacket patch.

The purpose of the program, according to the Council, ''is to get more adults to become active participants in sports, rather than being content with a spectator's role. The Council believes that the physical and mental benefits resulting from vigorous exercise contribute to personal health, appearance and performance.''

This belief is readily shared by Jeannette Westin, a 61-year-old, youthful-looking Vermont grandmother. She became interested in bicycling at age 40 and now cycles a minimum of 10 miles a day to keep physically trim. She rides year around, regardless of weather: during the winter she dons four layers of clothing, hiking boots, and ski socks to pedal her daily stint. She completed the requirements for the Presidential Sports Award in three months instead of the maximum of four.

When the energy crunch hit the United States, a 37-year-old Cleveland, Ohio, welder who spends a great part of his days in a stuffy auto body shop decided that he would help the common cause by leaving his car at home and cycling the nine miles to and from work. After a few weeks of this new routine, he went south on an annual hunting trip and was surprised and pleased to find that, thanks to adding regular exercise to his daily routine, he had got himself in shape for hiking around the countryside without his usual huffing and puffing.

For a 51-year-old Chicago stockbroker, a bicycle ride three or four evenings a week provides a vital escape valve — a chance to chase from his mind the pressures of managing portfolios and the worries of falling stock prices. After his ride he returns home, rejuvenated, to spend time with his family.

## PEDALING AWAY THE POUNDS

A young suburban housewife in Detroit pedals for a different reason. For her, bicycling is a means of practicing ''girth control.'' She finds that using a bicycle for trips to the supermarket, meetings at the school, and neighborhood coffee klatches helps keep her slim and trim.

Of course, this coffee-klatching housewife knows that unless she wants to nullify the weight-

control benefits of her dedicated pedaling, she must resist the temptation of cookies and sweet rolls at those morning neighborhood gatherings.

There is an undeniable correlation between exercise and weight control. If an individual can use restraint and moderation in managing his diet, bicycling can help him lose excess poundage. Scientists point out that by adding to his schedule a mere 30 minutes a day of moderate exercise, an individual can accomplish a weight loss of up to 25 pounds per year — assuming that he does not at the same time increase food intake.

The average adult male burns up between 2400 and 4500 calories a day, depending upon how much exercise he gets. Active persons can push their food intake up to 6000 calories a day without adding an ounce to their weight. A vital key, then, to effective weight control becomes a matter of metabolic arithmetic: keeping energy intake (food) and activity energy output (physical activity) in balance.

''This is true at all ages for both sexes,'' say scientists at the Department of Physiology and Biophysics at the University of Illinois who have studied the relationship between exercise and weight control. ''When the calories consumed in food equal those used to meet the body's needs, weight will remain about the same. When one eats more than this amount, one will put on fat unless physical activity is increased proportionately.''

To apply these principles to bicycling, energy expenditure tables compiled by the researchers indicate that a 150-pound person riding a bicycle at 5½ miles per hour will use up 210 calories per hour. If he pushes up his bicycling speed to 13 miles per hour, his rate of caloric expenditure will more than triple to 660 calories per hour.

With this information and a food calorie chart (available from bookstores, health agencies, and some insurance companies), recreational bicyclists can control weight by balancing caloric intake against expenditures (in pedaling output). Remember, one pound of body fat equals 3500 calories.

What you eat is as important as how much you eat when planning a diet that is complementary to bicycling and other forms of exercise. Pastries, deep-fried foods, chocolate, fatty meats, butter, and dairy products made from whole milk or cream are

rich in saturated fat. Egg yolks, liver, and other organ meats are high in cholesterol. These foods tend to raise the cholesterol level of the blood and encourage the development of atherosclerosis (hardening of the arteries), the forerunner of heart attack and stroke.

A Chicago pathologist, Ralph C. Greene, M.D., who serves on the board of the North Cook County division of the Chicago Heart Association, is an avid spokesman for regular physical activity as an aid to a healthy heart and good overall general health. Dr. Greene offers these dietary suggestions:

1. Substitute cereal, fruit, and/or toast for bacon and eggs and sweet rolls at breakfast (cocoa without cream is acceptable).
2. Substitute skim milk, sherbet, and skim milk cheese for whole milk dairy products.
3. Use soft margarine and polyunsaturated vegetable oils.
4. Trim fat from meat, and avoid gravies and cream sauces when possible.
5. Substitute poultry, fish, and veal entrees for lamb, pork, and beef.
6. Substitute fruit, angel food cake, and gelatin desserts for pastry desserts.
7. Avoid fondues.

*Most children (below and below, right) are naturally energetic; but if adults pass on their sedentary ways, youngsters will grow up deficient in stamina.*

## TO HELP THE CHILDREN

Vanity, though a strong and popular motivation for weight watching, is not the most pressing reason for dietary restraint and regular exercise. The American Heart Association, which recommends bicycling as one of the best exercises for a healthy heart, points to studies which indicate that individuals who are overweight and underactive run a much higher risk of heart attack and have a smaller chance of survival than their slim, active counterparts. It is a somber fact that 55 percent of Americans die from diseases of the heart and blood vessels — in many cases ailments associated with obesity and inactivity.

While many health conditions are inherited genetically, in a sense physical inertia also seems to have become hereditary; for we are passing on our sedentary ways to the generations that follow. The sad fact is that children are caught in the web of ''The Great American Unfitness Crisis.'' A regimen of regular bicycling — as a family activity — can strike at the roots of this malaise; and the sooner it is begun, the healthier the entire family will be.

Today's children, pampered by an automated society, generally get less exercise and are in markedly more inferior physical shape than were their parents and grandparents at a comparable period of life. Physical testing has pointed to deficiencies in children's flexibility and stamina and in the strength of their arms and shoulders. An estimated one-third of American boys and girls were overweight; and 29 percent of 12-year-old boys surveyed were unable to perform a single chin pull-up.

In large measure, this flab fad among the young is fueled by the sedentary nature of their normal life patterns. They are transported to and from school by car or by bus; during the evening they remain indoors, either engrossed in studies or mesmerized by the ubiquitous television set (which holds children in idle captivity for an average of 21 hours a week). Many parents seem content to promote intellectual development to the detriment of physical development.

Dr. Harry J. Johnson, chairman of the medical board of the Life Extension Institute in New York City, says that he has ''no patience'' with inflexible taskmaster parents who urge upon their children a steady diet of study. He wants them to tell their children: ''Forget your books for a while and get out and do something physical.''

Ideally, that ''something physical'' should be riding a bicycle or participating in some other form of recreational activity that is likely to continue beyond the school years. Certainly, such team sports

*Tandem riders in Florida (left and right) soak up the sun while benefiting from the therapeutic effects of cycling. You need not go on a vacation, however, to escape the fatigue of exhausting urban life; a brisk bicycle ride after work does wonders.*

as football and baseball can be a useful part of a youngster's overall physical development program — as well as great fun for many children. But their benefits are limited. Team sports depend on raising enough players to start a game. Often only a handful of would-be competitors make the team. And few youngsters continue such sports beyond graduation. "What I want to promote," says Dr. Johnson, "are the individual pastimes that continue after school days are long gone — the sports that last a lifetime."

## THE FATIGUE FACTOR

Besides promoting good physical health, bicycling can also make a significant contribution to psychological well-being by helping to relieve stress, hypertension, and mental fatigue. Many executives become so fatigued by a high-pressure, tension-filled day in the world of commerce that they feel as though they age about 30 years between the hours of nine and five. In a study of key executives, 43 percent noted fatigue as a major impediment, listing as its causes job pressure, voluminous workload, and increasing age. Studies by geriatric specialists show that fatigue is a significant barrier to a happy and full life among senior citizens. Unanimously, experts recommend vigorous exercise to bring about renewed vigor. After a hard day at the office — or classroom, plant, or laboratory — a brisk evening bicycle ride can be a remarkable restorative.

Psychiatrists attending the 39-bed psychiatric unit at Memorial Hospital, Long Beach, California, readily recognize the therapeutic benefits of bicycling. They prescribe bicycle rides in the park as therapy for mentally disturbed patients. Sociologists point to the bicycle as a great equalizer, noting that bicycling is a form of recreation that adapts itself so readily to group activity that it can be a "vehicle" for helping introverted persons overcome timidity and self-consciousness.

For others, the very appeal of bicycling is it ability to detach them — at least temporarily — from the exhausting grind of urban living. Like the long distance runner, they reach for that rare gem of solitude. John Auerbach, executive director of The Bicycle Institute of America, has described this singular state as a "blessed aloneness," noting that a bicycle affords the chance "to catch up with those private, precious hours we all need to open our minds and refresh our mental outlook, and re-establish a healthy balance of personality."

*There is no reason to discontinue pedaling just because there is snow and ice on the ground. A stationary exercise cycle allows for year-round conditioning.*

Possibly no one puts bicycling time to more productive cerebral use than Dr. Robert Cade, an eminent specialist in renal medicine who frequently rides to and from his job as professor of medicine at the University of Florida College of Medicine and as chief of renal medicine at the J. Hillis Miller Health Center at Gainesville. Dr. Cade not only finds in this pedaling stint a respite from day-to-day administrative problems, but he also uses his bike as a sort of pedal-powered mobile ''think tank,'' applying his time to creative thought as he attacks problems he sees in his professional capacity and in other spheres of life. Among the better-known results of his problem-solving are the inventions of Gatorade (originally designed to replace quickly the salt lost by athletes through sweating), a helmet lined with fluid (being adopted by many pro football teams), and a high-protein orange drink for persons who skip breakfast.

But the time spent pedaling need not yield profound thoughts or earth-shaking formulas in order for bicycling to be mentally beneficial. In fact, psychological attributes of bicycling can be quite elusive. Nonetheless, one man managed to express these in a vivid and poetic fashion. In testimony offered before the District of Columbia city council on regulations relating to bicycling, Nicholas Johnson, Federal Communications Commissioner, noted: "The air feels good on your body. Even the rain feels good. The blood starts moving around and pretty soon it gets to your head and, glory be, your head feels good. You hear things and smell things you never knew were there. You start whistling little original tunes to suit the moment and words start getting caught in the web of poetry of your mind."

### BIKE-A-THONS

As well as advising bicycling as one of the best exercises for a healthy heart, the American Heart Association also encourages bicyclists to ride for the hearts of others in those increasingly popular charity events called "Bike-A-Thons." Typical are the 472 bicyclists who turned out last summer in the Chicago area and, despite pavement-buckling 94-degree heat and strong west winds, pedaled determinedly over a 10-mile course to raise $14,000. Sponsored by the Wheeling (Illinois) Wheelmen Bicycle Club to benefit the Heart Association of North Cook County, the event measured how many times participants could travel over the course, collecting money from sponsors who pledged donations on a per-mile basis. Those who rode 100 miles or more during the 12-hour duration of the Bike-A-Thon were eligible for a League of American Wheelmen century patch. More than qualifying for this award was 16-year-old Ray Rich, who pedaled 174 miles in the 12-hour time limit.

Across the United States, bicyclists are rallying with typical camaraderie to ride for the good of their fellow man as they enter Bike-A-Thons to raise money for such worthy health causes as cancer and mental retardation. "The average person has no conception of how far a reasonably conditioned cyclist can ride in 12 hours of daylight," says Joe Weber, Jr., of the Arkansas Bicycle Club, which helped conduct a fund-raising Bike-A-Thon for the local chapter of the Cystic Fibrosis Research Foundation. "I've ridden a bike for some 55 of my 61 years," said Weber. "It's a strange and wonderful feeling to see the present interest in adult cycling. I hope it holds."

### A WORD OF CAUTION

If your pedaling takes you to where the air is rare — and there is much fine bicycle touring to be

*Tricycling can be just as good for you as bicycling if you have a balance problem. It is the pedaling that counts.*

enjoyed in the high country — there is one key word to remember: "acclimatization." The problem of altitude sickness can present itself when bicyclists, skiers, or hikers ascend from low-lying areas to mountains 9000 feet or higher. It can bring on general lethargy, accompanied perhaps by headache, insomnia, breathlessness, nausea, or loss of appetite.

Altitude sickness can be headed off. A member of Stanford University's medical faculty, who went to the Andes in South America to do extensive research into this condition, suggests that bicyclists bound for high places plan a gradual, leisurely ascent and, after arrival at high altitude, observe a rest period of one or two days.

Aspirin can help relieve minor symptoms, while a physician may be able to prescribe medication for further comfort. Certainly, anyone with health problems — especially if these involve the heart, lungs, or blood pressure — should consult a doctor before embarking on a bike trip into high country. In a rarefied mountain atmosphere, the heart is forced to work harder in order to get oxygen, and one's pulse rate is likely to increase.

Finally, for bicyclists who live in the snow-belt states there really is no reason to discontinue pedaling during the icebound months. With a stationary exercise cycle, one can adjust the tension as he progresses and can accomplish a daily training stint while listening to music, watching television, or reading. Dr. Irvine H. Page, a prominent cardiologist, once noted that his exercise cycle provided 20 minutes a day of "unadulterated, uncluttered reading." "I'm amazed," he said, "at the number of books I'm reading; and I'm getting quite a bit of exercise."

Every time a cyclist ventures out, he takes a calculated risk. In fact, the average American cyclist will fall several times a year. He has about two chances in five of experiencing an accident which causes injury or damage, and one chance in 25 that he will require medical treatment. The chances are less than one in 200 that he will collide with an automobile seriously enough to report it to the police, but these odds alone were enough to cause 1,150 deaths in 1973.

Even accidents that do not involve motor vehicles can be serious. There have been cases in which two bikes hitting head-on have resulted in a rider's death; in fact, 50 to 100 cyclists each year suffer fatal falls, usually the result of a blow to the head.

The bicycle is a natural answer to the environmental, energy, and physical fitness crises — but it is not without its limitations, the chief of which is the rider's safety.

## ACCIDENT STATISTICS AND YOU

According to some experts, bicycling has become more safe, while others claim it has become more perilous. Bicycle sales and fatalities have been rising rapidly for 10 years, and especially fast during the past three years. Whether one cites the number of bikes or the number of fatalities, statistics can be used to support either side of the bicycle-safety argument.

In the past 10 years, the rate of fatalities to 100,000 bicycles-in-use has fluctuated in the tight range of 1.50 to 1.75. By contrast, the rate in 1940 was 10.0. Even though bicycle deaths soared by 30 percent during 1972, a comparable rise in the number of bicycle sales kept the rate-of-fatalities figure stable.

The most significant trend in bike accident statistics pertains to the age groups involved. In 1960, adult and young adult riders accounted for 20 percent of the bicycle casualties; in 1972, this figure rose to 50 percent. Assuming that the number of accidents and the amount of cycling go hand in hand, the soaring accident rate illustrates the dramatic increase in adult bicycle riding as a means of transportation. Interestingly, the percentage of bicycle-automobile accidents resulting in fatalities rises sharply with age; the rate is four times greater for those over 45. than for children under 14. Differences in physiological recuperative powers can explain only part of this disparity; the higher hazard level of adult riding may explain some of the difference.

Accident statistics, however, are compiled from an average over a large number of people and accidents. You and your riding habits determine the actual risk you take. If you ignore safety, you accept these average risks, and take a chance at becoming a statistic. If you follow a few safe-cycling guidelines, you can have many miles of enjoyable and safe riding.

## NEW SAFETY LEGISLATION

Bicycle accidents are not always the fault of the rider. Mishaps sometimes occur because a bicycle is poorly made or badly fitted. The Federal Food and Drug Administration has found the following areas of product deficiency responsible for many bicycle casualties: pedal slippage, brake failure, component failure, lack of lighting and reflectorization, and protruding hardware and other sharp points or edges.

In fact, 17 percent of all bicycle related injuries have been found to be directly caused by mechanical or structural failure. Reacting to these statistics, the Consumer Product Safety Commission has set new standards, which become effective in 1975, for bicycles sold in interstate commerce, except for racing or custom-built bicycles. These standards delineate minimum and maximum limits for a bicycle's structural strength, design, and ease of assembly. Some of the new changes are:

**Reflectors:** Bicycles will have 10 reflectors, which must be able to bounce light back to its source at an angle of at least 40 degrees from the optical axis of the reflector, for a total spread of 80 degrees. The new regulations state that the reflectors must be durable and reflective. Tests and standards are specified. There will be two amber reflectors on each pedal, one large 2x3-inch rectangular reflector facing

*Cyclists find great pleasure riding through a park on a bicycle pathway, where separated from automobile traffic, they can forget about the menace of motor vehicles.*

Bicycle Safety

8

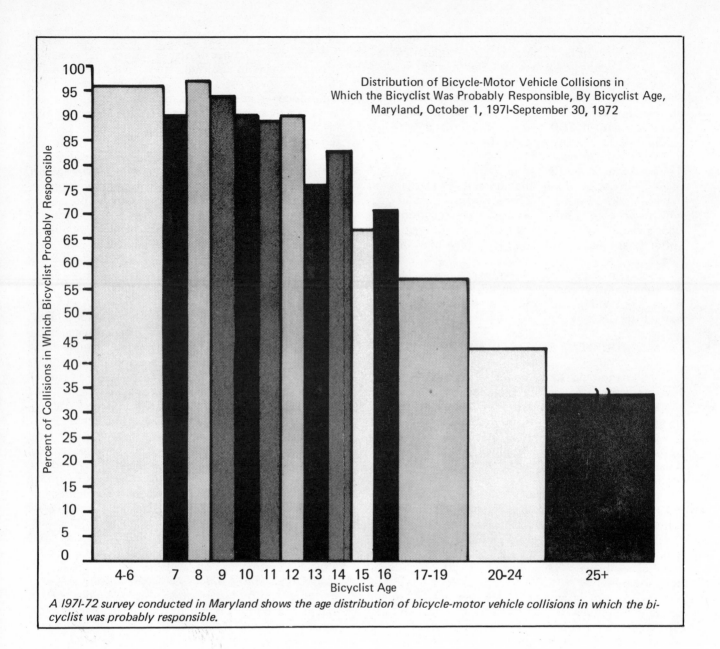

Distribution of Bicycle-Motor Vehicle Collisions in
Which the Bicyclist Was Probably Responsible, By Bicyclist Age,
Maryland, October 1, 1971-September 30, 1972

*A 1971-72 survey conducted in Maryland shows the age distribution of bicycle-motor vehicle collisions in which the bicyclist was probably responsible.*

behind and an identical sized large amber (or white crystal) reflector facing front. Additionally, the bicycle must have amber reflectors attached to the spokes of both wheels and must be visible from each side. New tires with reflecting sidewalls are permitted by the regulations as long as the tires meet new tire specifications.

**Brakes:** Caliper-type brake pads will have their surface area increased from the present dimensions of 1/2x1/2 inches to approximately 3/4x 2 inches. This will nearly double the brake's swept area. The new test procedure for brake compliance is based on the weight of the rider, type of brake system, and the gear ratio of the bike. Specifications include that a 150-pound rider going 15 mph on dry, level pavement must be able to apply 40 pounds of force to the brake lever at a point one inch from its open end, and

come to a complete stop in a distance of 15 feet. There are similar tests for coaster brakes,

**Road Test:** The bicycle must be ridden four miles by a person weighing at least 150 pounds. In the test, there are five passes over a 100 ft. "washboard" roadway. The bicycle must exhibit stable handling, turning, and steering during the test. After the test, the bike and all its components must still be functioning properly.

**Miscellaneous:** There are strength tests for the handlebar stem and seatpost, indicating the minimum depth to which they must be inserted for safe operation.

Projections from the top tube cannot extend more than 3-1/2 inches from the handlebar stem, to avoid the possibility of the rider hitting them in a sudden stop.

**VEHICLE MOVEMENTS BY PROBABLE RESPONSIBILITY IN BICYCLE-MOTOR VEHICLE COLLISIONS IN RELATION TO BICYCLIST AGE, MARYLAND   OCTOBER 1, 1971 – SEPTEMBER 30, 1972**

| Vehicle Movement | Bicyclist Probably Responsible | | | | Motorist Probably Responsible | Total |
| | Bicyclist Age | | | All Bicyclists | | |
| | 4-9 | 10-14 | ≥15 | | | |
|---|---|---|---|---|---|---|
| In motion; other vehicle not in motion | 11(4%) | 22(7%) | 16(13%) | 49(7%) | 7(4%) | 56(6%) |
| Struck other vehicle from behind | 0(0%) | 0(0%) | 1(1%) | 1(0%) | 47(28%) | 48(6%) |
| Intersected other vehicle traveling in same direction | 19(7%) | 55(18%) | 27(22%) | 101(15%) | 19(11%) | 120(14%) |
| Emerged from driveway, alley, parking lot, gas station, etc. | 103(40%) | 70(22%) | 15(12%) | 188(27%) | 8(5%) | 196(23%) |
| Came onto road from lawn or other non-roadway location and intersected other vehicle | 40(16%) | 31(10%) | 7(6%) | 78(11%) | 0(0%) | 78(9%) |
| Ran through stop or yield sign | 50(20%) | 78(25%) | 20(16%) | 149(22%) | 19(11%) | 168(20%) |
| Wrong way on one way street or in lane designated for traffic in opposite direction | 21(8%) | 51(16%) | 31(25%) | 103(15%) | 9(5%) | 112(13%) |
| While making a left turn, collided with oncoming vehicle | 4(2%) | 2(1%) | 3(2%) | 9(1%) | 47(28%) | 56(6%) |
| Unclassified | 7(3%) | 5(2%) | 3(2%) | 15(2%) | 12(7%) | 27(3%) |
| TOTAL | 255(100%) | 314(101%) | 123(99%) | 693(100%) | 168(99%) | 861(100%) |

*The research was conducted by the Insurance Institute for Highway Safety.*

Front wheel forks must pass a loading test.

Spoke guards for derailleur-equipped bikes are required.

Tires must have their recommended inflation pressure molded on the sidewalls and must not burst when inflated to twice that pressure.

Wheels must have a positive axle locking-device to prevent the wheel from falling off.

**Assembly and Packaging:** Shipping cartons for bicycles must state whether the bike inside is subject to CPSC regulations. It must also specify whether the bike requires home assembly. If it does, it must not require anything outside of the capabilities of an "adult of average intelligence." A clear and complete instruction manual must be included, along with a maintenance schedule and required procedures. A list of service centers must also be provided where the buyer can have work on the bicycle performed if he chooses. A list of required tools must be provided outside the box along with a drawing giving the minimum leg length required of the rider.

These are only a few highlights of the dozens of new regulations covering every aspect of a bicycle's design. A full list of the new regulations is available from the Consumer Product Safety Commission, Washington, D.C., 20207.

### FITTING BIKE TO RIDER

Making a bicycle safe, however, is not entirely the responsibility of the manufacturer. Even the best-built bike is unsafe to ride if it is not fitted properly to its rider. Wrong wheel and frame sizes,

*New bicycles should have large amber reflectors on the spokes of both wheels and must be visible from each side.*

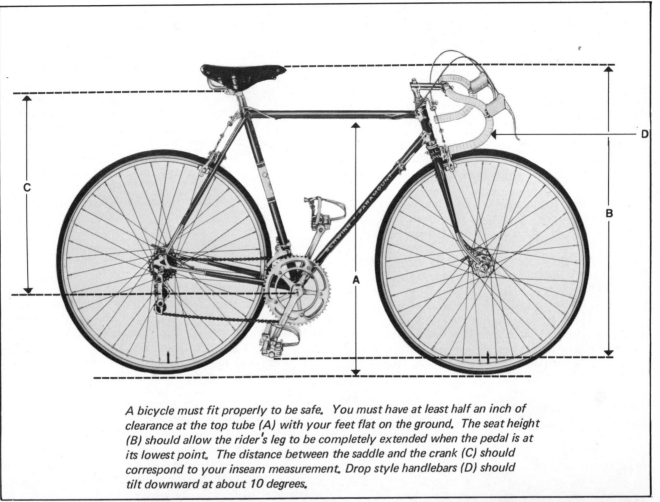

A bicycle must fit properly to be safe. You must have at least half an inch of clearance at the top tube (A) with your feet flat on the ground. The seat height (B) should allow the rider's leg to be completely extended when the pedal is at its lowest point. The distance between the saddle and the crank (C) should correspond to your inseam measurement. Drop style handlebars (D) should tilt downward at about 10 degrees.

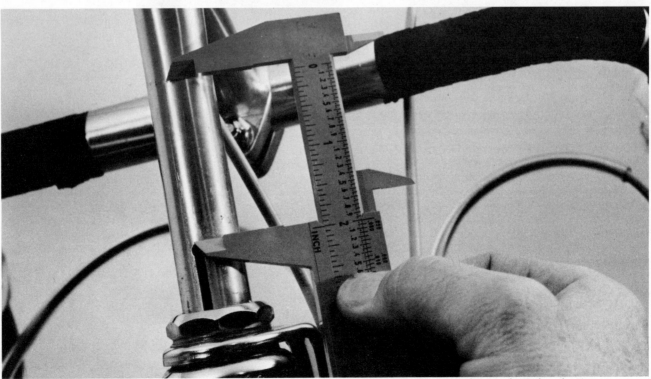

Under new regulations, the stem must have a permanent mark which shows the minimum safe stem insertion depth.

as well as improper settings of saddles and handlebars make riding both difficult and dangerous. As a matter of fact, research indicates that bad fit causes as many accidents as do bike defects and mechanical failures.

A Canadian study found that a child increases his chance of an injury by five times on a bike which is too large, and over three times on a bike which is too small. A bicycle should never be grown into but should be fitted to the present size of the rider. A bike of the correct size will allow the rider to straddle the top bar while standing flatfooted, with one-half to one inch clearance between the rider and the bar. When seated, with one foot on a pedal in the "up" position, the ball of the other foot should reach the ground when the bicycle is tilted just slightly to one side.

A bicycle should also fit its rider's characteristics. This means that there is no one best design of a bicycle, but that there is a design that is best for each person and that person's needs. For example, front and rear handbrakes, properly applied, can stop a bicycle going 15 mph in a five to ten foot shorter distance than can coaster brakes. An inexperienced, weak, or uncoordinated person, however, may not be able to stop by using handbrakes, or worse, may grip the front brake too hard and be pitched over the handlebars. Consequently, young children should use bicycles with coaster brakes, and all inexperienced persons should make judicious use of the front brake, by applying the rear brake first (usually the right hand lever).

The same principle applies to the type of gearing which is selected. For the young child or novice rider, a derailleur gear mechanism is too complex to use and may demand the rider's attention when he or she should be watching traffic. A tangled chain or slipping pedal due to misuse of derailleur gears has caused many accidents and injuries.

Like an automobile, the sportier the design of a bicycle, the more skill is required for safe operation.

## KEEPING YOUR MOUNT SAFE

You should inspect your bicycle periodically for any flaws or faults that could make it less than safe and reliable. The frame and fork assembly should be examined for cracks or bends. You should also check for broken spokes, wheels that wobble or do not spin easily, and less than perfect brakes. Any worn or deformed parts should be replaced promptly.

After any type of fitting adjustment, remember to tighten the appropriate parts securely. A sudden shift in the steering components can lead to instant loss of control. Check wheels, pedals, and grips as well. If the bicycle has caliper brakes, make sure that the rider's hand span is sufficient to operate them. Hand strength should be such that

with the exertion of a moderate amount of force the brake pads grip tightly.

Every cyclist should be aware of routine and continuous maintenance procedures and be able to identify problems that require professional attention.

Tire pressure should be checked regularly. Underinflated tires can make your riding unstable, fatigue you unnecessarily, and may cause damage to your rims. Over-inflation can reduce traction and increase the possibility of a blowout.

The front wheel is held in place by the front wheel nuts, which should be kept tight and checked as a matter of habit. Wheels that are out-of-round can be detected by a thump when coasting or by jerkiness when braking. Naturally, this condition affects brake performance and stability. Wheels wobbling laterally, usually caused by too much play in the bearings, can make control difficult.

Pedals should be kept in good condition and, when needed, be replaced with non-slip reflectorized pedals. Any reflectors on the bicycle should be kept clean, and lights should be visible at least 500 feet in front and 300 feet to the rear.

The importance of stopping is obvious. Caliper brake pads are inexpensive and easy to replace. Since different pad designs have different friction qualities, be sure to get the right ones for your bike. Make certain that the pads make full and complete contact with the rim. Bent rims, loose spokes, or worn wheel bearings prevent firm seating of the pads and reduce your stopping power. The cable adjustment must allow full contact of the pad on the rim before the hand grip touches the handlebar. If your bicycle is equipped with handbrakes, the pivot points on the calipers should be kept well oiled, and binding brake cables should be replaced. Be careful not to get oil on brake pads or wheel rims, as this will make your brakes ineffective.

A 25-pound bike's caliper brakes seem like power brakes in comparison with the coaster brakes of a 40-pound bike. If you have caliper brakes, be sure to apply both front and rear brakes simultaneously. Strong application of the front calipers only can lock the wheel and cause the rider to pitch over the front of the bike, or cause the bike to slip out from under the rider. Another important difference between caliper and coaster brakes is that the caliper type are ineffective when either the pads or the wheels are wet. The thin film of water that forms on the rim can be diminished by riding the brakes lightly.

Among the most important mechanical features on your bike are the steering bearings. They are probably subjected to more road forces than the wheel or crank bearings, and roughness or binding can hamper the bicycle's handling. Make sure your handlebars turn freely. Improper frame alignment can cause veering. If you notice that the front and rear wheels do not ride in the same track when pedaling straight ahead, take your bike to the repair shop.

Many accidents are caused by pantlegs or

*Many universities are constructing extensive bikeway systems to isolate riders from local traffic hazards.*

toes which become trapped in the front sprocket. Either tight pants or a pant guard, and shoes should be worn when riding, and keeping your chain or derailleur guard in place provides necessary insurance. A loose seat is a hazard that can send you sprawling, so keep your seat tight enough to prevent it from rotating or sliding.

## ACCESSORIES FOR SAFETY

A well maintained bicycle is a good foundation for the many accessories which can make your machine safer and more versatile. Lights, front and rear, are a necessity for night riding. Thirty percent of all bicycle fatalities occur at night; this is over 300 per year. To avoid being included in these statistics, you must be visible at night. Reflectors alone are inadequate, particularly on roads with high speed limits. By the time a car's headlights reach your reflectors, at such speeds, it is too late for the driver to react. When choosing between generator driven lights and battery lights, remember that the generator light operates only when the bicycle is moving. Because of this, the battery type light is preferred for

in-town, stop-and-go riding.

Another valuable accessory is the rear-view mirror. When riding in the legal manner, with traffic, a mirror relieves you of glancing back over your shoulder to check traffic. Looking over your shoulder can cause you to veer into traffic or not see a sewer grating or pothole, so the mirror is a valuable safety device. There are two varieties, those that mount on the handlebars and those that clip onto eyeglasses or hat visors. When buying the handlebar mounted type, look for one designed for motorcycles as these mirrors are more rigid and generally of better quality.

The best item for helping others to see you is the "day-glo" colored bicycle safety flag or pennant. These flags make you stand out in traffic, along the highway, and coming over the crest of a hill. Their bright color and waving motion warn approaching motorists of your presence. Other bright clothing, such as a day-glo orange hunting vest, jacket, or hat have similar advantages.

A final safety accessory to consider is a light helmet. About one-third of all severe bicycle injuries are head injuries. Beginners who are having difficulty, as well as stunt riders and racers, should always wear helmets, and commuters and recreational cyclists should consider wearing one.

There are also a few guidelines to follow when transporting things on a bicycle. Wearing a backpack while cycling can be hazardous. A light pack containing a few books or a lunch will cause no problem, but anything heavier than this can upset your balance.

It is better to purchase some carrying device like baskets or a rear carrier which mount directly to the bicycle. Try to keep heavy loads off the front wheel and fork because this can make steering and balancing difficult. Children should be carried only in a passenger seat specially constructed for that purpose. It should be rear mounted and bolted to the bicycle frame with hold-in straps and a foot shield. Generally, these seats are built only for children between the ages of two and five years.

## DEVELOPING CYCLING SKILLS

Maneuverability and stability are complementary yet opposing qualities of a bike; more of one means less of the other. Although, surprisingly, the complete theory behind the stability of the bicycle is not yet known, some forces acting on the front wheel have been identified. These include: gyroscopic, castoring, and center of gravity-lowering torque forces. The most important stability force, however, and the one which is more complicated in

Many bicycle groups are sponsoring "Cycling for Safety" races, designed to make motorists more aware of the increasing number of cyclists using the roadways.

its make-up than all the others, is the driver himself.

Learning to maintain complete control of a moving bicycle at all times is the first step towards safe riding. It is disturbing to discover that 10 percent of the people who responded to a National Safety Council Bicycle Survey stated that they fell down the last day they rode.

For those who are just learning to ride, falling is a common event. This is why a person should learn to ride *away* from traffic, in an empty parking lot, or on a dry, grassy surface away from any obstructions. The best bicycle to use is one that is just a little too small and has a "girl's" frame. Methods vary, but it is a good idea to learn the use of brakes early in the lesson.

The more experienced rider can practice and improve his skill by trying these exercises in an empty parking lot or school playground:

*The "day-glo" bicycle safety flag's bright color and waving motion warn motorists of a bicyclist's presence.*

*When riding in traffic, cyclists should stay to the right. Intersections should be approached with caution; cars turning right often cannot see cyclists to avoid them.*

1. **Balance**
   Comfortably pedal 60 feet within a three-foot wide lane, without leaving that lane and without braking hard or touching your feet to the ground.

2. **Pedaling and Braking**
   Mount the bike, pedal with the balls of your feet on the pedals and parallel to the ground (ankling), and stop the bike, without skidding, 10 feet short of some marked line.

3. **Straight Riding**
   Ride relaxed on a straight line, 100 feet long and only four inches wide, without touching your feet to the ground or riding off the line.

4. **Signaling and Turning**
   Look back over your shoulder to simulate checking for traffic to the rear without wobbling; demonstrate proper signals for turns in both directions with the left hand, and complete the maneuver smoothly with both hands on the bike.

5. **Obstacle Avoidance**
   Demonstrate your ability to judge limited space by alternating right and left zigzags around a series of 10 obstacles in a straight line, each about 5 feet apart. Accomplish this without touching your feet to the ground, braking excessively, sliding the rear wheel, or striking any of the obstacles.

6. **Figure-eight**
   Do a figure-eight, with each circle 20 feet in diameter. Stay in a lane only one foot wide, keeping both hands on the

bike and your feet off the ground. You should not brake during the entire maneuver. Then, try the same figure-eight much more slowly, taking at least 45 seconds, while staying in the one-foot lane.

7. **Turn-around**

   In a 12-foot lane, do a smooth turn-around to the left from the right side, and to the right from the left side, without excessive braking or touching your feet to the ground.

8. **Emergency Turn and Stop**

   From cruising speed, make a 90-degree turn and brake within 12 feet from where the turn started. Be able to do a right and left turn without losing control or touching your feet to the ground before you stop.

   If you ride a bicycle with a derailleur, practice changing gears smoothly and accurately, while keeping your eyes on the road. Never change gears while pedaling hard. Besides damaging the gears, the chain may slip and throw you off balance. When coming to a stop from high gear, you should always downshift to a lower gear before stopping. This allows you to accelerate rapidly with the least amount of wobble. This is an important ability when crossing intersections.

## SAFE RIDING

   Cyclists ride many different styles and sizes of bicycles in many different traffic situations. Every cyclist, therefore, should adopt his or her own code of safe riding habits based on the following factors: personality, physical capabilities, characteristics of the bicycle, and the nature of the majority of riding he or she does. Nevertheless, there are a few basic rules to which all reasonable cyclists should adhere whenever they venture out into traffic.

1. Remember that your bicycle is a vehicle and while driving it you are subject to the rules of the road. Ride with traffic. You may be nervous about traffic behind you at first, but a mirror and experience will help. Suppose you are riding at 15 mph and you happen to collide with a car going about 25 mph; the impact speed is 40 mph if you are going in the opposite direction, but a more merciful 10 mph if you are both going in the same direction.

2. Use hand signals, and remember that the use of the front caliper brake alone can cause problems. Notice that the rear brake is activated from the right side. This allows rear-wheel braking with the right hand when signaling with the left hand. Notice also that the left hand is closest to traffic when the cyclist is riding with traffic and staying on the right. Signals should be terminated in time to complete your turn with both hands on the bars.

Carrying a passenger on a bicycle designed for one rider is dangerous. The added weight and change in center of gravity causes the bicycle to become grossly unstable.

3. Keep your bicycle in good mechanical condition. If your bike is a clunker, do not ride it in the street.

4. Be an attentive and defensive driver. Get in the habit of looking before starting to pedal. Watch for pedestrians, other cyclists, cars, and buses. Try to keep an escape route in mind as you ride. Since traffic is on your left, it is usually better to veer right if you must. Unlike an auto accident, you are better off if you fall free of the bike in a collision.

5. Know the feel of your bike, and practice emergency turns and stops. At 15 mph it takes 20 to 25 feet to stop with either the front brake or rear brake alone, and about 15 feet or less using both brakes. Braking on a downhill slope from 25 mph may take five times these distances or more!

6. Ride in a single file on the street. When passing

*Children in Florida wait for their bicycles to be inspected for safety. Community programs that encourage children to practice bike safety insure their future as healthy cyclists.*

other cyclists, especially children, be prepared for them to wobble as you pass.

7. Wear clothing which is both light and tight. A cyclist needs all the visibility he can get, and floppy clothes can block your vision or get tangled in the spokes.

8. Never carry passengers on your bike. Besides blocking your vision and distracting you, passengers raise the center of gravity and make a bike much more difficult to handle. If you must carry packages, have some sort of handlebar bag or saddlebag in which to put them; always ride your bike with both hands on the handlebars.

9. At night, either light up your bike or do not ride.

There are many other safe cycling tips which you should remember and incorporate into your riding regimen. Be aware of specific hazards which plague cyclists in particular. Watch for sewer gratings which may trap bicycle wheels. Bumps, potholes, mud, loose gravel, and leaves or other obstacles can cause a bicycle to "spill." Bicyclists must be especially careful when avoiding these, because car drivers will not be expecting bicycles to swerve or stop suddenly. Rain affects autos and bicycles alike because the roads become slippery and visibility is reduced. Cyclists with handbrakes should be very careful because any water on the wheel rims or brake pads can more than double the stopping distance. One remedy for this is to ride a short distance with the brakes applied lightly. This will dry them somewhat and some braking power will be regained.

The urban cyclist also should be wary when riding along parked cars. A door opened suddenly, or a car pulling out can cause serious damage and injury. As a defensive rider, you should be constantly

Always look behind and signal when pedaling from a stop at a curb.

Be sure a driver in a car can see you in his rear view mirror and you can see his signals.

Signal a stop with an up-and-down motion of your left hand.

When entering a major road, look for cross traffic, signal, and proceed when safe.

Keep a decent interval and stay in line when stopping in traffic.

Always look behind and signal before turning left in an intersection.

Signal for a left turn well before entering the intersection. Move toward the left when safe.

Stay close to curb when approaching a crosswalk. Signal, slow down, and stop by the curb.

Slow down or stop before entering any intersection where auto cross traffic is a hazard.

Shift to low gear before starting a turn from a stop.

Always ride on the right-hand side, but do not go too close to the curb.

You must stop at every junction with a major road; be sure to signal your intended direction.

*In normal braking, signal with your left hand and keep your right hand on the handlebar.*

*You must be able to straddle the top bar comfortably with both feet flat on the ground.*

*Keep both hands on the handlebar when braking during an emergency situation.*

*Never assume that an intersection is clear; look both ways before crossing.*

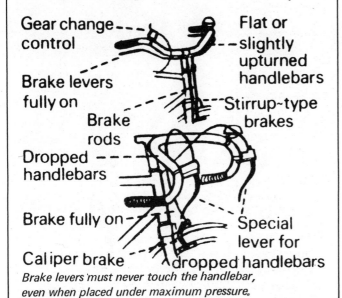

Gear change control

Flat or slightly upturned handlebars

Brake levers fully on

Brake rods

Stirrup-type brakes

Dropped handlebars

Brake fully on

Special lever for dropped handlebars

Caliper brake

*Brake levers must never touch the handlebar, even when placed under maximum pressure.*

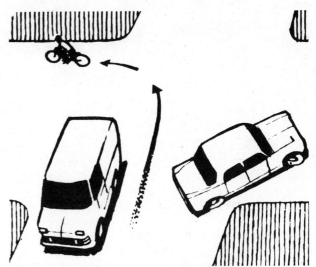

*Turn left with both hands on the handlebar, and proceed only when car traffic is clear.*

*Gladd Co.'s reflective leg bands keep pant legs a safe distance from whirling chainwheels, and when illuminated by car headlights make bikers visible at night.*

alert for evidence that a door is about to open, or that a car is about to pull out. For example, watch for exhaust fumes, the sound of an engine, or the sight of a driver in a parked car. Slow down, and use a bell or horn to signal your presence. Most of all, be *alert.*

Dogs can also create unexpected problems. Most dogs are content to run alongside a cyclist and make a lot of noise, and should be ignored. A particularly persistent dog can be discouraged by dog repellent spray. You should only resort to special measures if there is no traffic and if you are in

complete control of your bicycle. Kicking at a dog is not recommended as it may cause you to lose control.

The best way to avoid these occasional hazards is to plan your route before you ride. If possible, route your ride around the pesky dog, the rows of parked cars, and that left turn at a busy intersection. If you are fortunate enough to have bicycle paths, or even marked bicycle routes in your locality, use them whenever possible. If you are planning to use a route for commuting, ride it first on a weekend and make note of potholes, blind spots, and dangerous intersections. Try to plan your trips for times when traffic is light, and avoid "through" streets, especially if their speed limit is over 35 mph.

When planning rides in rural areas, remember that almost half of all bicycle fatalities occur in rural areas, on the open highway. The high speeds encountered there require you to be constantly alert and on the defensive. A car going 55 mph travels the length of a football field in 1.2 seconds, so you must stay out of its way because it will not be able to get out of yours.

## THE FUTURE OF AMERICAN BICYCLING

In the future, there will be improvements for the bicyclist. By 1980, there will be 200,000 miles of bikeways and bike trails in the United States. On August 13, 1973, the Federal Highway Act of 1973 was signed into law after being passed by both houses of Congress. The act heralded a new era for bicycles. It struck a blow against the philosophy that cars have priority to roadway space; bicycles were recognized as legitimate users of the nation's streets. City planners can no longer design roads for motor traffic, sidewalks for pedestrians, and leave

## BICYCLE SAFETY INFORMATION TEST

Instructions: If the statement below is true, draw a circle around the letter T; if it is false, draw a circle around the letter F. *(Answers on page 85.)*

1. Bicycle drivers should observe and obey all traffic signs, stop and go signals, and other traffic control devices    T F

2. Bicycles should be walked across heavily traveled streets.    T F

3. Bicycle drivers should carry bundles in one hand if the bundles must be carried upon a bicycle.    T F

4. Bicycle drivers should keep to the right when riding in the street.    T F

5. Bicycle drivers should give hand signals before making a turn.    T F

6. Before entering the street from a driveway, sidewalk, or alley, the bicyclist should stop and make sure that the way is clear before proceeding.    T F

7. Pedestrians are required to give the right-of-way to bicyclists driving on the sidewalk.    T F

8. When crossing an intersection a bicyclist should slow down, look left and then right, and proceed quickly if the way is clear.    T F

9. You should not drive in the street until you have learned how to control your bike under all conditions.    T F

10. Bicyclists should avoid driving at night, but if they do, they must have a white light on the front and a red light or reflector on the rear of their bike.    T F

11. It is wise to buy a child's bicycle just a little too big so that he or she can grow into it.    T F

12. When making a left turn at an intersection, it is best to move to the center of the street before turning.    T F

13. Buses are a special danger to cyclists because of their heavy exhaust fumes.    T F

14. A rear-view mirror on a bicycle is used to best advantage when changing lanes.    T F

15. Caliper handbrakes perform better than coaster brakes under wet conditions.    T F

16. There is some advantage for young boys to ride girls' bikes, and adult women to ride male-style bikes.    T F

17. A night cyclist, who makes several stops, is better off with a battery-operated headlight than with a generator type.    T F

18. With caliper brakes, the left hand controls the brake on the rear wheel.    T F

19. A bicyclist must yield the right-of-way even to motor vehicles that disregard traffic signals or signs.    T F

20. The principal dangers of riding with a passenger is that he can easily distract you or block your vision.    T F

*Many communities are constructing bike trails through their recreational areas for the enjoyment of all cyclists.*

tens of millions of cyclists to fend for themselves. Recently, hundreds of bills have been introduced and dozens passed in state legislatures for the design, construction, and maintenance of bike paths!

The steadily increasing number of cyclists and the rising number of bicycle-automobile collisions have indicated the necessity of these bikeways. Washington D.C., like many other large cities, has reported 6,000 bike commuters in good weather. New York City has 10,000 bicyclists in the city park system on a sunny day. Several transportation contests in Atlanta and Boston have revealed that the bicycle can often be faster than other modes of travel during rush hour trips of about five miles in length, to say nothing of fewer parking problems! The environmental pollution problems and now the energy shortage with rising gas prices have further turned the legislators' attention to pathways.

European studies have shown significant decreases in accident rates on streets where bikeways have been physically separated from motor vehicles. American cities that have provided bikeway facilities have found that there are far more users than were contemplated.

There are three different classes of bikeways. One type provides separate right-of-way for the exclusive use of bicycles; intersections where pedestrians and motor traffic are minimal. Another type of bikeway also restricts the right-of-way exclusively for bicycles, but allows a greater number of crossovers for parking, driveways, etc. The last type consists of shared rights-of-way, with signs posted to indicate the bike routes.

Through the continued development and construction of bicycle movement facilities, communities throughout the country can increase their residents' enjoyment of the bicycle as a safe, healthy, and efficient means of transportation and recreation. The full benefits available from bicycling will never be realized, however, until we can substantially reduce the number of people injured in bicycle accidents each year.

# ANSWER SHEET

1. TRUE   A bicycle is considered a vehicle when driven on public streets and highways and is, therefore, subject to applicable rules and regulations pertaining to vehicles.

2. TRUE   Bicyclists should stay as far away from cars as possible. At intersections, the bicycle driver should stop at the curb on the right, permit cars to proceed first, and watch for cars turning right. The best procedure is to walk the bike across the intersection.

3. FALSE   Packages should be carried in a basket or firmly attached to a luggage carrier.

4. TRUE   The "keep to the right" rule applies to pedestrians, boats, and rail traffic as well as to bicycles and motor vehicles. The only exception is in Great Britain, where vehicles still drive on the left.

5. TRUE   Signal well in advance; then get both hands on the handlebars to make your turn.

6. TRUE   Stop and be sure the way is clear.

7. FALSE   Sidewalks are for walkers, not riders. If you must use the sidewalk (never in busy downtown areas), it is best to walk your bike. Always give the pedestrian the right-of-way.

8. TRUE   Unless you are crossing a one-way street, traffic from the left is closer. Therefore look left, then right. Do not hesitate to dismount and walk your bike across.

9. TRUE   A wobbly bicycle driver is a safety hazard. Stay out of traffic until you can ride in a straight line, turn smoothly, brake without swerving, and mount and dismount confidently.

10. TRUE   Put your bike away at dusk; but if you must drive at night, be extra careful. Your bike must be equipped with a white light on the front and red light or reflector on the rear. Reflecting tape on your bike and clothing also helps you to be seen, as does light-colored clothing.

11. FALSE   A bike that is too big is difficult to control. Be sure to buy a bike that fits your child. Buy from a reputable dealer, who will make necessary adjustments and who is equipped to service your child's bike.

12. FALSE   The best way to make a left turn is to stay to the right, cross the intersection, and turn left. Only when there is absolutely no traffic should one attempt a turn from the center of the street.

13. FALSE   Although their heavy fumes are annoying, buses' chief danger is that they pull to the curb at corners, thereby encroaching upon the space that the bicyclist must use.

14. FALSE   A bicyclist must more often contend with cars in his own lane than cars in other lanes. A mirror mounted on handlebars or frame — or even on eye glasses — can save saddle shifting and the anxiety about motor-vehicle activity close behind.

15. FALSE   Wet rims and/or wet pads lead to a "no brake" situation. Riding the brakes lightly can correct the situation. Coaster brakes are internal and are therefore, unaffected by wet weather.

16. TRUE   In the many falls that an inexperienced boy rider takes, he is better off to fall free of the bike than to be entangled by the cross bar. Many serious female cyclists prefer the more rigid and inflexible frame of the male-style bike.

17. TRUE   The generator light operates only while the cyclist is in motion. A battery light shines until the battery expires.

18. FALSE   Braking with the front wheel only may cause the bicycle to slide from under the rider, or cause the rider to pitch over the bike. Since signals should be made with the left hand, the right-hand lever controls the rear brake.

19. FALSE   Cyclists are not legally bound to yield the right-of-way to cars, but obviously they would be smart to do so.

20. FALSE   Although there are many serious dangers involved in carrying passengers, the most serious risk is that a passenger alters the center of gravity, balance, stability, and controllabilty of a bicycle.

The energy crisis may yet prove to be a boon for the bicycle industry. The assumption is that the American public will turn increasingly to bicycles, not only as a recreational vehicle, but also as a practical means of transportation. As gasoline supplies dwindle and prices rise, it is tempting to think that an army of bicycle commuters will develop; such a development certainly would be better for the health and pocketbooks of commuting Americans.

A small number of bicycle riders already have made a practice of riding a bicycle to work, although many cities that have established special provisions for rush-hour bicyclists have been disappointed in the low turnout. America's love affair with the automobile will certainly linger for a long time yet, and the bicycle faces an uphill public relations campaign before its acceptance as more than a diversion for most Americans.

## BICYCLE COMMUTING IN OTHER COUNTRIES

European cities come to mind almost immediately when one suggests bicycle commuting. Pictures of the Netherlands or England or Germany always show thousands of bicyclists in the rush-hour streets. And remember the television coverage when the President visited China? There were thousands of bicyclists throughout the streets and plazas. Can the U.S. imitate the European and Asian experience?

There are significant differences, however, which account for the reasons this experience cannot be duplicated entirely in the U.S. In the first place, the distances between countries in Europe are quite small by comparison: a trip from one European city to another is often just hours away instead of days. Secondly, European suburbs are not the primary residence of most European people. A third difference is that European cities were originally built for the pedestrian rather than for the automobile. Multi-lane freeways are only a recent development in Paris, Cologne, or London.

A final factor concerns economics. For many Europeans, a bicycle is the only economically feasible means of transportation; gasoline costs more than a dollar a gallon. Most Europeans, whom we picture happily riding to work astride a trusty bicycle,

By avoiding loose fitting clothes and by wearing proper shoes and keeping dress shoes at the office, this commuter has successfully adjusted to bicycling requirements.

would gladly trade their bike for a Fiat or Volkswagon.

In contrast, the U.S. bicycle industry — until recently — was considered part of the toy business, and the only adults riding the street were older retired gentlemen on balloon-tired middleweight bicycles. When the U.S. finally did become bicycle conscious, people fell in love with the flashy 10-speed lightweight "racing bike."

All this is not to say that American bicycle commuting is an impossible dream, but rather that one should approach the prospect realistically and practically. With perhaps 80 to 100 million bicycles in the hands of Americans, the potential for large numbers of bicycle commuters is certainly present.

### IS BICYCLE COMMUTING PRACTICAL?

Bicycle commuting is eminently practical if you are in reasonably good health and if you live about 10 miles or less from where you work; bicycle commuting is, in fact, more practical than other forms of transportation. If you live 20 miles from

*As bicycles are recognized as practical transportation vehicles, more and more people will commute to work when the weather permits. Bicycle commuting, already popular in some cities, will certainly increase if fuel is rationed.*

# Bicycle Commuting 9

your place of employment, the bicycle is still quite practical. More than 20 miles (one way) may present some problem for the potential bicycle commuter.

A one-way bicycle trip of 10 miles in the city takes approximately one hour. Mass transportation usually requires longer than an hour when waiting and transferring time are added to the actual traveling time. The same trip by automobile sometimes takes less and sometimes takes more than an hour, depending on the route and the congestion on any given day. A 20-mile bicycle trip can take, at first, anywhere from an hour and a half to two hours. As you gain experience and confidence, this figure can be reduced steadily.

During the past few years, "commuter races" have been staged in a number of cities, pitting a bicyclist against both a car driver and a mass-transit user. The course has usually been less than ten miles and has been run during the rush hour. Predictably, the bicycle rider finished first, followed closely by the driver, with the mass-transit rider trailing far behind.

## CHOOSING A BICYCLE AND ACCESSORIES

Almost any bicycle can be used for commuting. A single-speed coaster-brake bicycle can be

*Whether at a railroad station or on a college campus, massive numbers of parked bikes testify to the steadily increasing popularity of two-wheel commuting.*

pedaled over flat terrain, but the obvious advantages of a 10-speed touring model with drop style handlebars, toe clips and straps apply not only to racing and long distance touring but also to shorter commuter riding as well. A light-weight bike will get you to your destination more quickly, but a heavy one will get you there, if that's what you have.

Insofar as accessories are concerned, some sort of a light is a must for those occasions when you have to ride home in the dark. A generator set with a powerful front beam and a highly visible rear red light has the advantage over a battery-operated light in that a generator light never suffers from battery failure. A rear battery light would be a good idea, however, to provide illumination when you are stopped at an intersection.

Under no circumstances should you attempt a bicycle trip at night without lights. You have to see and be seen to arrive home safely. Street lights may not properly illuminate potholes and other road hazards, and motorists seldom look for vehicles smaller than other cars. Anything you can do to catch the motorist's eye is a definite safety advantage.

Since you may also want to carry an attaché case, lunch, or a loaf of bread, your bicycle should be equipped with some sort of carrier or bag. Stick to the simpler utilitarian models rather than the big bulky baskets or camping bags.

## CHOICE OF ROUTES

Automobile drivers usually have a favorite route from home to work, and as a bicycle commuter, you will also search out the best way to travel to and from your office. If you can take advantage of a bike path, then do so by all means. Most of the time, however, you will have to share the road with motorists, and you may not always be able to avoid heavily traveled traffic arteries. Quiet residential streets may seem to be a good choice, but you will probably find that such a route contains too many stop signs or busy crossings. A route through a factory section may be relatively quiet if you are not traveling through it at the same time that a thousand other workers are entering or leaving it. A commercial street with many shops and stores may be nice in the morning, but intolerable in the afternoon when all the shops are open.

You may, in fact, find that a major traffic artery may be your best bet after all. If parking is prohibited during the rush hours, you may have half of the curb lane all to yourself. Moreover, the stoplights may be timed so that you can breeze through the majority of them. You will also find that you tend to travel between traffic rather than with the bulk of traffic, but be aware of the safety hazards of mixing closely with motor vehicles. If you have a choice between two major routes, pick the one with the lower speed limit. If suburban streets are included in your route, try to pick the streets with paved shoulders and lower speeds.

## ROAD AND TRAFFIC HAZARDS

You are probably familiar enough with the most common traffic hazards, but here are some rules which apply specifically to commuting:

• When you are riding between moving traffic and a line of parked cars, be especially alert for opening car doors and for cars pulling out into traffic. Learn to look ahead and to anticipate potential problems if you see someone sitting in a car or if you see smoke emanating from the exhaust.

• Cars turning right and buses or cars pulling over to the curb present problems in timing. Let the car or bus make the turn or discharge passengers unless you are absolutely sure that you can clear the intersection first.

• Chuckholes, storm grates, and railroad crossings all present special problems to the bicycle commuter. If you cannot avoid such areas, brace yourself on the pedals and handlebars and ease yourself off the saddle to minimize the shock.

• Obey all traffic signs and signals. Motorists assume that you will do what you are supposed to do, but even if you have the right of way, do not argue with a car, truck, or bus — you will lose.

## WHAT TO WEAR

Weather permitting, dress in comfortable sport clothes rather than your business suit and tie. Change clothes at work, and — if at all possible — see if you can find shower facilities. An hour's worth of exercise, a shower, and fresh clothes will make you feel great in the morning. Compare this ideal to the way you feel after being cramped in a car for an hour during heavy rush-hour traffic. In colder weather, of course, dress sensibly, paying special attention to gloves or mittens, warm socks, and head and ear protection. Avoid heavy and bulky clothes which have a tendency to trap perspiration and to make you feel clammy and uncomfortable.

## PARKING AND LOCKING YOUR BICYCLE

If at all possible, try to find a corner of your factory, office, warehouse, or storeroom where you can park your bicycle during the day. Leaving the bicycle outside for eight hours — even with a good lock and chain — is a bit on the dangerous side. Buy the best lock and chain you can afford, and always lock the bicycle even if you leave it unattended just for a minute to buy a loaf of bread. Otherwise, you could find yourself walking home, carrying the most expensive loaf of bread you ever purchased.

## ADVANTAGES OF BICYCLE COMMUTING

A list of the advantages of bicycle commuting sounds very much like the patent-medicine man's pitch. If a significant number of Americans rode bicycles to work regularly, the following changes could be expected: oil consumption would be reduced drastically as would auto-caused air pollution; and congestion would also be reduced, as a bicycle takes up a tenth of the space of a car.

These benefits would seem attractive enough to warrant government action on the establishment of bicycle lanes or paths for commuters. Bicycle paths heretofore usually have been limited to scenic routes which take you back to where you started. What is needed is some sort of provision for bicycle lanes that take people from residential areas to factory or office areas and then back home in the evening.

The rights and responsibilities of bicycle riders should also be recognized and enforced. The bicycle, theoretically, has a right to some of the road, but motorists seem reluctant, at best, to acknowledge this right. On the other hand, some bicycle riders are reluctant to stop at signs and lights that also apply to them. Rights and responsibilities are elementary conditions which must be established clearly before bicycle commuting can grow to any sizable proportion of daily urban traffic.

Bicycle commuting is very economical. Automobile usage costs around 12¢ a mile (a figure determined years before the recent soaring of gas prices). Bicycle usage, on the other hand, entails almost no additional outlay once the bicycle and appropriate accessories have been purchased. Bicycles also eliminate the costly repair of auto components.

Two undeniable advantages of bicycle commuting over driving an automobile are improved health and fitness. Imagine what would happen to you and your friends if you replaced an hour behind the wheel with an hour of pedaling! Cycling to work is a painless and practical way to obtain daily exercise, while actually accomplishing something you must do in any case.

## THE FUTURE OF BICYCLE COMMUTING

In the foreseeable future, the bicycle may prove to be one of the best alternatives for urban travel, especially as the shortage of fuel and the pollution wrought by automotive vehicles put greater pressure on society. In addition, bicycle commuting may become a significant way in which people can acquire a sense of well-being — not simply health. Western culture has created a "romance" with the automobile that has obscured the danger of automotive problems. Perhaps, someday, we will see the bicycle elevated to the status once reserved for the automobile.

## THE FUTURE FOR COMMUTERS

The future appears bright for commuting in urban areas. By the end of 1974, bicycle advocates had prodded some legislatures into adding provisions for bicycle lanes along new highway routes under construction in many widely separated parts of the country. Moreover, many urban areas had either built or were committed to building bicycle routes in cities, and some cities designated lanes of some streets primarily for cyclists.

There are some who feel, unreasonably, that the automobile has priority in moving people in urban areas, and who feel that bicycles interfere with smooth traffic flow. This is nonsense: the law already recognizes that pedestrians have priority in any situation where cars and walkers mix. And as traffic and transportation patterns change, public transportation vehicles are given special consideration in their movement through traffic by those who plan traffic control. In fact, on some streets in some big cities, only public transportation vehicles have access to some streets or lanes, or may turn in certain directions. Some city plans involve excluding private cars from some streets altogether.

All of this indicates that there is certainly room to include the bicycle in schemes for moving people with greater fluidity. There are two aspects of bicycle commuting that are ripe for change: one involves the commuter (or potential commuter) and the other does not. There is not much consumers can do about the state of bicycle design and technology, but, in fact, an improved design for an urban bicycle is required.

Although, as we have said, almost any sort of presently-existing bicycle can be used for commuting, there are problems. Most bikes are too big: big wheels go out of trueness; big bikes take more

space to store at work; big bikes do not stop as quickly as smaller bikes (this is partly a function of brake design). A smaller bike, with low center of gravity, smaller, sturdier wheels, better brakes (such as the new Shimano disc brake), and *all* operations performable without removing one's hands from the handlebars, is required. The industry has not as yet mass produced such a machine, but interested letters to the bicycle manufacturers might inspire them to market such new concepts in bicycle design.

The other aspect of commuting — the one in which the rider/consumer can play a distinct role — is in improving the facilities riders need for daily riding. For commuting to flourish, the cyclist requires better riding conditions in the urban situation, and he needs better lock-up or storage facilities at the work site.

Improving the situation calls for cities to improve the automobile — bicycle mix: the hazards for cyclists are great when bicycles must compete for space and right-of-way. Bicyclists need their own access into the central cities, designated lanes, or better, entire streets where autos are excluded. It would be reasonable to mix bicycles and buses on certain streets, since buses follow predictable lines without trying to occupy the whole street (this situation might improve bus scheduling, also). This bus/bicycle mix might only be necessary during morning and evening rush hours.

The other pressing need for the commuting cyclist is adequate parking in the city: there are simply not enough lamp posts and no-parking sign-posts around for people to lock their bikes to. Public bike racks are one solution and bicycle parking facilities provided by the employer are another. Some garages and parking lots provide space for parking and locking bikes — for a fee. Private and public parking facilities could be encouraged to provide bicycle parking. Everyone who lives or works in a city could be a lot happier if there was encouragement and support for larger numbers of cyclists. There would be fewer automobiles, less pollution, less-crowded buses, a less frantic pace going to and from work, less noise, fewer accidents, and more healthy people with better dispositions.

If we expect that municipal governments and private enterprise accomplish these changes on their own we will be sorely disappointed. Citizens' groups have been successful in bringing about public awareness and improvements in many segments of life in recent years. Improvements in automobiles, air standards, and consumer products are largely the result of concerted efforts by citizens' action groups. Such action is needed for the bicycle rider. If you do not have access to a chapter of the League of American Wheelmen or to an independent cycling club, then you could start a club or seek to use a community organization as a basis for starting a bicyclist's advocacy movement. It is not far-fetched to say that the bicycle might be the physical and social salvation of our cities.

*By the end of the nineteenth century, bicycle commuters dominated traffic along Michigan Avenue in Chicago. Still, crowds of curious bystanders lined the streets.*
*Courtesy of The Chicago Historical Society*

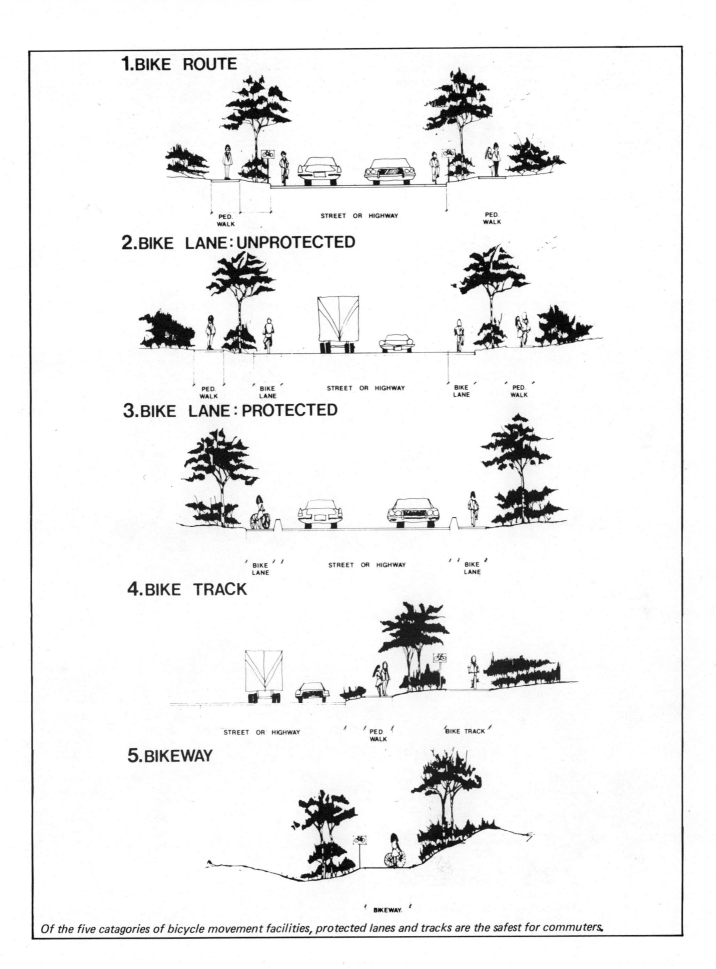

**1. BIKE ROUTE**

PED.
WALK

STREET OR HIGHWAY

PED.
WALK

**2. BIKE LANE : UNPROTECTED**

PED.
WALK

BIKE
LANE

STREET OR HIGHWAY

BIKE
LANE

PED.
WALK

**3. BIKE LANE : PROTECTED**

BIKE
LANE

STREET OR HIGHWAY

BIKE
LANE

**4. BIKE TRACK**

STREET OR HIGHWAY

PED.
WALK

BIKE TRACK

**5. BIKEWAY**

BIKEWAY.

*Of the five catagories of bicycle movement facilities, protected lanes and tracks are the safest for commuters.*

Bicycle racing in the United States is a very grueling, expensive, and largely unrewarding sport. In Europe, bicycling and bicycle racing are a way of life. Professional riders are national heroes and earn considerable amounts of money. Youngsters in Europe idolize bicycle racers as much as children in the U.S. idolize football or baseball stars. To most people in the U.S., bicycle racing is an esoteric sport of little interest. There are no professional riders in the U.S., and there is scant coverage of sanctioned bicycling events in the media. Indeed, U.S. riders are not considered to be on par with those from Europe — they simply do not have the atmosphere or competition of the European scene. (Occasionally someone from the U.S. does well in an international amateur event, but the fact remains that the United States is not a bicycling culture, at least at present). In the U.S., the bicycle is still regarded as a high-class toy, and bicycle racers are considered a little eccentric — like heel-toe walking racers, or tiddly-wink competitors.

Yet to those involved in bicycle racing, it is an engrossing, dedicated vocation. New spectators are amazed to discover that racers can, with equipment not too much different than an ordinary, adult pleasure-riding machine, produce and sustain high speeds for long periods — speeds two or three times faster than non-racers. Spectators discover that racing — road or track — has a tremendous variety of events and is highly strategic and dramatic. Spectators also discover that a cycling race of any type is almost never dull — unlike a baseball game — even if the times are not tremendously fast. One also becomes aware, as he gets familiar with the sport, that the racer, not the machine, wins the race. Unlike auto racing, bicycle racing focuses on striving and winning, rather than a flirtation with death.

## AMATEUR BICYCLE LEAGUE OF AMERICA

Outside of charity races or publicity races, the only "official" racing in the United States is amateur and is sanctioned by the Amateur Bicycle League of America (ABLA, or just ABL). To join the ABL, a man or woman joins an accredited local club. All amateurs in sanctioned events hold an ABL

Racers in Ohio's Tour of Kettering are among the best in the country. Most bicycle races are local events, but the big competitions draw the country's top contenders.

license that bears their picture and signature, their club affiliation, and the usual set of stringent regulations, along with an authorization to race abroad.

The ABL maintains a system that classifies riders by age. There are Midgets, Intermediates (between the ages of 13 and 15), Juniors, and Seniors (18 and up). The Senior class divides further into A, B, and C groups; you start in Senior C and remain there until you win a certain number of races, and then you move up. There have been efforts to organize a Veteran class, and some localities have this category in their racing programs; but Veteran and Senior B and C do not compete in the nationals.

Except for the nationals, almost all races within the ABL structure are conducted by individual clubs. These are administered by state or regional associations, which make up the yearly racing schedules and in other ways keep the structure regulated.

Some state associations will program a series of training races before the actual season begins; then the clubs take over, promoting, distributing entry blanks, making the rounds of potential prize donors, soliciting help from poster designers and local news media, and cajoling municipal bodies

*Instinct dominates the racer's mind as he goes into a final sprint to cross the finish line first. The brain ignores the body's messages of pain and fatigue; instead it compels the legs to move faster.*

# Bicycle Racing
# 10

*The most familiar road racing event is the massed-start race in which a group of riders start together, pedal for a predetermined distance with the first finisher declared the winner. Often, only half can finish the race.*

for permission for racing dates and places.

Though the system sounds loose, it is in fact imbued with tremendous survival powers. A given club's enthusiasm may wax and wane, but the more energetic members can always form another club, apply for an ABL charter, attract racing members, and take up the baton. Should a state association break apart, the neighboring state will usually extend its activities and become regional. Because there are always individuals who are willing to put out the effort, for the sake of something their neighbors may never understand, racing goes on.

## POPULAR U.S. RACES

The circuit is national, in theory and to some extent in practice. Any ABL card holder can enter any race. The vagaries of job, school, or bank account may shift a rider back and forth across the country, his 25-pound machine strapped to his car or boxed up on an airplane, train, or bus. In practice, the eastern, midwestern, and western riders tend to oscillate around the schedules in their own areas; but California riders have been turning up increasingly at Northbrook and farther east.

*Off through the heart of town, racers must be ready to surmount bad weather, road conditions, and other calamities that they may encounter during a long race, never deviating from their one purpose: winning.*

The bigger races attract them all. The bulk of racing is based on local events, some confined to a single club's racing team. And the calendar of major races is never the same from year to year. Yet a general pattern persists.

The Kugler-Anderson Memorial Race, held in Somerville, New Jersey, has been a road-racing institution since 1940 (it is named for its first two winners, both killed in World War II). In St. Louis, the George Wuchter Memorial is as prominent (Wuchter was hit by a car in training). There are others. The venerable Elgin-Chicago race is no longer

run ("It was becoming too popular," the authorities said, "and had to stop."), but the recently conceived annual Criterium of Old Town, in Chicago's Lincoln Park, has gained in popularity. The Tour of Kettering, in Ohio, and the Tour of New France, in Canada, attract a top-notch class of riders.

In California and the remainder of the West, racing activity is constant, though at times unpredictable. Western races are inclined toward track events. But in 1971, California hosted an event rarely seen in the United States — a multiday road race, run in stages, on the model of the Tour de

France. Races of this type are run over courses that wind for hundreds of miles across varying terrain, calling for actual changes of machines in some cases, if the rider hopes to beat all the combinations of difficulty on the course.

There are events in track racing that are analogous to multiday road races. But the restricted number of locations cuts down the possibilities for holding many races comparable to say, Northbrook's Midwest Sprints, which were renamed the Wastyn

Sprints following the death, several years ago, of Oscar Wastyn, the last of his generation of master frame builders in the United States.

## THE "B.A.R." RATING

Road racing is a sport that demands both technical and creative skills in all kinds of weather and requires stamina over hundreds of miles of rugged terrain. The "Best All Round" (BAR) rating,

*Long-distance racers must constantly replenish their energy supplies as they pedal. Energy must be replaced as it is lost; by the time hunger pangs hit, it is too late.*

maintained in conjunction with the ABL, is awarded to the most skilled of the road racers. Certain major races, carefully balanced for degree and variety of difficulty, award their high place finishers points toward the BAR rating.

Regionalized so as not to be biased in favor of the rider with the most plane tickets, the rating is a sought-after and respected prize, to be attained apart from victory in the nationals or a place on the Olympic team. There are those who feel the BAR means just as much as the national ratings, if not more. Others, however, feel differently. They disdain the road races, and prefer instead the subtle skills, lightning reflexes, and outbursts of unbearable energy-expenditure of track riding.

## TRACK RACES

Track racing provides a wide variety of events. A match race is a short-distance event with

*In a final burst of exertion, speeding racers force their bodies and machines toward the finish line, refusing to give up what it has taken them months to achieve.*

no time limit. The only object is to cross the finish line first. Track riders in a match race do not care how long it takes to win, as long as the opponent loses. But the track is short, and the man who commits himself too soon may get out of position just long enough for the other fellow to drop down off the high bank and flash by him.

One of the most excruciating sights in the racing world is to see two match-race riders standing still on their bicycles at the sound of the starter's gun, rocking back and forth on their machines, superficially motionless while perfectly balanced, eyeing each other, every muscle quivering, faces slowly turning red with strain, sweat splashing from their bodies, down over crank brackets, and onto the track in a pool.

More often, the match-race riders swoop and dart like hawks up and down the banks, then slow down, then hang there looking, then break into a sprint for the finish, trying to catch the opponent off guard. The track announcers call it ''cat and mouse,''

but it is more serious than that.

In pursuit racing, individuals, or teams, start out on opposite sides of the track oval. The first rider to catch the other wins. Team pursuit is especially exciting. In the miss-and-out event, the last man on each lap is out, until only two remain; they then sprint for the finish. In solo time trials, one person races against the clock .

## TO BE A RACER

Finding out about a bike race can be as easy as getting to your nearest bicycle shop. The bike shops have schedules on their walls, and the clerks will be glad to give you directions. Then you have to do what the racers do — get up for an 8 AM start time that may be miles away, or hurry through dinner to get to the track on a work night.

Getting to be a racer is no longer the catch-as-catch-can thing it used to be. In addition to the growing number of training programs under increas-

*A track racer does not accelerate to top speed immediately. Using strategy, he attempts to outsmart and outmaneuver his opponent.*

ingly knowledgeable racing directors, a number of universities have initiated bike-racing programs. Now, a woman also can have a decent coach and someone with whom to train.

A racer keeps at it. If you are a racer, you do not have much time to develop other interests or a demanding career. You cannot swim, because that is one of the many other sports that distorts your muscles away from the cycling ideal. Running or weight lifting is good, however. You must be disciplined. You cannot overeat certain foods; what you need are carbohydrates. You also should include green vegetables in your diet for their minerals to prevent muscle cramps. You should not smoke or drink, and you should not injure your hands or legs with contact sports. Man or woman, you must shave your legs to improve your aerodynamic surface and to make leg injuries incurred while racing easier to treat.

Mostly, you have to train yourself until your body is in that ideal aerodynamic shape, head down, shoulders up but lower than the back, elbows in, legs perfectly parallel, buttocks down on the saddle, weight almost evenly distributed on both wheels. Your eyes focus on that long gray line. They began to focus that way the day you woke in the middle of the night and realized that in a few hours you would compete in your first bike race and wondered how it would be.

## THE RACE BEGINS

The racer looks glamorous to the spectators as he steps to the starting line with his polished machine. The racer adjusts his helmet and gloves, tucks his colored jersey into his regulation tights, slips his cleated shoes into the two clips and makes the straps tight. In few sports does the person and equipment become so closely intermingled. Jim Hill, the late auto racer, once said he put his body, not his machine, through the race course: For an auto racer, this is only a metaphor, but not for the bicycle racer. Sustained racing is both physically and mentally exhausting, even when the racer is at the peak of his training. In a race, the machine becomes increasingly delicate and sensitive as miles and the hours pass — taking on an almost sentient responsiveness — while the racer becomes more and more mechanical.

The brain seems to separate from body and to narrow the focus of its attention. It must, for if it ceases to flog the body onward without heed to routine messages of pain and need, the racer will suffer something drastic. He will lose the race; but even worse than that, he will fail at a task for which he has spent so much time and effort and suffering, preparing himself in a mood of sometimes ascetic devotion.

Riders get hurt in races. But rarely do racers suffer as much from physical incapacitation as they do from the psychological wrenches of not being able to race.

Almost everyone who rides a bike likes to race somewhat, whether it be the kids on their bikes in front of the drugstore, or polite jockeying on the bicycle path, or the friendly ride in the country where it becomes clear that the object is to get to the next crossroad first. How, then, is the bicycle racer's experience qualitatively different from that of the bicycle rider who competes more casually?

The difference lies between the kind of person who rides and the kind who races. The people who jockey around on their recreational bikes cannot know how it feels to ride 150 miles in six continuous hours in the hot sun, each racer an integral part of a pack of his own kind, and yet each caught up in the solitude of his own drive and determination and discipline. The people who stand and watch the racers going by are perhaps thinking of the last time they commuted to work five minutes faster by "giving it a little something extra." Many of them cheer for the color of the rider's jersey or for the racing machine whose boldly splashed brand name is

*As racers come down the stretch, their months of training and dedication are revealed in the piston-like pumping of their legs, numb to everything but victory.*

the same as that on their own three-speed or 10-speed.

## THE RACER'S MIND AND BODY

The racer, meanwhile, has become mechanical and almost surreal. His body works like an engine, relentlessly measuring out the revolutions per minute. His eyes remain fixed on the line under his front tire.

Only if another line begins to converge on it does the racer's mind react. He maneuvers, as if by instinct, within the narrow limits of his chosen course, to move his own line away from the intruding one. If the limit is encroached, he shouts, ''Track! Track!'' never realizing that he is speaking. Before and after a race, he speaks a civilized language. During the race, one of the few things he continues to realize is that if the lines converge, his race is over — the program he has plotted out in his mind will not be completed.

He is one with the bicycle frame, the meticulously chosen tire weight and tire tread, the delicately filed-down stem that gets him a millimeter lower over the headset bearing cup. He may be a man or woman, but he is both a technician, and a racer. He has spent countless hours seeing himself completing the course.

One favorite racing story relates how a racer felt that he knew the course of a western mountain slope. He took a track bike to the top, pushed off without locking in his feet, and then raised his legs clear of the cranks. A track bike has no adjustable gears and no brakes. It has no freewheel, either; rear wheel and crankset go around together, mated by the chain. If he dropped his feet, the whirling pedals would break them. If he didn't make the switchbacks down the slope, he would crash.

A few moments later, he had completed his program. He also went on to win the race.

There is no accounting for this anecdote unless you have seen racers come into a downhill-gravel hairpin-turn, on a wet day and have seen the look in their eyes. They are not crazy, and few of them want to die. But very few of them are willing to interrupt the program.

## THE RACER'S MODES

The racer goes round and round, head down, feet flexing monotonously, sucking air through his nose. Meanwhile, inside him the monitors are speaking:

*With the frequency of bicycle races increasing and the prize lists growing, bicycle racing is growing in popularity, as Americans become interested in the sport long enjoyed and encouraged on every level by Europeans.*

*Bicycle racing is a supreme physical test. Each cyclist attempts to best his competitors, yet is caught up in a total, solitary, personal effort.*

My body hurts. Something is moving in on the left. The surface feels wrong. I have left my chosen line. The body hurts. The body is low on fuel.

The spectator watching the race sees that the fiercely spinning front wheel of one bicycle has met the whirling rear of another machine. In a twinkling, two bicycles and riders have shot away from each other like a dynamited eight-day clock, somersaulting through the air, rebounding from other machines until a whole pack goes down, hands still gripping bars, feet ripping free of pedals even though the shoe cleats were locked tight with straps.

Now the riders try to remount, instantly. You can see them — spokes ripped out with an elfin tinkle of pedal-end against taut steel, wheels wobbling as if in a clown act, one foot bare, jersey and shorts in shreds, handlebars twisted out of shape. A few yards down the road they fall and get up again, pulling angrily at the flat-tired machine, trying to bring it back to life.

They stand over the broken metal alongside

*Crossing the finish line first, an exhausted racer momentarily forgets his hours of pain and exhaustion and exults in his victory.*

the track, totally oblivious of their injuries. It is significant that they stay with the machine if it will not roll; they do not ever show an impulse to begin running after the disappearing pack. But strangely enough, they sometimes do get back in the race.

Some who come to the finish line dimly begin to realize that the bike is not their own. Groping back, they recall that someone with a bike was standing nearby when their own broke down. Sometimes voluntarily — occasionally by main force — this bicycle came into their hands. Now they remember. They look around in bemusement. Who will come to claim this machine? Who has mine?

Others have acquired parts in mid-race,

sometimes the same way, sometimes from a support truck. What is this unfamiliar wheel I have grabbed and locked in place when my own failed? They stare down at the hybrid bike which bears little resemblance to the equipment with which they trained so fanatically.

Racers in a race have modes within their programs. There is the position-changing mode as they realize their pace has become different from that of the surrounding riders. Special mental circuits cut through the prevailing haze, and they drift back carefully through the pack and out, or suddenly break forward, out through the balloon of moving air in which they all have been proceeding. With the

*Long months of proper diet, demanding exercise, no smoking, and ascetic self-discipline pay off at the final lap where the leader must pull away from the pack.*

position change accomplished, the mode cuts out, and the rider returns to the gray line under his face as he leans out over the bars. All the large remainder of the race is constant: the body hurts.

There is the feeding mode: Fuel is low. How far is it to the support man standing beside the road with the extended bag of fruit or the plastic bottle? Now. Reach. Take. Gulp down the tea steaming with honey, the secret mixture of orange juice and raw eggs. Or miss; or worse, near-miss. Feel the fuel bouncing at your fingertips, knowing that if you concentrate on that long enough to shift to a firm grip, you will lose track of the race. Better to utter an appalling howl of total deprivation and dash the bottle

aside, before it drops into the machine and disrupts the program. An observer might have said that the food was acceptably available. But the racer cannot violate the mode, which is set within his system in every detail, just as the various modes are set within the program, free to rotate but as rigidly positioned as bearings in a cage.

The observer thinks: Why is a grown person acting like a baby?

The racer thinks: Something is moving in on the right. The surface is good. The body is failing.

Later, after the race, the racer will wander aimlessly beside the road, muttering to himself, perhaps waiting for his soul to catch up.

## THE BICYCLE RACER

Racers, in their lives off the bicycle, have modes too. In the United States particularly, where they have to have jobs, or go to school, they frequently converse and interact with people.

Most of them are pleasant individuals, who can trot out as much mundane discourse as one might wish — making allowances for the fact that they rarely seem to concentrate very hard when they speak to you.

But the simple fact is that you cannot maintain 25-miles per hour (mph) for six hours every few days with a normal human body. The topflight racer rides 100 training miles or so every day, head down, feet revolving at 90 rpm when he is just idling along, at 120 to 150 rpm in a sprint. You see him passing cars out on the back country roads at six in the morning and nine at night. He can do 60 mph or better in a sprint downhill. Most racers who are seriously injured, collide with cars and trucks while training.

People in a race divide into three groups: those trying to find out if they will be racers, those who race, and those who consistently beat other racers. The latter group is an elite so small, that if they all took part in a single event, an observer would think it a skimpy turnout. He would soon notice, however, that there was something different, something very special, about the event.

Organized racing divides into two main types: road racing and track racing. Track-racing machines are superficially simple, but the rules of the various kinds of track races can drive the uninitiated spectator into a fit of bewilderment. Track racing is all done within easy eyeshot of the spectator. Road-racing machines bristle with apparatus — brakes, cogs, derailleurs, spare tires, pumps — but the rules are easy to follow. Everyone sets off at a common start line, runs the predetermined distance if he can, and first one back across the line is a winner. Road racing is strung out — there may be a race going by your window, and you may not realize it.

## TRACKS AND COURSES

If you would like to watch a track-racing program, you have a very limited number of tracks from which to choose. A bike track is difficult to build; it is a sharply banked smooth oval that takes up considerable real estate and has almost no other

*As bicycling grows in popularity, more American businesses are lending their support to cycling events.*

use. In the eastern United States, there is an aging track in Kissena Park, near the World's Fair site in Queens, New York City. In the Midwest, there is a track in St. Louis; an excellent one at Northbrook, just north of Chicago; and a good one at Kenosha, Wisconsin, about midway between Chicago and Milwaukee.

Milwaukee's Brown Deer Park has a little-known track that the Milwaukee clubs are trying to reactivate as a site for more than just sporadic attractions.

There is a concrete track in Detroit's Chandler Park that was barely finished in time for the 1969 national championships.

In the West, there are tracks at Encino and San Jose, both in California.

Some of these tracks are rarely used, for one reason or another, and rumors of abandonment sweep periodically through the racing crowd. The champion of them all in this respect is a track on privately owned land in Portland, Oregon. It was built for the 1964 Olympic trials and was the site of the 1970 Nationals. Other than these two major events, the track is rarely used for organized races. It is universally considered to be a very good track, but there are not many racers in Oregon.

Each year, the courses at which the U.S. national road-racing and track-racing championships are held are crowded with riders. The races run on up through their different classes, until one rider in each class gets to pull on a fresh star-spangled jersey. With it he earns the right to wear No. 1 in every race next year. As a courtesy, too, national champions do not have to pay entry fees at sanctioned races.

In bicycle racing, the blend of physical and mental discipline and the man-powered machine are put to the ultimate challenge; some uncertainty is always involved in this blend: Will the machine perform to its design capacities, and respond instantly to its riders commands? And even more difficult to predict is the question: Can the rider's performance match that of his machine?

*Road races can stretch out over enormous distances, but when the finish line gets close, riders fight head-to-head for first place. Some road races cover hundreds of miles and last several days.*

*Although the mounts are quite different, bicycle polo can match the excitement of the more familiar sport.*

Polo, once restricted to Europe's ruling classes, aristocracy, and landed gentry, and to America's most exclusive schools and clubs, has crossed the class barrier. In a version of the sport that is growing in popularity, not only have the players changed, but also the playing fields and rules have been modified. And, perhaps the strangest of all, horses' hooves have been replaced by bicycle wheels!

Bicycle polo had its origin in Ireland some 80 years ago; it was soon imported to the United States, where a charter club was organized at Milton, Mass., in 1897.

The sport experienced a series of rises and dips in popularity during the 20th Century, but it was kept alive mainly by the Aiken Preparatory School in South Carolina, which taught its well-endowed young students bicycle polo as part of their training for regular polo.

Only recently has the sport really begun to catch on in this country, as well as in England, parts of Latin America, and Canada. It is emerging as a game that demands skill, daring, and stamina, that requires a relatively small amount of equipment, and that provides a great deal of fun and excitement for participant and spectator alike.

Bicycle polo seems to have gained popularity at least in part because of inflation (polo ponies cost around $1000; and a polo great, Laddie Sanford, once paid $22,000 for one). Many of its adherents appear to be of affluent means — possibly aficionados of the traditional version of the game. Spectators at bicycle polo tournaments, in general, tend to comprise members of the social and international set.

But the game is also gaining enthusiasm among the general public, thanks to the surge in the popularity of bicycles. Clubs have been formed in various parts of the country. The sport has also caught on at many clubs in England. The United

# Bicycle Polo

## 11

States Bicycle Polo Association (USBPA), an organization dating back to the 1940's, was revived in 1970 by Carlos Concheso, a New York banker. The USBPA holds weekly practice sessions and sponsors weekend tournaments in New York City.

## PLEASING TO SPECTATORS

The rules for bicycle polo are similar to those for regular polo. Bicycle polo mallets are half-sized, and players can only hit the ball three times in a row, compared to an unlimited number of hits in regular polo. The field is about a third as large as for the traditional game.

In regular polo, a player can charge his pony into another player's mount to keep his opponent away from the ball. In bicycle polo, such contact — called "riding off" an opponent — is forbidden. "Bicycles get busted up, and they cost too much," explains Carlos Concheso. The USBPA also notes that ponies are somewhat resilient, whereas a bicycle is an "uncompromising animal which will tangle itself with whatever it can lay its pedals on."

Although the lack of contact is a disappointment to some players, as well as to "bloodthirsty" spectators, many observers feel that bicycle polo provides a much better show than the traditional version. The field is smaller, and spectators can follow all the action quite well from the sidelines. Englishmen often described traditional polo as "a game played by Peers on the far side of the ground."

Because any kind of bike is permitted on the field, the choice of equipment and the comparative effectiveness of various bicycles is a common topic for friendly debate. Many of the players prefer the minibikes with 18-inch wheels, which they feel provide optimum maneuverability. Others like the 27-inch touring bike, citing its speed as advantageous.

## EXCITING FOR PARTICIPANTS

Some players seem to develop as much affection for their "mounts" as do traditional polo players for their ponies. One member of the Southampton team has named his favorite bicycle "Black Beauty." A teammate explained that while "you can't train a bicycle the way you can a pony," the riders go through similar motions, "oiling, and grooming, and caressing and talking to them."

A special bicycle polo jargon has also developed. Players shout "Pump! Pump hard!" to urge on their teammates. A new tactic, developed by an American on the Buenos Aires team, has come to be called the "under the sprocket back-hand" shot. This maneuver, in which a player smacks the ball between the wheels of his own bicycle, has a counterpart in regular polo called "a millionaire's shot," so-named because few players would risk a hit that could damage their mounts.

Some bicycles have been modified to improve the game. The Cuban team, for example, developed handlebars that are cut down on the shot-making side to provide greater swinging room.

## ADVANTAGES OF BICYCLE POLO

Despite the risks of damaged bicycles and injuries, the bicycle polo player actually enjoys a number of advantages over the traditional polo player. First of all, he never has to shoot his bike. Secondly, if the bicycle is not damaged too badly, he can continue playing, or else wheel it off the field and get another. The unhorsed polo player must pursue his fleeing charge, often wasting many precious minutes of game time because no time out can be called unless the horse interferes with the game.

One veteran polo player, however, upon trying the bicycle variety for the first time, noted this disadvantage: "It's easier on horseback. You don't have to pedal the horse."

## RULES

Following are some of the general rules for bicycle polo, adopted by the United States Bicycle Polo Association on April 26, 1942, and amended on October 31, 1971.

### BICYCLES

1. Any type of bicycle may be used.

### THE FIELD

2. Maximum size of an outdoor regulation playing field is 110x80 yards, minimum 90x60 yards, when grass. Dimensions should be doubled for asphalt or concrete surfaces.
3. The field shall have two "quarter lines" (25 yards) and a "halfway line." Boundaries on the sides of the field are "sidelines," and at the ends of the field, "end lines." The end line between the goal posts is the "goal line."
4. An outdoor regulation grass field should have light blade grass (not crab grass) cut to a maximum of 3/4 inch in height.
5. The goals shall be 12 feet apart, at least six feet in height, and light enough to knock down if collided with.

### EQUIPMENT

6. The regulation ball to be used is the official outdoor polo ball. Its size shall not exceed 3-1/4 inches in diameter, weight shall be within 4-1/4 to 4-3/4 ounces.
7. Mallets shall have a shaft not exceeding 35

inches in length; heads may be any shape but may not exceed 12 ounces in weight. Metal insertions or additions are strictly forbidden.

### PLAYERS

8. Number of players shall be four on a side, with two alternates on hand. No player shall be allowed to play unless he wears a protective helmet or cap.
9. A player may be substituted for another during a period only if the latter player, because of sickness or accident, is unable to continue. In such case, the handicap of the player having the higher handicap shall be counted. Unlimited substitutions may be made between periods provided the four highest handicaps of players and substitutes be counted.

### REFEREES

10. There shall be a major Referee whose decision shall be final.
11. In all important matches 2 goal Referees and 2 sideline Referees should be appointed.
12. An official Timekeeper and Scorer shall be employed in all games and matches.

### TIME OF PLAY

13. A match shall consist of 6 chuckers of 7-1/2 minutes each with intervals of three minutes after each period and five minutes at half time.
14. Except where otherwise specified in these rules, play shall be continuous and no time shall be taken out for a change of bicycles, unless broken.
15. Each period of play except the last period shall, after expiration of the prescribed time, terminate as soon as the ball goes out of play over the side, end, or goal lines, or is in such a position that the Referee can stop the game without favoring either side. A bell shall be rung when each period has expired. Whenever Referee blows his whistle, the ball is dead.
16. The last period shall terminate, although the ball is still in play, at the first stroke of the final bell, wherever the ball may be, except in case of a tie.
17. In the event of a tie, the last period shall be prolonged until the ball goes out of play or is in such a position that the Referee can stop the game without favoring either side. After an interval of five minutes, the game shall be started from where the ball went out of play and continue until one side obtains a goal, which shall determine the match. This type of period shall be known as a "Sudden Death" chucker.
18. The side that scores the most goals wins the

*The rules of bicycle polo allow any kind of "mount" on the field. Many players prefer a minibike (above) with 18-inch wheels because of its extraordinary maneuverability, but polo participants who want more speed opt for the 27-inch touring bike.*

game. A goal is scored when a ball passes between the goal posts and over and clear of the goal line.

### STARTING THE GAME

Following are three accepted ways to begin a game. The committee responsible for organization of the tournament shall decide the rule which shall apply for that particular contest.

a. The Forbes Rule — Both teams take their positions in the middle of the field and the Referee bowls the ball, underhand and hard, into the center of the ground between opponents, who face him and none of whom stand within five yards of him.

b. The Corey Rule — Both teams circle towards the Referee on their respective sides of the field, 20 yards from Referee. Referee counts down from 5 to zero, then bowls the ball underhand and hard from sideline down halfway line between opponents.

c. The British Rule — Both teams take their positions; ball is placed on intersection of center line and halfway line. At Referee's signal one player from each side sprints from left side of his goal's mouth to try to gain possession of the ball, but must not cross center before ball is in play.

There is an exciting world of bike touring waiting for you; it is a world of sunshine and nature, of friendships and new experiences, of learning about the world and learning about yourself. On a bike tour you can pedal along a woodland trail where deer or pheasant are your companions, or ride up to a quaint country store for a snack and some casual conversation. For lunch you picnic in a meadow, while at your afternoon break you dangle your feet in a cold stream. At the end of the day you are as hungry as a logger, and nighttime finds you asleep within minutes after crawling into bed. The world of bike touring is do-it-yourself travel — with continents full of fun waiting for you.

Of course, not every minute of every tour is filled with sunshine and roses. There are hills to climb, rough roads to negotiate, and rainy weather to endure. The obstacles are part of the world of bike touring, but with a little knowledge and advance planning, they can be nothing more than minor inconveniences to be conquered.

Although riders have gone around the world on one-speed bikes, and though until recent years much touring was done on three-speeds, the ten-speed derailleur-equipped bicycle now completely dominates bicycle touring. Your touring bicycle should be something special to you. If it is not when you start the trip, it certainly will be at the end. No one can pedal hundreds of miles on 25 pounds of metal tubing and rubber tires without gaining some respect for the modern ten-speed. It is efficient; it is a joy to ride; it is the perfect match of man and machine; and it will get you where you are going if you do your part.

A bike for touring should be as light and as well made as you can afford, and strong enough to absorb the punishment of rough roads even when fully loaded. Ten-speeds vary from roughly 20 to 35 pounds. The 20-pounder is usually considered too light for touring, and the 35-pounder is a bit heavy. A cycle in the 25- to 30-pound range equipped with fenders, a rear carrier, water bottle, and tire pump should serve you well. If you learn to ride it well and

to do minor repairs, the world of bike touring will be open to you.

## WITH FRIENDS OR ALONE?

Although bicycling solo is efficient and flexible in that you never have to wait for anyone and that you can change your plans at the turn of a handlebar, most riders agree that touring is more fun with friends. If you do not belong to a riding group, inquire at your local bike shop about other riders from

*Touring knows no geographical, ethnic, or sex boundaries as lady riding through the Far East illustrates. On the other hand, one thing touring does demand is proper gear: a light but strong derailleur-equipped bicycle — mounted with sturdy waterproof bags — is a necessity.*

*Not every bicycle tourist can expect to view the splendor of nature such as the riders (left) experience along Icicle Canyon Road near Leavenworth, Washington. Yet, there is no better way to appreciate the world around you than to see it from a bicycle.*

# The World of Bicycle Touring
# 12

*The friends you ride with should possess similar interests and riding ability. Since every trip offers moments of stress, those people who can laugh at minor adversities make the best touring companions.*

your area. Inquire about local bike clubs, and check nearby American Youth Hostel groups. For a list of all the AYH councils, you can write to American Youth Hostels Inc., National Campus, Delaplane, Virginia 22025; then contact the local council for details about their bicycle program. You might also wish to contact the International Bicycle Touring Society, 846 Prospect St., La Jolla, California 92037; or the League of American Wheelmen, 19 South Bothwell, Palatine, Illinois 60067.

The friends you tour with should possess nearly the same cycling ability, and should share common interests in the things to see and do. Your group should also agree in advance about where to spend the night and whether to cook your own meals or eat out. Above all, select friends who get along well. There are always some stresses and strains during a trip, and the companions who can smile even when things are not going well are the ones whom you should choose.

The family and friends you leave behind can write to you during your trip if you leave them a copy of your itinerary. The best way to receive mail is to have it sent in care of general delivery to the towns along your trail. You can also have mail sent to hostels and motels you plan to visit. Ask friends to mail letters far enough in advance that you will be sure to receive them, and have them mark their letters "Hold for 30 days, then return to sender."

## WHEN NIGHT APPROACHES

When you are in strange surroundings and night is coming on, it is only natural to wonder about where you will lay your head. You may want to take potluck on meals and sightseeing during your tour, but it is a good idea to plan carefully concerning your bed for the night. You can choose your overnight accommodations from camping sites, hostels, and motels. Which you select determines how much you should carry on your bike and in your pocketbook, and how you can spend your free time.

Camping is the least expensive and the closest to nature, but it does require some equipment and some expertise. You will need sleeping bags, ground cloths, and foam pads or air mattresses. A sleeping bag with two pounds of down — a total weight of about three pounds — should prove adequate for summer trips. Tourists seem about equally divided between foam pads and air mattresses; but to save some weight, get the short models that reach only to your knees. If you can sleep without a pad or a mattress, so much the better.

If rain is a possibility, include some sort of a shelter: a backpacker's tent, a plastic tube tent, or a large sheet of plastic with which to improvise a shelter. Try to keep the weight of the shelter less than three pounds per person. You also need a cook set and a small stove, as you will want to eat some meals in camp; but numerous pots and pans are unnecessary. One sauce pan plus a skillet will suffice for a small group. Of course, each person must possess a plate, cup, and eating utensils — stick with aluminum for lightness.

You need a stove because many campgrounds no longer allow open fires or even charcoal fires. Campers' favorite stoves are models which use gasoline under pressure, or ones that utilize liquified gas cartridges. The first type gives a hot fire with cheap fuel, but it demands an extra supply of gasoline, can present lighting problems, and may exude gasoline fumes into your duffle. Cartridge stoves deliver a hot fire quickly, but cost more. Be sure you carry extra gas cartridges or buy new ones before you find yourself with a half-cooked meal in the middle of nowhere.

Naturally, if you plan to camp, you must be able to set up your tent, cook a meal on your one-burner stove, and do the other necessary camp chores. Camping during a tour gets you in close contact with a natural environment, gets you away from civilization, but it does require more time and expertise.

To stay at a youth hostel you need a valid hostel pass, a sheet sleeping sack, and the willingness to perform a few chores. Anyone can secure an

AYH pass: If there is no group near you, write to the AYH National Campus, Delaplane, VA. 22025. The youth pass (for those under 18) costs $5.00, and the adult pass costs $10.00. There is also a family pass — which is valid only in the United States and Canada — for $12.00.

Upon joining AYH you receive, in addition to your pass, the handbook showing the location of all U.S. hostels. The handbook also gives the dimensions if you want to make your own sheet sleeping sack, which is nothing more than your bed linen; it is not a sleeping bag. On the other hand, you can purchase a sheet sleeping sack from the Metropolitan New York AYH Council, 1554 First Avenue, New York, N.Y. 10028. The muslin model weighs 22 ounces and costs $5.00, and the nylon model weighs six ounces and costs $6.25. Each hostel has a complete kitchen, but each hosteler is expected to carry his own plate, cup, table service, and dish towel.

The most important assets at any hostel are a big smile and a willingness to pitch in. Everything is self-service from cooking dinner to sweeping up the bunk room; do not expect to be waited on. There are, nonetheless, plenty of compensations: companionship, songs around the fireplace, and fellow travelers to answer your many questions about the road ahead.

Hostelers are expected to abide by the hostel customs — common sense traditions that make it possible for groups to live together harmoniously. Sleeping arrangements at most hostels are double bunks in men's and women's dorms. Some hostels do have rooms for families. The hostel tourist must carry a bit more than the person who stays at motels, but much less than the camper. The cost of hostels is normally $1.50 or $2.00, with a few charging $3.00.

If you elect to stay in motels or hotels, you can get by with the smallest amount of duffle — except in your pocketbook which had better be stuffed. Nevertheless, if you are willing to do without some of the frills and if you have time to shop around, you can often find a motel at modest prices. The bike tourist who stays at motels usually finds that civilization is near at hand. This means a larger selection of restaurants and evening activities. The motel route costs more, but provides many conveniences.

## KEEP IT LIGHT

It always amazes those who have never gone bike touring to learn how much can be carried on a bicycle. The aim, however, is not to load yourself down, but rather to keep your duffle as light as possible. The moteler can get by with 20 pounds and the hosteler with a few pounds more. The camper's duffle probably weighs in at 25 to 35 pounds.

First, take what you need to keep your bike operating. Since the most common ailment is a flat tire, carry a tube patching kit, and make sure that the rubber cement has not dried. You also need tire irons to get the tire off the rim. Do not use a screwdriver for this job, or you will end up with more punctures than when you started. Always start a tour with new tires and tubes, and carry a spare tube on longer tours. Thorn resistant tubes all but eliminate punctures, but they are much heavier than standard tubes.

Brakes and derailleurs often require minor adjustments. Take the tools that came with your bike, or carry a six-inch adjustable end wrench. Since some tools use American measurements and some are metric, various sets of bike tools are not all interchangeable. For this reason, you are safest with an adjustable wrench. A small screwdriver (or one on your pocket knife) is also a must. A chain tool can be invaluable. With a few extra chain links, you can repair a broken chain and be back on the road in minutes; without the chain tool and links, you would be stranded. On longer tours, carry some extra nuts

*There are advantages to riding solo, but group touring is often more fun. This group — like most — is composed of diverse people joined by their interest in seeing the world on a bike.*

*The cyclists who take short rides in nice weather need not worry about carrying extra gear; but if you venture far from civilization or ride through cold, rainy, or hot climates, be sure you carry the proper clothing and protective equipment you need.*

and bolts, a section of brake cable long enough to fit your rear brake, some brake blocks, and lubricating oil.

By far, the most important thing in bike maintenance is knowing what to do and how to do it. There are many good books on bike repair. Many AYH groups conduct bicycle maintenance clinics in which you learn the fundamentals of bike repair. Major repairs are best left to the experts, but with a little study and practice you can learn to do many jobs which will save you time — and possibly your tour.

Practicing preventive cycle maintenance is the ideal. Check your mount every day for nuts that are loose, brakes out of adjustment, and bearings that need oil. Lubricate your bike regularly, and keep it out of the sun and rain when possible. Finally, ride it with consideration; riding through chuck holes may not have an immediate effect, but the cumulative results can be disastrous. Remember, if your bike falls apart, your trip does the same.

## CLOTHES

The clothes you take are determined by your personal preferences, by the climate in which you will be cycling, and by the places you plan to visit. There is no reason why a bicycle tourist cannot be tastefully attired at all times. Many people carry dress clothes on their tours, which not only allows them to visit nice restaurants, but also is great for their morale. After a hot, dusty day on the road, there is nothing like taking a shower, getting all dressed up, and going out for a night on the town.

Select double knit and permanent press materials for your wardrobe. Coordinate the colors — fairly dark colors with a pattern have proven best — so that you can mix or match your outfits. Socks and underclothing should be of a quick drying type.

The universally accepted warm weather cycling togs for both men and women are shorts and cycling jerseys or other short-sleeved knit tops. Knee socks look much better with shorts than a pair of droopy gym socks. For cooler days or for evenings in camp, a warmer outfit — such as knickers or jeans with a long-sleeved shirt or sweater — is required.

Dress clothes for girls consist of a wrinkle-free dress or a skirt-blouse combination. A dressy sweater, a few pieces of jewelry, and a colorful scarf round out the outfit. Pants suits are another possibility, but they are usually a bit bulkier. Men may want to carry slacks and a sports jacket, or they may opt for slacks with a dressy shirt or a sweater.

Shoes are heavy, and you should take only one or two pairs. The first pair should be suitable for cycling and walking; the second for dress and walking. A windbreaker jacket for cool mornings of cycling and chilly evenings, swim clothes, pajamas, cycling gloves, a hat with a small bill to keep the sun out of your eyes, and perhaps a sweater complete your wardrobe.

Pedaling in the rain is a unique experience; rain coats, rain capes, and ponchos do a fair job of keeping your torso dry, but they let your legs and feet get wet. Rain chaps, available from backpacking stores, can be a big help. Rain suits and foul weather gear keep out all the rain, but they often feel like a steam bath inside. If the weather is warm, you can try riding in your shorts and jersey; the bike's fenders prevents the road dirt from spraying you. Nevertheless, if you do not dry out during the remainder of your ride, change into dry clothes as soon as you reach your destination.

If your bicycle tour is planned to venture far from civilization, you can forget about taking dress clothes. What you need are rugged clothes suited to the terrain. This might include light, loose fitting outfits for sun protection in hot climates; warm wools for mountain camping; good rain protection and plenty of dry socks for wet regions; and even mosquito head nets for insect country.

## MISCELLANEOUS EQUIPMENT

Although you need some sort of a toilet kit, rule out the bulky leather types. Instead, try a cloth bag with a drawstring or a small plastic kit. Carry cosmetics in tight-sealing plastic containers, and reduce the weight of your gear by carrying small sizes of toothpaste, etc. A small towel or a few bandanas will suffice. Battery-operated razors are generally successful, while tubes of concentrated soap are very handy for personal use as well as for laundry and dishes. It is a good idea to carry some lotion to counteract the effects of sun and wind.

The amount of sporting equipment you can take with is, of course, limited. If you like fishing, try one of the new telescoping rods. For a lively romp after a day in the saddle, a frisbee game is hard to beat. These plastic discs are light, unbreakable, can be used to stiffen the inside of your saddlebags, and can even substitute for a plate in an emergency.

For diversion in the evening or on rainy days you may want some letter writing material, a paperback book, a deck of cards, or a portable chess set. A flashlight is indispensable. You should also carry a first-aid kit and a small sewing kit. Take an extra pair of spectacles and a supply of any medication that you use.

Cameras do not travel well by bicycle. You can take your camera, but give it some extra protection. You may want to carry it around your neck, using a light strap to hold it securely to your chest; or in a small knapsack on your back; or in a handlebar bag, spring mounted with elastic stretch straps.

## LOADING YOUR BICYCLE

The best procedure, by far, for loading gear on a bicycle is in tough, waterproof, nylon or canvas bags. These usually consist of saddlebags (pannier bags) which lay across the rear carrier, and a handlebar bag which fastens to a special bracket on the handlebars. The bracket holds the bag a few inches away from the handlebars, and does not interfere with your grasp of the bars. Other bags can be attached over the front wheel, to the top tube, or to the back of the saddle. Campers usually attach their sleeping bag and tent to the top of their rear carrier.

Veteran bike tourists pack their saddlebags to show the top of each item. Using this verticle packing system, they need only lift the saddlebag flap to see everything. For extra protection, pack items by groups in plastic bags; grouping items together helps keep them orderly. For example, you might keep bedtime items — like pajamas and sheet sleeping sack — together. Many riders reserve their handlebar bag for gear that might be needed quickly during the day: rain protection, first-aid kit, bike repair kit, and food snacks.

Two riders (above, left) can communicate easily, but when a group beyond three ride (above), everyone should know the ride plan.

If you plan to tour on a tandem, be aware that there are fewer places to pack things than there are on two singles. Tandem touring is wonderful, but it does call for special planning.

Perhaps, when you get all your duffle assembled, you will find that there is no way it will fit into your bags. You can either eliminate some items or else carry them in a trailer. Lightweight, well-designed bike trailers are now on the market, but only strong riders should attempt pulling them on longer tours. Trailers are best where traffic is light, where there are few hills, and where the road surfaces are smooth.

Assembling your equipment for a bike tour can be an enjoyable project, but start early to have time enough to get everything done and yet keep it pleasant. If you are talented with your hands, you might consider making saddlebags, handlebar bags, and a drawstring toilet kit. Many manufacturers of outdoor equipment sell fabrics, slide fasteners, snaps, and other hardware needed to create first-rate gear carriers.

## GETTING READY FOR THE ROAD

The longest journey starts with but a single step. Chances are that you will start your trip with a light heart and plenty of enthusiasm. You will start losing your bounce, however, some miles down the road if you are not in condition. The secret to enjoyable touring is to get in condition before you start.

The world of bike touring may have its demanding days, but overall it is not a sport that

The veteran tourist (above) uses every possible place on his bike to carry duffle for a long tour. One of the tricks to proper packing is starting early enough to get everything done without a last-minute rush.

New graphic road signs (right) tell the tourist at a glance what facilities are available along the way. Riders (far right), often stop at interesting places along the road to absorb some history, or just relax and enjoy the surroundings.

**First Aid**

**Lookout Tower**

**Trail Shelter**

**Picnic Area**

**Showers**

**Viewing Area**

120

demands that you be a super athlete or that you go into a spartan training program before a tour. What you must do is a great deal of riding. Try to pedal a few miles every day, and take longer tours on weekends. On some of these weekend rides, be sure to carry full saddlebags to get the feel of riding a loaded cycle.

Riding every day gets your legs and lungs in top shape. There are other benefits such as breaking in the saddle and familiarizing yourself with the bike. These rides also give you an opportunity to practice bicycle maintenance and to make minor fitting adjustments.

## WITH A GROUP ON THE ROAD

If your group numbers only three or four, you will have few communication and logistical problems. As groups grow to five or more, however, a few special precautions are in order. Group cycling is fun, but make sure that you all end up at the same campground and that the cooking committee knows who is supposed to buy the food.

Assemble the group of riders in the morning to decide what route to follow, where to stop for snacks and lunch, and where to spend the night. It is especially important that everyone know the evening destination (some leaders have every rider write down the name and address of this spot). Meeting for lunch in very small villages presents few problems as there are not many stores. In larger towns, however, you should make more precise arrangements.

Occasionally, members of the group may

have divergent ideas about what activities they want to do. Some may want to stop at a museum, while others may want to take a swim; still others may want to eat lunch at a special place. All of these different desires can mean that the group will not even travel the same roads. If the leader has a responsible group, if they all know the destination, and if they stay in groups of at least two or more, there should be no problem.

If the group is composed of mature people, very little is needed in the way of road organization. Younger riders, however, need to be better organized. A plan that is often used is called the locomotive and caboose method. The locomotive is a person who knows the route or can read maps. His job is to lead the way and to direct the group through tricky turns. No one gets in front of the locomotive. The caboose brings up the rear. This person should have first-aid and bike repair kits, and the knowledge of how to use them. No one gets behind the caboose. During a typical day on the road, the locomotive and caboose may be miles apart; but they can still control the group, while giving the riders the freedom that is the essence of bicycle touring.

## TRICKS OF THE ROAD

One of the best tricks to making bike touring enjoyable is to get an early start each day. Riding in the cool of the morning with the dew still on the leaves and the birds singing in the trees is a joy to the heart. Although getting up early may not be your idea of a good time, the alternative is to find yourself hurrying along during the heat of the afternoon to reach your destination. It is much better to get up a bit earlier, have a simple breakfast, and get in two-thirds of your biking before lunch. Then you can eat a leisurely meal, rest, see a few sights, and still pedal to your stopping place with time for a shower or a swim before dinner.

Try to arrive at a campsite with at least two hours of daylight remaining to set up your camp. Since most hostels open in the late afternoon, plan to arrive — if you do not have reservations — between 4 and 5 pm. If you have reservations, you can arrive a bit later, but allow yourself enough time to check in and cook dinner. You can arrive at a motel most anytime as long as there is a vacancy.

Many bike tourists find that a noontime picnic can be one of the most enjoyable periods of the day. The backdrop for your lunch may be a mountain range, a forest, or a broad river. A few items of equipment will make your lunches go more smoothly. A square of plastic on which to lay food, a personal cup in which to mix fruit drinks, a pocket knife for slicing and opening, and a salt shaker all come in handy.

The lunch itself may be from your saddlebag or from a local store. Lunches can be sandwiches, fruit, hard-boiled eggs, carrot and celery sticks,

potato or corn chips, and a host of other things. Be certain, of course, to sample the local specialties when you pedal through an area.

Most bikers like to snack during rides. A wide range of suitable items are available from the supermarket, sporting good stores, and health food stores. Some of the choices are fresh and dried fruits, nuts, cookies, fruit cake, candy bars, honey, crackers, pretzels, and jerky. Riders must always carry their own water bottle to drink from whenever they are thirsty. Your body is your power source when you are on a tour, and it does not work well when hungry or thirsty. So eat and drink often, and keep your energy coming in abundant supply.

*When touring (far left), get an early start each day; it assures that you will arrive at your evening destination relaxed. Riding in the cool of the morning (left), is not only exhilerating, but also a smart way to tour.*

## PROTECTING YOUR BIKE AND BODY

One unfortunate aspect of the bike boom has been a tremendous increase in bicycle thefts. Since no one wants a tour to be cut short by a bike rip off, it is important to take some precautions.

The most secure protection for your bike and duffle is someone watching them; it is the only way to safeguard the contents of your saddlebags. Other possibilities are to check your loaded bicycles at a railroad station or hostel, or to lock them in a motel room.

You can lock your bike itself with any of a large range of chains, cables, and alarms. Your bike

shop attendant can inform you of the features of each locking device and tell you which offers the maximum protection. A reliable locking device may well cost $10.00 or more and may weigh two pounds or more; but if it does its job, it is worth every penny and every pound.

When locking your bicycle, be sure to secure the frame and — if possible — both wheels to a solid object. Try to leave your bike in a lighted spot, where there are people circulating. If you are riding in groups of two or three, one person can run an errand while the others watch the cycles.

If you ever have run a rapids by canoe or raft with a real expert, you know how this person can read the river and spot potential problems in advance. To be a safe cyclist you must be able to do the same. For example, you are cycling along a side street, and you see several cars parked on either side of the street ahead. Slow down. The chances of a car door opening, a car pulling out, or people dashing across the street are sufficient to warrant caution.

Suppose that you and a friend are making good time down a rural road. Ahead you see some youngsters hiking along with their dogs. Slow down: Both children and dogs are unpredictable.

On one of your tours you must travel a few miles on a road filled with heavy auto traffic. Of course, heavy traffic means that you must be doubly cautious about vehicles turning in front of you or pulling in front of you from side streets. Caution and the law dictate that you ride as far to the right as practical. But be alert; there may be storm grates that can grab your front wheel, or water diversion ridges that can throw your front wheel and send you flying. The litter and trash along busy roads is another hazard. Glass and metal chew up your tires, and larger junk can send you tumbling.

Yet another situation finds you cycling through beautiful mountain country. Light traffic and good roads combine to dull your caution. Then you find yourself traveling at 40 to 50 miles per hour down a steep grade that leaves little room for error. Before starting a steep descent, check both brakes to see that the brake blocks contact the rim squarely, but that they do not touch the tire. Put your hat on squarely, and secure your sunglasses. During the descent, keep your eyes moving to spot potential road hazards. Make any evasive actions smoothly and far in advance — quick turns at high speeds spell disaster.

There are many theories on how best to apply handbrakes, but most riders agree on a few basics. Apply the brakes before a turn, not during a

There are many different ways to secure your bicycle, but none is better than someone watching it at all times. If you must leave your bike for awhile, be sure to lock it (above) by chaining both wheels and the frame to a solid object.

A reliable locking device (right) may be both heavy and expensive; but if it does its job, it is worth every penny and every pound.

turn. Apply both brakes in unison. Do not clamp your brakes on and then hold them on; if you do, your rim will heat up and blow your tube.

When cycling with one or more friends, you must develop a sense of togetherness in riding. Each rider must think and anticipate for the entire group. Communication between riders is also important. When you spot road hazards, yell ''glass ahead''; when you pass, holler ''on your left''; and tell your friends in advance what you plan to do with instructions like ''stopping.''

For safe cycling, put reflectors or reflector tape on your bicycle. Wear bright jerseys that include some white, and carry safety flags. Since orange triangles are recognized indicators of slow moving vehicles on the highway, many bicycling groups either tie orange triangles to their backs or hang them over their rear carriers to warn passing motorists. As mundane as bicycle safety may seem, it must be given top priority on a trip.

### THE CANINE CHALLENGE

Historians tell us that the dog was the first animal domesticated by man. The dog has been man's friend and companion ever since, but when bicycles enter the picture, this friendship sometimes ceases.

No one system is guaranteed to protect you from all dogs. Many dogs feel compelled to run out and bark at anything that passes. Such canines can often be sent on their way with a loud command: ''Go home.'' Other bowsers are fascinated by whirling ankles and feel obliged to take a few nips. Dismounting on the opposite side from the dog and walking your bicycle some distance usually takes all the fun out of the game, and the dog goes home.

For truly vicious dogs, more drastic actions are needed. The aerosol spray used by postmen, plastic squeeze bottles filled with lemon juice, bicycle pumps, and switches have all been used with varying degrees of success. Even noise makers are sometimes effective in distracting a dog until you can make your getaway.

### PLANNING YOUR TRIP

There are several basic plans you must make before beginning your bicycle trip. A few of these are: where to go, how long to stay, and how to get the bikes to the jump-off point.

The simplest way to transport your bike to your starting point is to carry it on a bumper rack attached to your car. If you want to carry multiple bikes, try a roof-top rack or a rack that holds bicycles in the bed of a pick-up truck.

If you must ship your bike by air or train or bus, you may be asked to remove the handlebars, turn in the pedals, and place the cycle in a carton. By removing both wheels and taping them to the side of the frame, you can further condense the size of your package. Whenever you ship a bicycle, pad the derailleur. If you ship the bike in a carton, you can include accessories; but if you ship the bike unboxed, be sure to remove pumps and water bottles.

For most people, the length of their vacation determines the length of their tour. Only those lucky people with plenty of time must be careful not to plan too ambitious an effort. One or two weeks is a good first journey. Later trips can stretch to a month or two if you can get away for that length of time.

A bicycle will take you just about anywhere you want to go. High mountain passes, deserts, and swamps have all been crossed by people on bicycles. Most people, however, want to stick to paved roads during their trip, negotiating a few miles of gravel road if they must. Nevertheless, some riders even go out of their way looking for ''rough stuff,'' cycling over jeep trails and cow paths. If you like the challenge of climbing a high pass and the well-earned downhill run, head for the mountains. Those who dislike climbing had better head for flat country. It is a rare trip, though, that does not offer a few climbs.

Climate can also affect your choice of bike touring regions. Some people like the cool mountains, while others prefer warm coastal areas. In general, springtime tends to offer the greatest chance of rain in North America. Summers offer fine cycling, except in those areas where heat and humidity combine to wilt everything — including bike tourists. Fall is the ideal touring season, while winter rules out cycling in many northern areas, but opens up areas in the southwest.

Your single most important consideration when planning your tour is deciding what you like to see and do. The various sections of North America offer museums, sports, scenery, history, and nostalgia in diverse flavors. Your first job, therefore, is to select a general region you would like to visit. Then collect some maps and general travel literature — easily secured by writing to the state or provincial travel department — of your chosen area.

You may want to write to specific state or county parks to check on reservations. National parks do not reserve campsites, but the superintendent of a specific national park can answer most of your inquiries. Detailed information about local festivals, exhibits, and fairs can be secured by writing to the local chamber of commerce.

Give special thought to your nighttime arrangements. The youth hostel handbooks, campground directories, and motel listings are quite helpful. The *Canadian Youth Hostel Handbook* can be purchased for $1.50 from the AYH National Campus, Delaplane, Va. 22025.

There are a number of ways to map out your tour. You can cycle in a wide loop, and finish at your starting point; such tours are the easiest to plan because nonbike transportation is kept to a minimum. Another approach is to pedal to a point from

Touring bicyclists (above) begin their
journey by loading their bikes on a roof-top
car rack. Then they drive to the jumping-off
point and start pedaling.

Cyclist (right) checks her gear; if she packed
wisely and efficiently, she will have no
trouble finding what she wants. A vertical
packing system is best.

The modern ten-speed bicycle (far right) is a
joy to ride, even fully loaded with saddle-
and handlebar bags. The derailleur-
equipped bicycle is a perfect match of man
and machine.

which you return to your home by commercial transportation.

Frequently, bike tourists decide to take a motor vehicle — usually referred to as the sagwagon — with them. Sometimes one person volunteers to drive for the entire trip, or else all the licensed drivers can take turns driving. A sagwagon can leave the group in the morning and drive immediately to the day's destination to reserve campsites or to buy food. Another procedure is to have this vehicle move forward in several jumps during the day, which allows the sagwagon to help the bikers who have problems.

## MAPS AND REFERENCES

Once you select the area for your tour, start thinking about specific routes. Two reference books that may be helpful to you are the *North American Bicycle Atlases.* The original *Atlas* ($2.50), with a blue cover, contains 90 tours of one- to four-week durations and 62 weekend or one-day rides. The latest edition ($3.15), with a green cover, contains 90 long tours and 80 shorter ones, all of which are different than the ones in the original *Atlas.* Both are published by The American Youth Hostels, Inc., Delaplane, Virginia 22025.

Check your library for books that list local bicycle tours. County maps are best for cyclists because they show the many lightly traveled scenic side roads. The county engineer's office in the county seat will often send you such a map at no charge.

The ideal roads for bicycle touring are ones that are paved with wide shoulders and light traffic. These are not the highways that are featured on service station maps. Rather, they are the side streets and rural roads that meander throughout most of America. On these quiet roads you can shed the frustrations of the city and enjoy a relaxing vacation.

## HOW FAR — HOW FAST

When you start to plan your day-to-day itinerary, you face many decisions, not the least of which is how far to travel each day. First, keep the mileage low during the early part of the trip. Even if you are in good shape, there is no point in over-extending yourself physically during the first few days.

Second, never seek to break mileage records. Even if you can ride 75 to 100 miles in a day, do not try it on a tour. If you do, you will miss

*Bicycle riding spans the generations (left). Several manufacturers make infant seats for bicycles, but be sure that you can pedal a fully loaded bicycle before you add the weight of a child to your tour.*

seeing the country and meeting the people, and that is what the world of bike touring is all about. Most experienced tourists plan on 25 to 50 miles per day. Beginners or families with small children are generally happier doing 10 to 25 miles daily.

Third, give yourself an occasional layover day to visit a special spot, to engage in some sports activity like surfing or fishing, or just to rest up, wash up, and write a few cards. You will probably average eight to twelve miles per hour for the time actually spent in the saddle. If you can average ten miles per hour, you will pedal only five hours to cover 50 miles. This allows plenty of time to see and do all the things you wanted along the way.

The fun things to do en route are just about endless. You can browse in an antique shop, have a glass of cider at a road-side stand, watch a fishing boat unload its catch, or see some cowboys move a herd to a new range. You miss such things if you cycle too many hours of the day. Relax, and enjoy your trip.

## WHERE TO TOUR

To help you select an area and a route for your bicycle tour, we will take a look at several regions for general cycling conditions, climate, terrain, where to stay, and things to see and do. Our appraisal of bike touring regions will start in eastern Canada and proceed clockwise around the continent, later covering some of the interior that we missed on the peripheral swing.

## EASTERN CANADA AND THE ISLAND PROVINCES

The Canadian provinces of Ontario, Quebec, and New Brunswick offer wonderful summer touring. There are plenty of hills, but also much flat pedaling. Outside of the major cities there are miles of rural roads through countryside dotted with lakes and streams. Campgrounds, hostels, motels, and small inns abound, but be prepared for rain and cool days even in summer.

The flavor of France is quite heavy in certain areas: shopkeepers speak French, signs are bilingual, and restaurants feature French cooking. Whether you visit a sophisticated city restaurant for a Parisian style meal or a country cafe to sample the delicious cooking of rural France, be certain to try some of this delightful fare.

An easy ride that just drips with history stretches along the St. Lawrence River from Kingston to Cornwall, Ontario. Highway 2 stays fairly close to the River, skirting a number of campsites where you can swim and spend the night. The total ride is about 140 miles of flat road. The two most significant historic sites are Old Fort Henry near Kingston and Upper Canada Village. Both offer glimpses of fascinating colonial history; you will see

people in period costumes performing the crafts of earlier eras.

A 360-mile ride from the city of Quebec north to Lake St. John, then east to the St. Lawrence River, and back to Quebec is a good one to make in July or August — but only for fairly experienced cyclists. Plan on a two-week trip, staying in campgrounds and motels. For still more rugged riding, tackle the Gaspe Peninsula, where you will find fishing villages reminiscent of France. Cottage crafts are still practiced in this region. Highways 10 and 6 in Quebec and Highway 11 in New Brunswick can occupy the experienced cyclist for two to six weeks; if your time is limited, concentrate on Highway 6.

The island provinces of eastern Canada have fine cycling amid farms, forests, open grassland, and windswept rocks. Take a ferry or plane to reach Prince Edward Island, Nova Scotia, or Newfoundland. Make arrangements well in advance to be sure that you and your bike arrive in the right place at the right time. You can spend the nights in campsites, hostels, or motels.

Prince Edward Island is small, but it is great fun for a one-week ride. A circuit of the Island includes Port Borden, St. Peters, Cavendish, and back to Port Borden. Southern Nova Scotia has both English and French regions. You can circle the southern portion or do just the east or west coast. You can even tour a portion of either coast, using Highways 8, 10, or 12 to cross the interior.

The northern portion of Nova Scotia is called Cape Breton Island and has fewer towns. If you ride in this area, you encounter some unpaved roads, but there is ample reward for your hardship in the magnificent scenery. Most Newfoundland touring is done in the southeast. You can take a good tour in the Placentia, Trinity Bay, Conception Bay, St. Johns area.

## NEW ENGLAND AND MID-ATLANTIC STATES

For many years, a bike trip almost automatically meant a tour through New England. The many low-cost hostels, motels, and hotels in this area have always been a big drawing card. New England, however, has much more to offer: colonial history, mountain scenery, and miles of coastline that varies from the rocks of Maine to the sands of Cape Cod. Since much of the New England countryside is quite

colors. Families with school-age children must do their New England pedaling in the summer, and that is a fine time. Adults, however, should try to visit this area after Jack Frost has done his paint job. The last weeks of September and the first weeks of October are usually the choice times. Not only are the maple trees in all their dazzling splendor, but also the roads, hostels, motels, and restaurants are uncrowded.

The mid-Atlantic states can be hot and humid during the summer; you may, therefore, want to consider spring or fall for your tour. The terrain varies from flat to rolling to mountainous. In Pennsylvania, the regions around Valley Forge, Lancaster, or Gettysburg are most interesting. The Lancaster area is in the heart of the Pennsylvania Dutch country, where the hearty food of the early German settlers can still be sampled. These areas, as well as Washington and Philadelphia, tend to be crowded during the tourist season.

Three historically significant sites are connected by the Colonial Parkway in Virginia: Jamestown, where the first permanent English settlement in the New World was established; Williamsburg, with its beautifully reconstructed buildings; and the Yorktown Battlefield, where you can relive the conclusion of the Revolutionary War.

Farther south, you pedal the flat coastal roads of the Carolinas, or the winding hilly roads of the Great Smoky Mountains. The back roads between Maryville, Pigeon Forge, and Richardson Cove, Tennessee, offer the sights and sounds of the mountain people who have contributed much to our heritage in music and folklore.

## FLORIDA AND THE GULF COAST

Florida and the other Gulf Coast states provide year-round touring. Summer may tend to be warm, but these areas are great for touring when the northern states nestle under a blanket of snow. The rural roads of northern and central Florida are replete with orange groves, lakes, and swamps. Remember, however, that it can be cool in north Florida during winter.

You can plan your tour to cover some out-of-the-way areas and also to visit some of the major tourist attractions, but expect heavy traffic in the tourist areas. Cycling in Florida is flat, with plenty of

hilly, quality low gears on your bike are important.

Most bike touring in Maine occurs along the indented coast, concentrating on the Bar Harbor and Acadia National Park areas. In New Hampshire, the Franconia Notch region north of Woodstock has many attractions and plenty of hills to climb. One can bicycle the full length of Vermont on State Route 100, an off-the-beaten-track meander that takes you through breathtaking countryside.

Massachusetts provides great cycling — flat riding for New England — along the Connecticut River Valley. You can extend this trip into New Hampshire, Vermont, and Connecticut. Try the Massachusetts coast area around Gloucester or Cape Cod or the enchanting islands of Martha's Vineyard or Nantucket. You will find terrific seafood; all sorts of art, gift, and nautical shops; and miles of seaside for walking, fishing, swimming, and sailing. The choice riding in Connecticut is in the west around New Milford, Litchfield, and Canaan. New York State is more crowded, but there is good cycling in the Finger Lakes area and in the vicinity of Alleghany State Park.

We could not leave New England without some discussion of the fantastically beautiful autumn

motels and campgrounds available. One of the most unusual rides in the United States covers the route from Homestead to Flamingo, Florida, in the Everglades National Park. Here you experience life in the tropics: unusual birds, trees and plants, and perhaps a glimpse of an alligator. Be prepared for rain and insects, however.

The states along the Gulf of Mexico beckon riders during the spring when the azaleas are in blossom. Write to the Mobile, Alabama, Chamber of Commerce for the prime times. Be sure to sample the fabulous seafood and some of the French and Creole specialties.

There are good riding areas near Pensacola, Florida and Mobile, Alabama. Of special interest is the region around New Iberia, Louisiana, the Evangeline country made famous by Longfellow's immortal poem. Here you can see rice fields and sample crawdad dishes.

For a most unusual ride in either spring or fall, pedal all or part of the Natchez Trace Parkway. This parkway — which, in general, follows the historic trail of the same name — stretches from Natchez, Mississippi to Nashville, Tennessee, passing through a corner of Alabama en route. A real back-to-nature trip with abundant hardwood forests, birds, and small game to be seen, the Natchez Trace Parkway forbids truck traffic, making for pleasant bike riding.

## THE SOUTHWEST AND PACIFIC COAST

The sand, sagebrush, and sunshine along with legends of cavalry soldiers and Indians combine to make the Southwest an interesting and romantic area in which to cycle. Since there are still miles of uninhabited territory in the Southwest, plan on carrying some emergency food and filling your water

bottles at every opportunity. This region can dish up some tough pedaling; check your maps closely for elevation changes.

The northern portions of New Mexico (around Taos and Santa Fe) and of Arizona (around Flagstaff and Prescott) invite the summer bike tourist. This high and cool country, with stands of ponderosa pine and scrub juniper, offers sights of Indians, working cowboys, and perhaps a few rattlesnakes. Be prepared for summer cloud bursts, some of which will be complete with hail and lightning.

The winter months beckon the bike rider to southern Arizona and New Mexico. The White Sands National Monument and Carlsbad Caverns in New Mexico are good choices. In southern Arizona the square formed by Tucson, Nogales, Douglas, and Willcox enclose countryside with plenty of sun, hills, and Old West history.

The Imperial Valley of southern California is

*Two bicycle riders (above, left) find that one of the most enjoyable aspects of touring is stopping for a break at some scenic spot.*

*Although a bicycle can take riders just about anywhere they want to go, most people, like these three (above), opt for level dirt, gravel, or paved roads and bikeways.*

another spot for good winter cycling. Primarily high-production farm country, Imperial Valley is dotted with towns and fine motels; you can cross into Mexico for a visit if you wish. The cycling in this region is flat.

Bicycling has long been popular in the Pacific Coast states, which is no wonder considering that much of the area has a year-round cycling climate. From north to south you will find divergent scenery and weather. Lodgings include a myriad of motels, a fair number of hostels, and campgrounds that vary from primitive to luxurious.

The Los Angeles-San Diego megalopolis has year-round cycling weather, but the traffic can be wicked. Your best bet is to move inland from the coastal area, and ride the back roads through the oak covered hills in Los Angeles, Orange, and San Diego counties.

The forty-niners carried their packs on their backs over 100 years ago when looking for gold in the western foothills of the Sierra Mountains. You can soak up some of this nostalgia by carrying your duffle on your bicycle through the Mother Lode Country, along California Highway 49 and its many side roads. A favorite adult ride is through the California wine country of Napa, Sonoma, and Mendocino counties north of San Francisco. Concentrate on the area around the towns of Santa Rosa, Calistoga, Napa, and Sonoma. West of this region you will find excellent pedaling in the Point Reyes National Seashore.

Bicycling along the Pacific Coast is a truly thrilling experience. Always travel from north to south to take advantage of the prevailing winds. The coastlines of Oregon and of California north of San Francisco are fantastic. On your right are the crashing surf and perhaps some sea lions sunning themselves. On the left are the windswept, grassy hills or perhaps stands of arrow-straight redwood trees. Riding along the coast in Oregon and California can be cool and damp even in summer, but you are sure to encounter some sunny days as well.

Washington offers good cycling in the Olympic Peninsula, but be prepared for rain: those rain forests did not get their name by accident. On the other hand, biking through the maples and giant western red cedars is a unique experience. The entire Puget Sound area — especially the San Juan Islands — offers miles of good pedaling.

## WESTERN CANADA AND THE PRAIRIE PROVINCES

Two areas of western Canada are outstanding for bicycle touring. The first is Vancouver Island and the Straits of Georgia. The ride from Victoria (with its old English flavor) to Nanaimo and by ferry to the city of Vancouver is a relatively flat ride, and is recommended for novices. The central part of Vancouver Island is more for the experienced bike tourist. A fine tour takes you from Port Alberni to Courtenay, and then by ferry to Powell River on the mainland of British Columbia, and back to Vancouver.

The second highlight of bike touring in western Canada is the run from Jasper to Banff, which takes place entirely in national parks. The mountain scenery rivals that of the Swiss Alps.

Although you must make some stiff climbs, you will not have to cross any major mountain passes. The wide shoulder on each side of the highway is great for bicycling, and you will find a youth hostel every 30 to 40 miles.

Eastern Alberta, Saskatchewan, and Manitoba are for the biker who likes light traffic, solitude, and small towns. Many people who ride across the continent use Canadian routes. If you want a long tour in this area consider the ride from Lethbridge, Alberta to Moose Jaw, Saskatchewan and on to Winnipeg, Manitoba. A more northern route starts in Edmonton, Alberta and proceeds to Saskatoon, Saskatchewan and ends at Winnipeg. You will see wheat fields, forests, and plenty of water fowl (especially ducks) as you cross the endless Canadian prairie.

The Ontario side of the Great Lakes is mainly forested. There are few towns and a limited

selection of roads. This is riding for experienced bike tourists, who are prepared to camp much of the time, and ready to face rain and mosquitos.

## THE MIDDLE WEST

The rural portions of Minnesota, Wisconsin, and Michigan have much to recommend them for a summer or fall ride. You will pedal by woods, lakes, and pastures full of fat herds of dairy cattle; take a tour through a cheese factory; and listen to tales of the legendary logger, Paul Bunyon.

Wisconsin has the only bikeway in the country that crosses an entire state. It starts in LaCrosse on the Mississippi River and proceeds south and east to Kenosha on Lake Michigan — a ride of 295 miles. Yet another Wisconsin ride starts in Bayfield on Lake Superior and goes south to

LaCrosse — about 280 miles. Cycling on either the Wisconsin or Minnesota sides of the Mississippi River can be rewarding, and can be continued south into Illinois or Iowa.

You can cycle from Lake Michigan to Lake Huron across the lower peninsula of Michigan. Start your ride at Glen Arbor and travel east to Traverse City, Grayling, Curran, and end at Harrisville. This is a relatively easy 170-mile trip.

Ohio is best known for the Tour of the Scioto River Valley, a 210-mile weekend ride spon-

*Riding through Findley State Park in Lorain County, Ohio, cyclists (below) pedal past some superb natural scenery. Ohio is best known to bicycle tourists for the 210-mile Tour of the Scioto River Valley.*

sored each spring by the Columbus AYH Council. It is the most popular bike ride in the United States, with over 3000 riders participating. Write to: TOSRV, P.O. Box 3165, Columbus, Ohio 43210, for details. You can, of course, make the ride from Columbus south to Portsmouth on your own any time the weather is warm enough. For a folder on bikeways in Ohio write to: State of Ohio, Box 1001, Columbus, Ohio 43216.

Indiana offers covered bridges in Parke County, and beautiful fall colors in Brown County. The town of Peru in Miami County is known for keeping alive the spirit of the circus. Illinois provides miles of paved farm roads — between fields of corn and soybeans — that take you through Springfield, New Salem, Decatur, and Charleston.

If you go bicycling in the Great Plains, you will find a land of wide open spaces, tall grass, and clean air. Since there are not many cities, however, do not look for bright lights and evening entertainment. Trips in this area must be camping or camping-motel tours. Spring and fall are the best times to cycle through the Plains, with the summers — which can be quite hot — being a possibility.

In the Dakotas, the countryside is flat to rolling, except for the Black Hills where you will find steep mountains. A very interesting ride in western South Dakota takes you from Mt. Rushmore to the Crazy Horse Statue and on to Wind Cave National Park. Expect mountain pedaling.

The Flint Hills of Kansas remind you of the days of the great cattle drives. And, indeed, you may see some genuine cowboys working a herd. Ride from Council Grove east on Highway 56 to Osage City; then south on Highway 75 to Yates Center. Pass to the south of Toronto Reservoir and on to Cassoday and back to Council Grove for a round trip of 240 miles of fairly easy cycling.

## ROCKY MOUNTAINS

It is rather obvious that pedaling in the mountain states demands low gears and strong muscles, but not every trip in this area must include mountain passes. You can select river valleys and foothill areas that are less strenuous. Although towns are widely scattered in this region, you can hit a settlement quite regularly if you plan your trip carefully. You should probably figure on some camping (this is prime camping country), but there are more and more youth hostels appearing in the Rocky Mountain region.

*Smart bicycle tourists (left) never try to break mileage records. They want to view the scenery and meet the people: the basic reasons for traveling on a bicycle.*

The ride in Montana from Missoula to Philipsburg, Wisdom, Hamilton, and back to Missoula is reserved for top-notch riders. This ride of about 300 miles crosses the Continental Divide twice. You will encounter fine scenery, good fishing streams, and you will certainly be away from the crowds. A summer ride.

The Grand Loop in Yellowstone National Park brings you in contact with some of the wonders of the world. Yellowstone tends to be crowded in the summer, so try late spring or early fall. On the 132-mile jaunt you will see geysers, paint pots, a natural bridge, and Yellowstone Lake. Campgrounds are arranged to allow you to stay in one each night for a fine one-week mountain tour.

A ride in Colorado that combines an easy portion with a tough portion starts in Denver, proceeds north to the small town of Lafayette, and goes on to Boulder. So far the trip is fairly level, but when you proceed to Nederland, you will start climbing. Continue north to Rocky Mountain National Park, where you will see true alpine country with delightful clumps of brightly colored mountain flowers. Since you will also encounter high mountain passes, you may wish to use a sagwagon. Continue on to Grand Lake to conclude your Colorado tour.

Utah offers mountain cycling as well as good cycling through farm country. The majesty of Zion and Bryce national parks has long acted as a magnet for bike tourists.

## TOURING THE WORLD

Despite the fact that North America offers exciting bike touring, many riders succumb to the lure of far-away places. For them, Europe, Asia, and Africa are as irresistible as New England in the autumn is to many other tourists. With air transportation costs no longer prohibitive, bike riders can reach their destination quickly and easily. Once there, they can begin to savor all the delights inherent in bike touring — enhanced by the sights, smells, and sounds of foreign cultures.

Advance planning is even more essential for a trip abroad than it is for a domestic tour. While you cannot — and should not attempt to — plan where you will be each minute of the day, you should at least obtain confirmed reservations for overnight stays in large cities. Accommodations in smaller towns can be left to chance. If, however, you plan to attend some special event or to catch a particular train on a particular day, you should arrange to have your tickets in advance.

Whatever you plan, avoid trying to see too much in too short a time. Such travel leads to the typical American tourist syndrome of rushing through a number of countries so quickly that it becomes impossible to appreciate what each has to offer. Bike touring affords the unusual opportunity of meeting new people with differing lifestyles; do not cancel these benefits by pedaling your heart out just to keep pace with your itinerary.

## BEFORE YOU LEAVE

Different countries require different legal documents before they will admit you; be sure that you know the requirements and that you possess whatever is needed before you leave home. Most European nations do not require visas, but you will need a passport. Apply for a passport at a special passport office, courthouse, or post office — then allow from five days to three weeks for processing and delivery. The passport costs $12.00 and requires two full-face photos and proof of citizenship. If you travel outside of Europe, a visa may be necessary.

Arrange for receiving mail by instructing friends to send letters in care of general delivery ("Poste Restante" in most of Europe, but "Lista de Correos" in Spanish speaking countries). Letters should be sent at least ten days in advance of the date you will be in a particular location; American Express and Cooks Tour offices will hold mail for you, but hostels generally will not.

Carry your funds in travelers checks, with some big denominations to avoid constant trips to the bank, and some small denominations to take care of any contingency. Your budget, of course, is a personal matter, but plan on spending at least $8.00 per day on any European bike tour. Be sure to keep a close eye on your money throughout your trip, placing it under you sleeping bag or pillow at night, or even buckling a money pouch around your middle before you go to sleep.

Never even consider a foreign bike tour if you are not in good health and fine physical condition. Having a physical examination before you leave is always a good idea; your doctor can give you the necessary innoculations and any special medication you may need. An extra supply of any prescription medication you require is a wise thing to take along — with a letter from your doctor explaining the drugs and their use. Carry an extra pair of glasses, prescription sunglasses, or contact lenses. In addition, take a first-aid kit, water purification tablets, insect repellent, sun lotion, and motion-sickness pills.

## ACCOMMODATIONS

The same three general categories of overnight accommodations exist abroad as in the United States and Canada: hostels, campgrounds, and motels or hotels. The hostel pass which you buy in the United States is valid in any of the nearly 5000 hostels in 48 countries; but family, organization, and special youth passes are not good outside the United States and Canada.

European hostels vary greatly in nearly every respect. Some are located in the major cities, while others are out in the distant countryside. In some you will be awakened by military-like commands over a public address system, where in others the same task is accomplished by strolling guitar players. The food in some hostels is just average, but in others the fare is outstanding. There are modern hostels that provide as much hot water as you can use, but you will find hostels in ancient buildings with equally primitive plumbing.

Similarly, there are differences in the age restrictions among hostels in various countries. For example, the age limit in Switzerland's hostels is 25; in Luxembourg's, 35; while in Moroccan hostels, there is no age restriction at all. Most European hostels charge between 80 cents and $2.00 per night, and most usually limit stays to three nights. The accommodations are not luxurious: a bunk bed with blankets, down-the-hall toilet facilities, and a kitchen — though most European hostels serve meals.

Camping in Europe is designed mostly for automobile travelers, but bike tourists are not excluded. The campsites — generally privately owned — are called *Kampierenplatze* in German and *Terrain de Camping* in French. Rest rooms and, generally speaking, showers and a small food store are provided. The majority of European campsites are located in Germany, Spain, France, and Italy.

There are hotels in virtually any country you plan to tour; they range from nearly unimaginable luxury to almost unthinkable decrepitude. While some hotels remain bargains, you can expect to pay about the same as you would for equal accommodations in the United States. To save a little money, you might consider staying in a guest house or pension, which are fairly common in Europe. These small establishments — often operated by a family — can be charming or plain, serve meals or not.

If you find yourself in a foreign country without a place to stay overnight, do not panic. Check with the local visitor's bureau for out-of-the-way inns or guest rooms. They may also know of dormitory-type sleeping quarters in a nearby school. If the visitor's bureau cannot help, check with the police or with various religious groups.

## MAPS AND GUIDE BOOKS

Once you know where you are going, you should examine guide books, reference materials, and maps to make your detailed plans. An information sheet called "Hosteling Independently Abroad" (available free from the AYH National Office, Dela-

*Cyclists traveling through foreign nations (above) should avoid the typical American tourist syndrome of rushing through a great number of countries. Stop frequently to appreciate what different cultures have to offer.*

plane, Virginia 22025) contains much useful information.

The International Youth Hostel Federation publishes two volumes of the *International Handbook* annually. One volume deals with Europe and the Mediterranean; the other with the remaining nations which provide hostels. Each handbook lists every hostel in each country, with address, telephone number, dates the hostel is open, number of beds, and eating facilities.

The Michelin maps and guides are quite popular, but be sure to purchase guides that have "English Edition" printed on the cover. These guides provide interesting insights into the history and culture of a region, as well as ratings of local restaurants and hotels.

The Kummerly and Frey maps (distributed by Rand McNally) have detailed renderings of the Continent and the British Isles. They contain scales in both miles and meters; the height of passes is shown in meters. Rand McNally publishes the *Road Atlas of Europe*, a collection of excellent maps of 28

countries in the British Isles and on the Continent, plus maps of 18 major cities. Contrary to what most Americans expect, service station maps in Europe are not free.

### BICYCLE SHIPMENT

You can either ship your bicycle in advance of your tour, or take it with you when you travel. If you ship your cycle via air freight, you should send it at least one week before you depart. Normally, the air freight company will require that you box your bicycle before shipment.

If you decide to take the bicycle with you, you can either make advance plans or else simply show up at the airport at the time of departure with your bike alongside. To make advance arrangements, call the airline and get their instructions concerning bicycle shipment. Usually, the company will tell you to box your bike and will inform you of the restrictions on size and weight. While often this is the safest approach, plan-ahead bike tourists often find that their plans go awry: They arrive at the airport only to be told that they have done something wrong in boxing their bicycles and cannot be accommodated.

The tourists who simply wheel their vehicle up to the check-in counter often are told that they must box their bikes, which means that they must have their tools ready to remove the pedals and

## THE BRITISH ISLES

A common language is not the only lure the British Isles extends to the American bike tourist. The charming English countryside and the beautiful Irish seascape make for delightful riding.

From Land's End on the southwest tip of England to John o' Groats in northern Scotland stretch 700 miles — many of which are ideal for bicycle riding. Stay clear of London; the traffic is so heavy that pedaling is no pleasure. If you want to tour southern England, take a train from London to Red Hill and cycle to the seaside resort town of Brighton. From Brighton, tour inland to Winchester, Salisbury, Dorchester, and then back out to the coast. An ancient Roman road then takes you to Exeter. You can continue this tour further southwest until you reach Land's End.

A northerly tour takes you to Oxford, Stratford, and Coventry — some of the most interesting and historically significant points in all the British Isles. The west coast of Wales is fairly rugged country and should be tackled only by good cyclists. The Lake District in northwest Britian provides an excellent bike tour as well as good areas for hiking.

The Scottish Highlands present difficult terrain for bike riding (challenging hills and rainy weather), but the countryside is worth the effort. Ride from Glasgow to Loch Lomond for a 30 mile tour; continue on to Fort William, Loch Ness, Inverness, and John o' Groats for a longer and tougher tour.

The Emerald Isle, while offering good biking, possesses distinct disadvantages for the touring cyclist. Expect rain — which makes the already rough Irish roads even rougher. On the other hand, the light traffic and quiet charm of the countryside more than compensate for your troubles.

## THE CONTINENT

France — especially south of Paris — offers superb cycling. You can spend a week or two pedaling southwest from Fontainebleau to Nantes in a giant crescent-shaped tour. Or start in Le Puy or Roanne, enjoying the scenery, cheese, and wine as you make your way toward Angers. If you arrive in France from Britain, be sure to tour Normandie and Brittany — a region known for its seascapes, folk

handlebars. On the other hand, sometimes cyclists are allowed to load their unboxed bikes onto the baggage trucks — the safest procedure of all. If you decide to take a chance on this method, however, be sure to pad the derailleur, turn the pedals in, and disconnect the handlebar (tape it to the top bar).

When you want to ship your bicycle during the tour itself, check to see if the train you will take has a baggage car. If it does, you can generally take your bike with you, but you must load it — and unload it — yourself. Buses also carry bicycles — either on a roof rack or suspended from the front of the bus. Whether you ship by train or bus, remove pumps and water bottles beforehand and expect to pay extra for the shipping service.

festivals, and buffeting winds. Strong and experienced cyclists can tackle the French Basque country, cross the Pyrenees at Puerto de Ibanate (3000 feet in elevation), and continue on into Spain and Portugal.

Much of Spain is too hot for summer tours, but the northern region and the coastline are quite suitable year-round. Many other regions provide good touring during the spring and fall. While major roads are paved, most others are gravel. The Mediterranean coast offers miles of glistening beaches and charming small towns, but you can find yourself on cobblestone pathways between Valencia and Barcelona. The Spanish-Portuguese border area provides pleasurable pedaling on back roads through cork oak forests.

Portuguese touring is rugged, and therefore limited to good cyclists. There are steep mountains in the north, hot weather in the south, and bumpy — even cobblestone — roads are frequent throughout the country. Lisbon's heavy traffic rules it out for pleasant riding, but the interesting countryside and low prices are distinct Portuguese attractions for the touring cyclist.

## CENTRAL EUROPE

Germany is a cyclist's delight, possessing picturesque countryside and fantastic food. Moreover, there are miles of bike paths which parallel main roadways. Stay away from the northern coast and its cold winds. The ride up the Rhine River from Koblenz offers historic castles, hillside vineyards, and excellent food. If you desire some rugged riding through back-road beauty, try the tour through the Black Forest. A tour of the Moselle River (also starting at Koblenz) holds the promise of several days of good riding through vast vineyards.

Denmark is delightful for touring cyclists; in fact, many riders consider it the best touring country in Europe. There are no mountains, and there are plenty of interesting sites and fine accommodations. Copenhagen is a good place to start; from this fascinating city, you can pedal southward to the islands of Falster and Lolland or go west to the island of Fyn. West of Fyn is Jutland — the mainland of Denmark — which offers miles of back roads for pleasurable pedaling.

Sweden is less flat than Denmark and prices are among the highest in Europe, but there is fine pedaling on paved roads through rolling forested countryside. Take a train out of Stockholm to avoid heavy traffic; but be sure to visit the historic island of Gotland, which offers good pedaling along its coasts in addition to fascinating sightseeing among its ancient buildings.

Holland is also flat, and there are many excellent bike paths for touring cyclists. Moreover, since nearly everyone in Holland pedals a bicycle,

you will never feel out of place. From Amsterdam, ride north to Alkmaar, south to Aalsmeer, west to Haarlem, or east to Arnhem.

Switzerland does present some tough mountain pedaling, but a good rider can enjoy spectacular scenery. Even an average tourist can pedal the Swiss valleys and lakes. The ride around Lake Geneva offers up to a full week of delightful riding. The perimeters of Lake Zurich and Lake Constance also provide fine cycling, and the ride up the Rhone Valley is another good adventure in bicycling.

There is marvelous bicycling in Austria — if you are prepared for some mountain pedaling. The

town of Innsbruck in the Austrian Tyrol presents traditonal folk dances of the mountain people. Vienna is in a flatter portion of Austria. Take the lowland route to Vienna from Salzburg, passing through Linz.

## CONCLUSION

The truly adventurous cyclist may be interested in tours through the less-developed areas of Asia, Africa, South America, the Philippines, Australia, and New Zealand. None of these are outside the pale of possible pedaling. Nevertheless, these are portions of the globe reserved for the strong and experienced rider, who knows how to take care of himself far from the luxuries of modern civilization. If you are interested in touring remote countries, research your trip carefully, starting with the *North American Bicycle Atlas* and *International Handbook;* both publications are available from the American Youth Hostels, Inc., Delaplane, Virginia 22025.

*Pedaling past an antebellum mansion in Florida (below, left), tandem tourists take in the tropical surroundings. Touring the Grand Canyon (below), provides some of the most breathtaking scenery in the United States.*

Once you experience the pleasure and sport of two-wheel travel as the way to get from here to there, it is almost inevitable that your thoughts should turn to cycle camping — exploring the byways of America and living close to nature in some lovely and remote spot.

The temptation to plunge immediately into a two-week adventure is almost irresistible; but unless you are an experienced cyclist with a number of years of camping experience under your belt, you should ease into bicycle camping by starting with a few weekend excursions. Get to know your capabilities and your limitations — both as a cyclist and a camper — and, equally as important, get to know your camping gear.

The tendency of most beginning campers is to load up on gear that "might come in handy." Vehicle campers have more leeway, but even they can find themselves needlessly cramped by excess paraphernalia. Go-light cycle campers, who depend on "people power" to get to their destination, must be more careful. Bicyclists soon find that too much gear — or the wrong type of gear — makes for an endurance contest rather than the pleasurable experience camping is supposed to be.

The ability to go light but right has been simplified in some respects during the last decade. New synthetic materials are lightweight but exceedingly sturdy; and new designs in packs, tents, sleeping bags, and outdoor clothing help to take the "rough" out of roughing it in some far-off wilderness.

### GETTING OUTFITTED

As go-light camping has increased in popularity, more and more manufacturers have fought for their slice of this booming phase of the camping industry. Quality products, designed by experts, are often copied and produced in other countries where labor is less expensive. Production short-cuts and inferior materials make it possible to offer imitations of the quality originals at bargain prices. Unfortunately, it is often difficult for the novice to differentiate between the two. The picture is further confused by an increasing number of quality items imported from Europe, where cycling and other aspects of go-light camping have been a way of life for years.

While it is true in most purchases that you get just what you pay for, quality and, therefore, reliability are not always as important as they are in camping gear. Bicycle camping equipment from reputable manufacturers will last for many years — if properly cared for — and will serve you well, with little likelihood of failure when you are far from home.

Investing in reliable camp gear generally involves a considerable cash outlay, but it is possible to keep your budget intact without sacrificing comfort and convenience. Many outfitters and stores specializing in lightweight gear offer equipment rental service. Using rental equipment provides another advantage: For example, there are a number of lightweight tents that are suitable for cycle camping, and it might be difficult to choose the best model for you, especially if you have little experience in go-light camping. By renting various models for several weekend trips you can determine, on the basis of actual field tests, which one you should purchase.

Often, in fact, such rental equipment is sold at the end of the camping season for a reasonable price. If it has been kept in good repair (and most of it is), such equipment provides one way to stretch your outfitting budget. Moreover, watch for end-of-the-season sales; you can save as much as 10 percent, and on high ticket items 10 percent can be a substantial saving.

Another approach to saving money on high quality gear is to make your own equipment from kits. Sleeping bags, stuff sacks, jackets, parkas, rain gear — even tents and packs — are now available in kit form. These kits include precut fabric, thread, trim, and all necessary hardware, along with detailed instructions for assembly on your home sewing machine. The designs and materials are the same as those found in top-notch commercial products. It is

# The Basics Of Bicycle Camping
# 13

*Bicycle campers (left) carry their gear in panniers. Available in different sizes to hold large or small loads, bike panniers fit over the rear luggage rack. Some models can be converted for attachment to a backpack frame.*

*Bicycle camping can be great fun, but it demands proper equipment: tent, cooking kit, sleeping bag, etc.*

possible to save about 50 percent of the cost of a ready-made item by doing-it-yourself, but surveys indicate that most people do it themselves for the creative pleasure such work provides. Kits are available from Holubar, Eastern Mountain Sports, and Frostline.

The basic gear for cycle camping includes a lightweight shelter or tent, sleeping bag and pad, camp stove and cooking kit, repair kit, and packs in which to stow all your equipment. Generally speaking, most backpacking gear is ideal for the cycle camper, inasmuch as both find weight a critical factor. While a cyclist can cover more ground in less time for the same expenditure of energy as a backpacker, he still has nearly the same weight

limitations — about 50 pounds. While heavier loads can be toted by both backpacker and cyclist, it is neither advisable nor necessary to do so in most instances. Keeping gear pared to the essentials leaves you unencumbered and free to enjoy the pleasures of the trip itself.

The only major difference between backpacking and cycle camping is in the packs. Large rucksacks or backpacks with frames are not recommended for cycle camping. You do not want to overload the bike, and using a backpack on a bicycle violates a cardinal rule in this type of camping — keeping the center of gravity low and balanced properly to avoid spills.

Once you assemble the basics — and add food, clothing, first-aid kit, and personal items — you should load your gear and take a shakedown cruise at least a day before you start on your camping adventure. Pedaling a few miles around your neighborhood will tell you whether you should rearrange some of your duffle. Next, head for the back yard,

and go through all the motions of setting up camp and preparing a meal. In this way, you can tell if you have overlooked some small but essential item such as matches, can opener, or salt. In addition, you get enough practice in setting up and striking your tent and in operating your stove that you will not look like an amateur on your first trip.

Since part of the charm of camping is that no two trips are ever exactly alike, your equipment checklists will never be precisely the same. You should include a swimsuit, insect repellent, and possibly a jointed fishing rod if you are planning a summer tour in lake country; but take a wool shirt, perhaps a down vest, and heartier food for a fall tour through the New England mountains. Checklists of essential and nonessential camping gear abound in the outdoor literature — some so detailed as to be insulting to anyone over six years of age. Every camper should prepare his own checklist; even friends traveling together may have different notions as to what is essential. As you gain experience, you

*A poncho tent can provide adequate protection during mild weather, and is light and easy to carry.*

may find the carefully prepared and detailed list no longer necessary — the basic list becomes firmly fixed in your mind.

## SELECTING YOUR TENT

The majority of ultralight tents are made of nylon; it is the most durable and lightest fabric available. A few two-man canvas tents are still made, but such models are fast disappearing from the scene.

Cotton tent fabrics, treated with a water-repellent finish that enables them to shed heavy rains, permit moisture inside the tent to escape through the pores of the material. In contrast, nylon fabric must be coated with urethane in order to shed heavy rains, and waterproof fabric does not breathe. However, with adequate ventilation along the sides and with netting-screened vents at each end, moisture can escape readily. Except in areas of extremely high humidity, coated nylon tents are quite satisfactory, keeping out rain and insects and at the same time preventing the occupants from stewing in their own juices.

Nevertheless, coating the nylon fabric increases both the tent's weight and cost. A few manufacturers have produced lightweight nylon tents of water-repellent or water-resistant nylon that are "breathable" and relatively inexpensive, but, unfortunately, nylon treated in this fashion only protects against light misty rains. During a summer downpour in a nylon tent you might just as well not have any tent at all.

Waterproof nylon tents with breathable cotton water-repellent roofs weigh slightly more, but are simple to erect and require a minimum of poles, stakes, and guy lines. Camp Trails — one of the pioneers in lightweight gear — offers a unique solution by installing laminated foam on the interior roof panels of the tent, which acts as a thermal and condensation barrier and provides a comfortably dry interior with all the advantages of a completely waterproof tent. If you anticipate cycle camping in spring and fall, as well as in the summer months, such a tent would be a good choice.

The most sophisticated, and the heaviest, models for cycle camping are those in which an external fly of waterproof nylon is pitched over a tent with a breathable uncoated nylon roof. The fly is pitched so that there is an air space between the fly and the roof. Consequently, water vapor passes through the permeable tent roof before it can condense, and then either dissipates in the air space between or condenses on the fly and drips to the ground. The air space keeps the tent about 10 to 15 degrees cooler in summer and that much warmer in the colder months — a factor to consider where temperature are extreme.

There are three construction variations to the basic form of tent: the double-shell, full-fly, and top-fly. In the double-shell design a breathable tent is suspended inside a waterproof exterior shell and the two are pitched together as a unit. The full-fly design is perhaps the most versatile; since the waterproof fly is fully detachable and can be carried by another camper, the weight load can be divided between the bikers. In mild weather — and where insects are not troublesome — the fly alone may be used as a shelter. In the top-fly variation, the fly is attached at the ridgeline to the breathable tent roof, then extended out to provide the necessary air space.

In all of these tents, the floor and lower part of the walls should be of waterproof nylon to prevent water seepage from below. Those of better construc-

tion are provided with a "bathtub" floor — the flooring is extended up the side walls and then stitched. This method of construction eliminates needle holes along the ground line where moisture could penetrate. Stitching in waterproof fabric can create minute points of entry for moisture. Many manufacturers, however, have eliminated this problem to a major degree by using cotton-wrapped poly thread in their nylon tent constructions; the cotton, when wet, expands to fill the needle holes. Should you ever encounter any leakage along the seams in your tent, there is a special seam sealant available.

Although you can still read in the outdoor literature that you should dig a drainage ditch around your tent, this practice is as outmoded as high button shoes and celluloid collars. Modern tent design with waterproof floors make ditch digging unnecessary, and, as a matter of fact, ditching is forbidden in some areas.

The most practical tent for cycle camping is the two-man A-shape tent, with low sidewalls or pullouts to provide full use of the floor area. These two-man tents are usually about 5 x 7 feet, with a height at the front of about 3½ feet and sloping to about 3 feet at the rear. Since weight is the all-important factor, the silhouette is low to reduce the required amount of fabric. Some two-man tents offer greater headroom, but they weigh more.

As yet, there is no perfect tent design, but there are enough variations on the basic design to provide a choice between the advantages of lighter weight or increased comfort. Similarly, you have a choice as to the type of frame which supports the tent. Early models had a jointed aluminum pole at the center front and rear, with the sides stretched taut by attached guy lines. To overcome the annoyance of maneuvering past that center pole, some manufacturers offer an inverted V frame at the front of the tent and, in some instances, at the rear as well. Although weight differences among frames and support lines may only be ounces, these ounces can have a profound effect on your cycle camping comfort.

Reliable tents of this basic design are available from Camp Trails, Eureka, Eastern Mountain Sports, Gerry, Browning, Orvis, and Stag. Do-it-yourself tent kits are available from Frostline and Eastern Mountain Sports. Prices range from about $50 to $100, depending upon the sophistication of the tent model.

Many go-light bicycle campers — who limit their excursions to mild weather — never bother with a tent. Instead, they carry some type of tarpaulin or fly which can be rigged as a shelter or as a cover for equipment and supplies. Tarps suitable for cycle camping are made of waterproof vinyl-coated nylon or of polyvinyl reinforced with nylon threads, with rustproof grommets placed along the four edges so that the tarps may be lashed together or suspended in a variety of ways. One or two telescoping

*A quality sleeping bag can mean a major investment, but a good bag can provide years of comfort.*

aluminum poles relieve you of finding trees which are spaced the precise distance apart for rigging such tarps.

When cost is a major consideration, a heavy-duty dropcloth of four-mil plastic can be used as a shelter. Versa-Ties or Visklamps along the edges are used instead of the grommets found on conventional tarps. Although plastic tarps are quite easily torn, they are inexpensive and light enough so that you can carry several replacements; be sure, however, to dispose of any torn plastic and not leave it to clutter the wilderness, for it will never rot or disintegrate.

## SLEEPING IS IN THE BAG

The number of sleeping bags on the market is enough to boggle the mind of the beginning bicycle camper. Available in a variety of shapes and sizes, there are sleeping bags with different types of linings and covers and insulated with a variety of materials.

Fortunately for the beginning cycle camper, bag selection is somewhat narrowed by the weight

and size limitations imposed by the mode of transportation. The bike camper needs a sleeping bag that provides the greatest insulation value per ounce of material, and one that can be compressed into a small bundle. Unless your body metabolism is such that you normally put on a sweater when others are comfortable in a light summer shirt, you do not need a heavyweight sleeping bag — that is, one suitable for temperatures down to zero.

A sleeping bag is a lifetime investment which starts paying dividends the first night you use it. Although there are continuous design improvements, a good bag does not go out of style or lose its usefulness after a few years. It is worthwhile to buy the very best you can afford, even if you have to skimp elsewhere in your camping budget to do so. The price of a sleeping bag is largely determined by the type and amount of insulation used and by the manner in which the insulation is assembled in the finished bag. The insulation material, of course, does not warm you; it merely traps your own body heat in dead air spaces and prevents it from being dissipated. At the same time, quality insulation allows body moisture to escape in order to eliminate that cold clammy feeling.

Ounce for ounce, prime northern goose down is the most efficient insulation available; prime duck down and some of the newest synthetic fibers — Dacron Fiberfill II from DuPont and Celanese PolarGuard — also do an excellent insulating job.

Although down compresses into the most compact package for easy carrying, the down filaments spring back with just a brisk shake to provide the original loft when your sleeping bag is unrolled in camp.

Prime northern goose down is, of course, the most expensive insulation material initially, but a superior down bag — selling for about $100 — will actually cost you less than $5 a year for at least 20 years of comfortable outdoor sleeping. Dacron II has almost as much insulation value as down, requiring 1.4 pounds of insulation to provide the same warmth as one pound of down, and its compression factor is 90 percent that of down. A synthetic fiber, Dacron II is easily machine washable and dryable, and unlike down it will retain its loft and insulation properties even when wet. PolarGuard exhibits many of the same qualities as Dacron II, and both are less expensive than down. Since the synthetic fibers dry more quickly than down, they are particularly valuable in climates with sustained high humidity.

Despite the significant virtues of the synthetics, experienced outdoorsmen still choose down over any other insulating material. One reason they

*A rectangular sleeping bag offers maximum freedom, but is not as warm as other shapes.*

do is the wider comfort range of a down bag. You can be comfortable in a down bag at zero degrees and at 65 degrees. The cellular structure of down enables it to breathe, transmitting your body moisture through the down filaments and out through the outer covering of the bag.

Unless you are a particularly restless sleeper who needs plenty of room to toss around, a mummy bag is your best choice. It provides more warmth for less weight since there is less air space to be heated by your body warmth. A rectangular bag offers maximum freedom, while a tapered rectangular or barrel shape bag is an effective compromise between the two extremes. If you are undecided about which type of bag is most suitable for you, rent different types of bags for several weekend trips before making a final purchase decision.

The manner in which a bag is put together has a definite bearing on its ability to keep you warm. If you shop for a sleeping bag, you will notice racks of bags with elaborately stitched scroll patterns. Stitching is not done to increase the attractiveness of the bag, but rather to prevent inferior insulating material from shifting and clumping together. The best of the synthetic bags have, at most, one or two lines of stitching sewn through from lining to cover. The insulation batts of top-notch bags are bonded together before they are inserted into the bag to prevent any shifting of the insulation.

*Some campers cannot squeeze all their gear into panniers. A bicycle luggage carrier is very handy when traveling over flat terrain.*

Down bags designed for moderate temperatures are usually quilted in large square puffs to prevent the down from shifting and creating thin spots in the insulation. Down bags made for a wider temperature range are assembled in several different ways to prevent shifting. Overlapping V-tubes, box baffle, slant box baffle, and double layers of quilting are all efficient ways of providing maximum dead air space within the bag, while eliminating thin spots through which body heat can escape.

Lightweight bags are usually lined and covered with durable rip-stop nylon, and there are some models lined with a closely woven cotton or cotton/Dacron blend. The latter are particularly well suited for those who tend to perspire heavily, since cotton is more absorbent than nylon. Washable sleeping bag liners are recommended to prolong the life of your bag. Although many of the synthetic bags may be machine washed and tumbled dry, it is much easier to wash and dry a liner.

Down bags should either be dry cleaned by a firm skilled in handling down, or they may be washed in some instances. However, neither dry cleaning nor washing may ever be necessary if you take reasonable care to keep the bag clean. Always use a liner and a pad beneath the bag. Carrying the bags in waterproof stuff sacks and airing them frequently during and after use keeps them in like-new condition. Some campers have used quality down bags for over 15 years without ever having them cleaned.

If you are planning to camp without a tent, do not let a salesman convince you that you need a bag with a waterproof bottom. Both cover and lining fabric should breathe to allow moisture from inside to escape. Look for sturdy and smoothly operating zippers — most of the latest models have nylon self-repairing zippers. Full-length zippers allows you to open the bag fully for airing and for ventilation at night when the weather is mild. Moreover, many of the latest models can be mated with a like model to form a double bag.

Quality bags always have a baffle filled with insulation behind the full length of the zipper to keep out the cold air. Bags for all-weather use usually have some sort of hood arrangement for additional warmth, and some of these models have a built-in pillow pocket into which you can stuff a down sweater or jacket at night. The so-called "head tent" found on inexpensive bags is merely an extra flap of material into which the bag is rolled for carrying, but it may also be used as a pillow by rolling it around an outer jacket.

Quality bags are available from a number of manufacturers, including Eddie Bauer, Browning, Gerry, Black, Alpine Design, Stag, and Coleman to name but a few. Sleeping bag kits, available from Frostline, offer a fine way to own a quality down bag for the cost of a better synthetic bag.

Although air mattresses are still on the market, they are gradually being replaced by foam pads. Air mattresses do not insulate you from the cold ground, require inflating every time you set up camp, and frequently succumb to punctures. On the other hand, 1½-inch thick foam pads provide resiliency for a comfortable night's sleep while providing a barrier between you and the cold air from the ground. Full-length as well as ¾-length models are available; the shorter foam pads are excellent when you are trying to eliminate as much excess weight as possible. Most pads are covered on the bottom with waterproof fabric.

## SACKS AND PACKS

Anyone who does any bicycle camping needs packs in which to carry clothing, food, repair kits, and personal items. The bike panniers which fit over the rear luggage rack are available in different sizes to accommodate large or small loads. Many have outside pockets for quick access to frequently used items. Prices vary from about $20 to $50 for the most sophisticated models, which can be zipped together to serve as a piece of hand luggage or attached to a backpack frame should you decide to explore on foot.

As with any other camping equipment, you get just what you pay for. Some canvas models are available, but for the most part pannier bags are made of waterproof coated nylon which is durable yet light in weight. The weight factor is crucial; the 50-pound limit includes everything on the bike except, of course, the rider.

Zippered bags may be slightly more expensive than buckle models; both are equally serviceable. Zippered closures must have a storm flap over each zipper to seal the contents from the weather and dust. Buckled closures must have an ample over-flap to accomplish the same purpose. There should be some sort of interior stiffener in each pannier to prevent objects from poking into the rear-wheel spokes, and the panniers should be

shaped so as not to interfere with the cyclist's heels as he pedals.

The center of gravity should be kept low for road stability, and each pannier must be packed so that the total weight is equally balanced on each side of the bicycle. Otherwise, you will be fighting a cycle that is off-balance — a dangerous procedure. Pack the weightiest objects at the bottom of the main compartments, then distribute the balance of your gear. Finally, check the weight of the panniers to be sure that they balance. After a few trips, you will be able to balance the load without using a scale.

Usually, a waterproof stuff sack containing sleeping bag and pad is fastened to the top of the rear carrier. The pannier pack manufactured by Gerry, however, incorporates the top stuff sack into the complete unit. The two side pockets of the Gerry model do not provide as much space as some others on the market, and you may want to consider competitive models before you buy. Large panniers are particularly important if you hope to take some extended trips; large panniers can accommodate small loads, but the reverse never works.

A saddle or seat pack is usually reserved for your bike repair kit and for spare parts that you feel are essential, but this is also a good place to stow the first-aid kit, flashlight, and chain lock for ready access. Although panniers for the front wheel are available, they can interfere with sensitive steering.

*Packing all of the necessary equipment for a camping trip (far right) is no easy task, and requires considerable practice. Riders (right) have their gear balanced well and display road flags for safety.*

If you feel you must use them, pack only the very lightest gear in them and be sure to keep the load balanced between the two.

Handlebar packs — useful for sunglasses, brimmed cap, rain jacket or sweater, lunch or snacks — should be fastened in such a way that they do not interfere with full use of the handlebars or brakes. Some of the models have a clear vinyl window at the top for insertion of your map — a definite convenience. Look for a handlebar pack which has either a metal support or interior stiffener to prevent the pack from sagging or interfering with either the tire or brake cable.

Packs are usually available in a choice of colors — red, blue, yellow, and international orange — and although some people may have a personal preference for one color or another, the yellow and orange are most readily visible under all light conditions. If the pack that appeals to you in terms of construction and design is available in yellow or orange, purchase it for safety's sake. Panniers and packs are available from a number of manufacturers: for example, Eddie Bauer, Cannondale, Eastern Mountain Sports, Gerry, Camp Trails, Cascade Industries, Touring Cyclist, and Bellwether; look to Frostline for do-it-yourself kits.

Backpacks are not recommended for cyclists. If you feel that you must carry a pack on your back, by all means confine it to a teardrop-shaped day pack or small sack, with webbing shoulder straps and a waist strap to keep it from shifting. Carry only light items in such a pack, or you will raise the center of gravity to such an extent that you will endanger your safety on the road.

An alternative to carrying your camp outfit on the bike is to carry it behind you on a luggage trailer. A luggage carrier does not affect the maneuverability of the bike nor increase wind resistance, but the carrier's weight — 22 or 24 pounds unloaded, depending on the model — can be a drag when you are traveling over hilly country. With the recommended load limit of 80 pounds, a luggage carrier could turn touring into endurance riding. If you can avoid the temptation of loading such a carrier to the limit, it could be extremely useful for extended flat-land cruising.

## CAMP COOKING KITS

Although some outdoor writers still wax poetic about the mystique of the evening campfire for preparing meals and go into great detail about fire building and campfire cooking, the truth of the matter is that campfires are fast becoming obsolete. The wilderness areas are being rapidly depleted of available dead wood, and what little is left should be left for emergency or survival use.

Lightweight backpacker stoves take up little

*Camping meals are generally simple, but freeze-dry foods are easy to prepare and allow for some variety.*

space and work efficiently, enabling you to have a meal cooking in the time it takes just to gather wood. American camping manufacturers offer a number of one-burner stoves which are fueled by propane or butane disposable cylinders. Cylinders, however, which have been depleted of their fuel must be carried out of the wilderness and not left to litter the landscape.

The European mountain climber's stoves are the most appropriate for cycle camping. These stoves may burn white gas, kerosene, or denatured alcohol; some require pumping up of pressure in the fuel tank, while others require preheating. It takes little skill however, to operate any of the lightweight stoves if the instructions are followed precisely.

Gloy's Pocket Stove weighs 15 ounces, is small enough to be carried in your pocket, and requires ½-pint of denatured alcohol for an hour's cooking. The Svea 123, with a tank capacity of 1/3-pint of white gas, provides 45 minutes cooking time, with a total stove weight of 20 ounces. Optimus offers two models — the one-burner 8R which burns white gas and weighs 1½ pounds, and the two-burner 22 which comes in three versions for burning white gas, kerosene, or alcohol.

For the ultimate in convenience, freeze-dry and dehydrated foods should make up the major portion of meals during cycle camping trips. These foods require little cooking time or skill, and some are ready to eat after adding boiling water for rehydration. Rich-Moor, Trail Chef, Oregon Freeze Dry Foods, Chuck Wagon, Smilie, Stow-A-Way, and Wilson all offer a wide variety of these lightweight trail foods, from high-energy snacks to desserts. Since freeze-dry main dishes are beginning to appear in great variety in supermarkets, you should have no

trouble replenishing supplies in towns along your route.

Since camping meals are simple, cooking kits need not be elaborate. Individual mess kits comprising fry pan, small kettle, cup, and dish are all that is necessary. Larger cooking kits are available for groups of two, four, or more, and all have the advantage of the individual components nesting compactly together. Such cook kits are widely available, though quality may vary considerably. While all go-light campers try to eliminate any excess poundage in their outfits, cookware that is too thin and light can be a hassle. Sturdy aluminum ware does not dent as easily as the thin versions, and better cookware reduces the danger of food being scorched and burned.

Look for fry pans and pots which have detachable handles with secure fastenings. Larger cook kits usually include plastic or aluminum serving plates, but with individual mess kits the amenities of separate plates are overlooked. Since every camper carries a pocket knife, only a fork and spoon need to be carried. Waterproof matches, small containers of spices, and other food preparation accessories can be carried inside the nested cook kit.

A bar of mild soap serves for dishwashing and laundry as well as for personal needs. A scouring pad of nylon or copper mesh that can be rinsed clean of all food particles and a sponge that can be sterilized by boiling complete the list of cleaning equipment.

Always carry some drinking water on your bike during the day. A number of the panniers have outside pockets which can accommodate one-quart plastic water bottles. These are much more satisfactory than the round canteens on shoulder straps — just try having a canteen bounce against your side for an hour or so! The quart bottles can be refilled as you travel, while a folding plastic water carrier for additional water at your camp site takes up little space and adds little weight to your outfit. Water purification tablets are also a must when the quality of the water is uncertain.

Lightweight plastic bags in assorted sizes are useful in camp and on the road. Sandwiches prepared at breakfast time stay fresh until your lunch stop; snack foods can be carried in a jacket pocket or handlebar pack without mess; damp washcloths or swim suits can be stowed in a pannier without dampening the rest of your clothes; and dirty laundry can be kept separate from the clean clothes. Used plastic bags should be retained to hold litter until you can dispose of it in a trash receptacle.

## CLOTHING AND SAFETY ITEMS

Clothing is a matter of personal choice, as long as you keep within the general guidelines of comfort and safety. Clothing that is too tight restricts your freedom of movement; on the other hand, clothing that is too loose can catch on the pedals or sail in the wind.

Knit warm-up suits move as you do, yet fit close to the body for a trim appearance. They are available in nylon, cotton/synthetic fiber blends, and all-cotton knit. Cotton is more absorbent and preferred by those who perspire freely, but such outfits take longer to dry when laundry is done by hand. Of course, if your route takes you through towns, you can launder all-cotton warm-up suits quickly at laundromats.

A change of underclothing and socks, a nylon windbreaker or sweater, and lightweight cycling shoes are the mainstays of a bicycle camper's wardrobe. If your legs are well tanned, cycling shorts are ideal for summer tours; but if your skin is sensitive, it is best to wear lightweight long-sleeved shirts and long pants. A brimmed hat that can be rolled up and stuck in a pack adds to your comfort on the road.

Two-piece rain suits are generally preferred over ponchos or capes that tend to flap in the breeze and drip moisture on your exposed pants legs. Many of these suits can be folded and carried around the waist in a self-contained pocket. Urethane-coated nylon is completely waterproof and light in weight, but since this coated material does not breathe, condensation of your own body moisture may leave you almost as wet as if you wore no rain gear at all.

Recently, 100-percent waterproof rain gear has been imported from England which eliminates the condensation problem. BUKFLEX "no sweat" rain gear by Peter Storm is a knit fabric that allows

*Since bicycle campers must carry plenty of gear in a limited amount of space, going light but right demands special equipment.*

water vapor to be dispelled while keeping out the foulest weather. More expensive than the coated nylon, this rain wear might be worth considering in some parts of the country where rain and high humidity are prevalent.

Select clothing that is light in color for maximum visibility even in dim light. Reflective tape on windbreaker or rain jacket makes for greater visibility on dark stormy days and add an extra margin of safety for night cycling, even though you have a headlight and rear reflector on your bike.

## GOOD CAMPING MANNERS

When camping, make sure that the sites are left with no evidence of your having been there — no litter, no chopping of branches, and no digging of trenches. Avoid riding bicycles over marshy ground where there is no trail. If the ground cover is sparse, fragile roots can be chewed up, starting a chain reaction of soil erosion.

When you wish to suspend ropes from trees to support tarps, loop the rope around the tree; never use nails. Keep your camping groups small to minimize the impact on the natural flora and fauna, and keep the noise level down so that you can appreciate the wilderness sounds.

Respect the wild plants and flowers, leaving them for others to enjoy. Avoid the cult of existing on wild foods; you should be able to recognize wild foods and know how to prepare them should an emergency arise in which your survival might depend upon them, but many of these wild foods are also the prime sustenance of woodland birds and animals. If you eat the wild foods, you jeopardize the survival of the wild creatures.

Observe animals from a distance, and keep a tidy camp with no food scraps to lure them. Above all, never feed animals your food; once they become dependent on handouts, they may not survive on natural food. Some of the larger animals — bears particularly — have become so conditioned to handouts in national parks that they have become nuisances and even renegades. When this happens the animals must be removed or destroyed, thus depriving everyone of a segment of the outdoors scene.

Wilderness toilets and shallow pits for disposal of waste water from laundry, dishes, and washing should be dug well away from a lake or stream and, of course, downhill of the water supply. Never wash clothes, dishes, or yourself in a lake or stream — unpolluted water is scarce enough already. For a temporary wilderness latrine, a shallow hole in the first six inches of soil, where bacteria are most active, is best. The hole, naturally, should be covered after use.

When you are ready to leave a camp site, take a good long look around: Is this a spot you would like to come upon at the end of a day's travel? If not, better improve your camping manners!

As pedal-powered vehicles have been refined to meet basic transportation requirements, most manufacturers have adopted a single, popular configuration — the bicycle. Bicycles are two-wheel, chain-driven vehicles with either coaster or caliper brakes in men's or women's frame styles, and often with shift controls on the handlebars, stems, or downtubes. In the common conception, all pedal-powered vehicles look pretty much alike.

But the pedaling concept is like a kaleidoscope. When you shake up the basic configuration to match vehicles to specific demands, you can create designs in fascinating array and infinite variety. No two need ever be exactly alike. There are pedal-powered cars with sleek plastic bodies, some having four wheels and others three. There are folding bikes, handy transportation that can be collapsed conveniently for unobtrusive storage in closet and car trunk. There are tricycles in all shapes, sizes, and colors; and for cyclists with an acrobatic bent, there are unicycles. Twisting the kaleidoscope from one extreme to the other, you will find sleek track bikes that are built without gears or brakes; they are designed to achieve every ounce of speed of which a pedal-powered machine is capable. On the other hand, there are exercisers for pedaling in place — bicycles that go nowhere. Finally, there are tandems — bicycles built for two riders.

## PEDAL CARS

Talk about pedal cars and most people think you are discussing children's toys. Yet, some of the pedal cars are serious vehicles built to serve the adult market; and for limited distances over reasonably flat terrain, they provide the best possible answer to the fuel crisis — short of walking.

Consider the Pedicar from Environmental Tran-Sport Corporation of Windsor, Connecticut. This handsome pedal-powered car sports a full coupe body that keeps you dry on rainy days. The body is of tough durable ABS and is painted international safety yellow so that you will be highly visible to motorists.

The 125-pound Pedicar is designed for one adult, but it also includes a jump seat for a child. A linear-torque drive system lets you operate the two pedals singly, simultaneously, or alternately. The transmission provides five forward speeds, neutral, and reverse.

Another interesting pedal car is the three-wheel PPV built by PPV of Sterling Heights, Michigan. This topless vehicle shifts through a three-speed transmission that lets you change gears at any time, whether you are pedaling, stopped, or coasting. The body is made of impact-resistant polyethylene, and the seats are bucket style. The brake operates by a grip lever mounted on the steering handlebar, and the unit also has a parking brake.

True, these vehicles have serious limitations regarding speed and hill-climbing ability. They are, nevertheless, ideal for short trips on the flat streets of cities and small towns.

## FOLDING BIKES

If you are short on storage space and must keep your bicycle in the closet, or if you like to keep a bike in your trunk for vacation side trips, you will find a host of folding bikes that will meet your needs. Bikes of this type come in all sizes right up to 27-inch frames, but the most popular models are those with small wheels — obviously, they pack more compactly.

Folding bikes are rather expensive when compared with regular three-speeds and less-expensive ten-speeds. For their size, they are quite heavy, usually weighing around 32 to 35 pounds. The weight factor limits their utility for long trips, and most people buy them strictly for short jaunts.

## TRICYCLES

Many people believe that tricycles are for the exclusive use of children. The tricycle, however, is a versatile machine whose full potential is often realized by adults. There are some inherent attributes

*It takes two working riders to ride a tandem pleasurably. Although tandems are best used by two cyclists of approximately equal weight and strength, this is not a hard and fast requirement. When both riders maintain their fair share of the pedaling, tandem riding can be one of the most enjoyable bicycle riding experiences.*

# Pedal-Powered Vehicles
# 14

of tricycles that can be very appealing to people who either have no desire to or are incapable of riding a bicycle. First, tricycles balance more easily — you do not have to learn to balance a tricycle, and you can come to a complete stop without losing your balance. Secondly, they steer easily — bicycles require fairly complicated coordination for turning, whereas tricycles will go where pointed. Thirdly, the inherent stability of tricycles allows you to carry a large amount of "cargo" without the extra burden of balancing an unstable vehicle.

There are some theoretical disadvantages to the tricycle which, though real, generally present no hardship to the rider. Tricycles are quite heavy in adult sizes; hence, they are more useful in relatively flat areas. Better adult tricycles come equipped with gearshifters: These permit you to ride up slight inclines with less exertion. Also, there is a limit to the stability of the tricycle: Its greater mass and triangular base may lead to tipping when turning at higher speeds. You can avoid this tendency to tip by moderating speed on turns and by taking the turn as widely as possible (sharp turns tend to keep the mass of the vehicle moving in its original direction). Another consideration is that a tricycle is more difficult to transport in a car or truck or on a bicycle rack because of its weight and relatively cumbersome dimensions.

None of these limitations alter the usefulness of tricycles, especially for aged riders, riders with certain handicaps, or riders with weight problems.

Most bicycle dealers can obtain a tricycle for you. Few dealers carry a great number of tricycles, or any at all, in stock. Most of the tricycles available are made in the United States, so it should not take long to get one delivered. An alternative to buying a whole new tricycle is purchasing a tricycle conversion assembly. This is nothing more than the rear portion — the rear wheels and associated gears — of a tricycle, onto which almost any two-wheel bicycle may be added, minus, of course, its rear wheel. The advantages of a conversion are substantial: It costs less then purchasing a whole new vehicle, provided that you already have a bicycle; it may allow you to keep a favorite bike and extend its usefulness; it may eliminate the inconvenience of disposing of an old bike; and it may allow re-conversion of the trike back to a two-wheeled bicycle.

If you have no bike, or have never ridden, an adult tricycle may be your passport to the healthful enjoyment of cycling.

## UNICYCLES

What child who ever attended the circus ever came away without wanting a unicycle? Unicycles are fun, and they are great for trick riding once you master them. Instead of balancing in two directions, you have to balance in four. Do not look to a unicycle for more than recreational purposes; they are not for long-distance riding, for picking up packages, or even for traveling from one place to another at reasonable speed. Look to unicycles when you want a sophisticated toy, not when you want transportation.

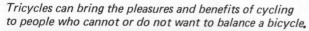
*Tricycles can bring the pleasures and benefits of cycling to people who cannot or do not want to balance a bicycle.*

## TRACK BICYCLES

Boats, airplanes, automobiles — even trains and tractors — whatever the mode of locomotion, those people with sporting enthusiasm have sought to race them, and bicycles are no exception. Bicycles built specifically for racing look just like lightweight 10-speed touring bikes until you approach closely enough to see that there are no gears or brakes. Obviously, on a bike for racing, you want every ounce of muscular effort transmitted directly into forward motion. The nature of gearing is to let you pedal with less effort over a longer time to cover the same distance. In racing you want to cover the distance in as little time as possible, so you must be willing to put forth the maximum effort over the shortest time.

Like racing machines of other types, bicycles for the track are highly sophisticated, well-tuned machines. They feature handmade frames, usually of double-butted Reynolds 531 tubing. A responsive ride is of utmost importance. The bike must follow every bodily movement of its rider; in fact, it must be able to become an extension of the rider himself.

## TANDEMS

Finally, there are the tandems, bicycles built for two passengers. Among the best are touring models that feature 15-speed transmissions and lightweight frames. There are racing tandems that have extremely lightweight frames and no brakes or

*Track bicycles are extremely specialized machines. They are designed for maximum speed through maximum effort.*

gears. And, of course, there are inexpensive tandems, although these bikes are very heavy and must be considered appropriate only for short-distance transportation.

Do not look on a tandem as a bike that can accept a passive passenger. The second rider has very definite responsibilities in powering the bicycle — it takes two working members to ride pleasurably. Tandems are best used by two cyclists of approximately equal weight and strength. When this condition exists, tandem riding can be one of the most enjoyable bicycle riding experiences.

*The Paramount, by Schwinn is representative of the finest lightweight, 15-speed, touring tandems available.*

No bicycle company in the world makes all the necessary parts of a bicycle. Bicycle companies either make only frames and buy all the other components or they buy everything and assemble and distribute. Some bikes are labeled by the manufacturer, some by the distributor — this applies to components as well. These facts should not be surprising or alarming: the same is true in the automotive industry; auto makers buy a lot of their car's components.

One should recognize, however, that the incorporation of this system in the bicycle trade means that most bikes in a given price range are pretty much alike — there is not a great deal of difference between a Peugeot, with Simplex derailleurs, Mafac brakes, and Lyotard pedals, and a Gitane, with identical accouterments. Both are excellent factory-made, middle-priced bikes with good components. If you changed the decals on the frame you could not tell the difference. The purpose of this chapter, then, is to give a healthy sampling of what is available and where it comes from.

## AMERICAN MANUFACTURERS

Until the "bicycle boom" of recent years, U.S. manufacturers were largely concentrated in the children's bicycle market. By the early 1970s, U.S. companies began to diversify their lines into the adult market and began to devote more money for advertising in that market. Of all the U.S. manufacturers, only Schwinn (in their Paramount series) has made a bicycle comparable in design and quality to the best European equipment. Most U.S. production however, — Schwinn's included — aims at medium-priced adult bikes, bikes for children, and a few utility bikes. In these markets, U.S. equipment is generally quite good: naturally, to compare a low- or medium-priced U.S. bike with an expensive one from Europe is unfair. Purchasing one of the domestically produced bikes indicated in this section, will usually give you very reliable two-wheeled transportation.

*Bicycle factories are primarily assembly plants, since no bicycle manufacturer fabricates all the components and parts necessary to make a complete bicycle. This is advantageous, since many brands share the same components.*

## AMF (AMERICAN MACHINE AND FOUNDRY) WHEEL GOODS DIVISION
**Box 344**
**Olney, Illinois 62450**

AMF is a large supplier and manufacturer of a great variety of sporting goods. In bicycles, AMF manufactures and distributes a complete line of children's and adult sizes and styles — coaster-brake, three-speed, and derailleur models (in addition to an adult tricycle and an exerciser).

AMF is the proprietor of the venerable "Roadmaster" label. In this series you will find adult-sized bicycles in the medium-priced range, in addition to high-rise and moto-cross models in children's sizes. AMF also makes many of the same machines for private-label distributors, including Firestone, Western Flyer, and others.

Bicycles made under the parent label can now be serviced at any Sunbeam Appliance Service Company (SASCO) service center through AMF dealers. SASCO maintains 63 service depots in 30 states and, through contract with AMF, provides repairs and service for AMF products. Service procedures for private-label bikes should be determined with the private-label dealer.

For 1975, Roadmaster bicycles come in 12 colors and black and white. AMF dealers also can provide a wide range of accessories and replacement parts distributed by AMF.

## BROWNING
**Route 1**
**Morgan, Utah 84050**

Browning — the company that makes firearms — has in recent years, expanded into other sporting goods, including fishing equipment and very good, middle-priced adult bicycle equipment. Their bicycles include one grade of men's and women's three-speed bikes, at under $120.00; women's five-speeds, at about $125.00; three grades of men's-

# Bicycle Makers And Models
# 15

*BROWNING GRADE V*

*COLUMBIA ARLINGTON*

style 10-speeds, ranging from $145.00 to $235.00.

All of the Browning bicycles are equipped with high-grade European and/or Japanese components (Shimano, Mafac, Sturmey-Archer), and a small, but adequate selection of add-on accessories — lights, tools, carriers, etc. — are made available through Browning dealers. Browning guarantees their frames through their dealerships or through a Consumer Relations Department at the Morgan, Utah, address.

## CHAIN BIKE CORPORATION
**350 Beach Street**
**Rockaway Beach, New York 11693**

Chain Bike Corporation markets a complete line of bicycles, from 10-speed adult models to high-rise and other children's models. The 27-inch-wheel

*ROSS GRAN EUROSPORT*

adult bikes come in two models. This line is manufactured in Allentown, Pennsylvania, and is marketed under the ''Ross'' label and under various private labels. Prices are moderate. The adult 10-speed Ross Eurosport is a good buy at under $100.00

## COLUMBIA MANUFACTURING COMPANY
**Westfield, Massachusetts 01085**

Columbia, founded in 1877, is the oldest bicycle manufacturer in the U.S. Though the firm markets extensively under private label, notably the ''Vista'' line, Columbia promotes its own name more aggressively than some other U.S. manufacturers who also private label.

Columbia 10-speed models come with both straight and turned-down bars, in a variety of men's and women's sizes, with different sized wheels.

The Columbia 10-speed (Lexington Super) hovers around the $100 mark. By comparison, the three-speed models cost only about half as much and should be considered if you are looking for an inexpensive utility bicycle. The Columbia-built Vista line carries a higher price tag. The remainder of the Columbia line is quite expensive and includes a number of well-constructed high-rise models, juvenile sidewalk models, tandems, unicycles, a folding adult triwheeler, and home exercisers. Selection of frame sizes and colors is varied.

### JOHN DEERE

John Deere, world renowned for their agricultural equipment, has entered the bicycle manufacturing arena with a small, but comprehensive line of excellent bikes. There are six models in the line. All are of popular quality and price, that is to say, medium-priced with standard high-quality components. The six models include the following: There is the top-of-the-line men's 10-speed in black with silver trim; a five-speed, white, so-called "Universal" model is in fact a "Mixte" frame design, suitable for men or women. There are men's and women's three-speed models in Deere's famous green color. These four models are all hand-brazed and lugged. Finally, there are boys-and girls'-frame high-rise models in bright yellow that can be adjusted for size as the child grows. This is a small, but thoughtful line of bicycles.

## HUFFMAN MANUFACTURING COMPANY
7701 Byers Road (Miamisburg)
P.O. Box 1204
Dayton, Ohio 45401

Huffman, maker of the Huffy line, is one of the largest bicycle manufacturers in the U.S. In 1972, it produced just over two-million bicycles at factories in Ohio and California. The company also makes lawn and outdoor equipment. Huffman bikes can be purchased under the Huffy label or private-label at K-Mart, Federated Stores, Sears, and Western Auto stores.

For 1975, there are ten 10-speed models, five of which have women's as well as men's versions. There are three five-speed models with men's and women's frames. One new five-speed model, the "Straight Five," employs the new Tok-heim five-speed transmission, which is radically different from traditional three- and five-speed gear changers. Then there are three 3-speed models and one coaster-brake model, both types in men's and women's styles. There is a youngster's line of high-risers and a child's line for smaller children. An adult tricycle, a tandem, and a balloon-tire model fill out the 1975 line.

## MURRAY OHIO MANUFACTURING COMPANY
635 Thompson Lane
Nashville, Tennessee 37204

Murray Ohio is the largest bicycle manufacturer in the U.S. It is a prime supplier of bicycles to Sears, J. C. Penney, and other mass merchandisers, and it also markets its own label. Like Huffman, Murray also manufactures lawn and outdoor equipment which it sells through large retail outlets. Murray also has been one of the largest tricycle and wheel-goods makers and suppliers; though in 1973 and '74 this aspect of the business was played down, and greater emphasis was put on the adult market.

Murray bicycles are quite similar to Huffys and Columbia bikes in quality, equipment, and price. The line includes adult styles and sizes — and many styles for youngsters.

*HUFFY HIGHGEAR*

*MURRAY OHIO 2-6440*

## SCHWINN BICYCLE COMPANY
**1856 N. Kostner**
**Chicago, Illinois 60639**

Though the Schwinn name is probably the best-known in the U.S., it is not the biggest, much to many people's surprise. Schwinn bikes are sold only with the Schwinn label and only at franchised Schwinn dealerships. These facts, plus the reliable, good quality service, and guarantee one gets with Schwinn products, all account for Schwinn's widespread reputation.

Schwinn has the largest, most comprehensive line of bicycles of any U.S. manufacturer. The top of the line is the Paramount series — these include track racing, road racing, and touring models (special orders are also taken). The Paramount is the only production bicycle in the U.S. comparable or superior to similar European equipment (this is the bike of the U.S. Olympic track-racing team). Paramount frames are hand-brazed from Reynolds 531 light-gauge, double-butted tubing; the judicious chroming and excellent enameling are well-done, Paramount bikes are expensive — around $500.00

— but considering their equipment and quality, this price is usually lower than European bicycles of the same quality.

Schwinn's other 10-speed models also perform well, and they too exhibit Schwinn's traditional durability and quality. Typical of the lower-priced 10-speeds from Schwinn is the "World Traveler," a Japanese import built to Schwinn specifications. This model has dropped down handlebars and a one-piece steel crankset with dual plateau chainwheels having 39 and 52 teeth. The free-wheel five-gear cluster has 14 to 28 teeth. Sidepull caliper brakes are featured with safety and conventional brake levers on the handlebars. As is typical of many Schwinn bikes, the "World Traveler" is a little heavier than its competition, but it is built to last.

In 1974, Schwinn introduced the "Sprint," which features a curved seatmast resulting in a shorter wheelbase. This shorter wheelbase produces outstanding handling and steering response. Schwinn also introduced last year the approved "Letour," which is imported from Japan. The "Letour" features a lugged frame and a decidedly "continental" appearance.

The Schwinn adult triwheeler is also worth mentioning because it has been fitted with a differential drive system so that both wheels drive and brake. This provides a sure ride and eliminates the tendency triwheelers have always had of wandering from the steered path. At the top of the Schwinn adult trike line is the AT1-8, a handsome model that boasts three-speed gearing, a feature that is appreciated by persons who ride their tricycles over uneven terrain. The tricycle features a removable vinyl-covered wire basket and a dual brake system — coaster brake for the rear wheels and caliper for the front.

Schwinn is well represented in the children's market too. For youngsters age six to nine, it offers the 20-inch "Bantam," a sturdy little bike with a frame of heavy-gauge welded steel tubing. A particularly nice feature of the "Bantam" is that it features a removable top tube. This means that you can convert it into a girl's bike, an ideal feature if the bike will be handed down from one child to another.

Even smaller is the Schwinn Sting-Ray "Pixie," a 16-inch model that comes complete with training wheels. Like the "Bantam," the "Pixie" has a removable top tube. As the designation Sting-Ray implies, this is a sporty little bike, complete with chrome fenders, banana seat, and semi-high-rise handlebars.

Another useful Schwinn design is seen in the "Breeze" and "Speedster" 26-inch single-speed models for adults. The women's model is the "Breeze," and it comes in 17- and 19-inch frame sizes. The "Speedster," for men, has frame sizes of 17-, 20-, 22-, and 24-inches. The heavy-gauge steel frames are sturdy and dependable, if somewhat weighty. These are bikes designed for years of trouble-free service, even under rugged conditions.

SCHWINN PARAMOUNT

The Schwinn guarantee offers to replace any defective parts, with no time limit. Bicycle frames are covered and are replaced free of charge for a period of one year. The Schwinn guarantee is impressive in that it clearly states who pays for what, and for how long.

**STELBER INDUSTRIES**
**33 West Hawthorne**
**Valley Stream, New York 11580**

Stelber has manufacturing plants in the U.S., Austria, Portugal, and Germany. The U.S. line of bicycles is sold under the Iverson label. Stelber makes adult models but emphasizes its sporty high-rise models. These bikes are sold primarily by mass merchandisers rather than bicycle dealers.

The Iverson guarantee states that all units are warranteed for 90 days, with the frames covered for one year as long as the bicycle is in the possession of the original purchaser. To utilize the guarantee, you are asked to send only the defective part back to Stelber. If the part is judged to be defective, you receive a new one.

## IMPORTED BICYCLES

By 1972, approximately 40 per cent of the bicycles sold in the U.S. were imported. By the end of 1974, there was a definite slow-down of bicycle purchases — and all other purchases, for that matter — which reflected general economic difficulties, rather than disenchantment with bicycles. Indeed, if the bicycle experience of Europe and other parts of the world teaches us anything, it is that the bicycle will be in even greater demand as economic problems persist.

With a few exceptions, foreign bicycle manufacturers are not as well-known to the public in the U.S. as are the domestic makers. The imported bikes — about five-million a year — find their way to retailers through importer-distributors. Some retailers import directly themselves.

European firms also make private-label bicycles, as do U.S. firms, either directly for retailers, for wholesalers and jobbers, or for distributors. Additionally, foreign manufacturers may find themselves with surpluses, make an agreement with U.S. importers, and send the bicycles to the U.S. on a

165

one-time basis. This may leave the buyer with an "orphan" and servicing difficulties. But unlike imported cars, bikes in this category are rarely exotic and use standard equipment in the same dimensions as that on other bikes.

Although there is no precise count, it is estimated that there are now almost 300 brands of imported bicycles on the market. Nearly every country in the world has a bicycle manufacturing facility. Central and South America have about 20 bicycle factories, Japan also about 20, Taiwan 5, India about 7, etc. Europe has the largest concentration of manufacturers of frames, parts, and accessories. In 16 European countries, there are over 150 bicycle manufacturers, some turning out a handful of machines annually, others turning out carloads. Total worldwide bicycle production is estimated at 30-million units a year.

Ten countries, however, account for over 90 percent of the bikes imported into the U.S. They are (in order of quantity) Japan, Taiwan, Austria, West Germany, France, England, Italy, Korea, Belgium, and the Netherlands. A smaller number of units also come from Portugal, Poland, Canada, Spain, Norway, and Sweden.

As might be expected, the quality of imported bicycles varies widely. Import quality ranges from some of the very best to some of the very worst. Of the "big ten" countries, Taiwan and Korea generally specialize in producing the least expensive bicycles and quality usually corresponds to price. Some Japanese manufacturers provide high-quality bicycles — a great improvement over their earliest offerings of many years ago. Manufacturers in the European countries have consistently offered high-quality bicycles, but they also produce bicycles for the low-price market.

The following review highlights some of the bicycle brands you may find advertised and promoted. Keep in mind that it would be an impossible task to list every brand you could conceivably encounter. When you are confronted with an unfamiliar name, ask the dealer about its origin, why he chose to stock it, whether it will be assembled, what the situation is concerning parts and service. Also be sure to check the warranty. Knowing the answers to these questions could prevent some unpleasant surprises after you have paid your money. And, if the

C. ITOH 4711

physical surroundings permit, do not be bashful about asking for a test ride. This may be the quickest way to judge the overall quality of the bicycle. It is, certainly, the acid test for any vehicle to which you are going to trust your safety and well-being.

# JAPAN

Japanese bicycles — for years the cheapest and flimsiest bicycles on the marketplace — have undergone a fantastic metamorphosis. Now bicycles and bicycle components from the Land of the Rising Sun are among the finest in the world. With their new quality image, coupled with some of the largest and most modern plants in the world, the Japanese manufacturers will be a potent force in the American bike market for years to come. And although it is a little too early to predict that Japanese bicycles will follow the same development as Japanese electronics, it is indeed obvious that Japan is making a serious run at the American bicycle market.

Japanese bicycles no longer are uniformly sold with private labels; they are imported under their own distinct names and are actively advertised and promoted as such. A review of some of the Japanese brands you are likely to encounter follows:

## C. ITOH & CO.
**270 Park Avenue**
**New York, New York 10017**

Bicycles with the C. Itoh label are representative of the finer Japanese models. The Itoh line includes 10-speed models for under $100 to models selling in excess of $300. Several of these models feature die-cast construction of the frame tubes, which is supposed to eliminate weak points in the frame and make the frame lively and responsive at the same time.

One of the better-known Itoh 10-speeds is the PSD, a low-priced model with a frame of seamed carbon steel. The frame is fully lugged with pressed-steel lugs, and fork and stay dropouts are forged steel. Brakes are of the center-pull variety. The SunTour derailleurs have a pantograph arrangement that is designed to assure trouble-free shifting in hill-climbing situations. Chainwheel and crankset are three-piece steel.

C. Itoh even invades the youth market in a rather sophisticated way. The bike in question is the Itoh 4711, a 24-inch 10-speed with downturned-handlebars and 17-1/2-inch frame. The finish features three coats of pearl-colored enamel and all cranks are steel cottered. A Shimano Lark all-steel derailleur is employed. Pedals are steel rattrap with reflectors and do not include toe clips and straps. Shift levers are stem-mounted and brakes are of the sidepull variety. The 4711 is aimed at boys who are ready for something a little more "professional" than a utility three-speed.

# NISHIKI AND AZUKI

The Nishiki and Azuki bicycles are manufactured in Japan and imported into the U.S. through a number of distributors, the largest being West Coast Cycle and Supply, 1241 East Watsoncenter Road, Carson, California 90744. Nishiki and Azuki bikes are respectively the higher- and the lower-priced line from a single Japanese company.

The higher-priced of the two lines — the Nishiki — includes a complete selection of adult 10-speeds ranging in price from slightly over $100 to over $300 as well as high-rise and juvenile models. The higher-priced Nishiki bicycles are noted for craftsmanship, good components, and overall finish. The "Custom Pro," the "Road Compe," and the "Professional" are manufactured with double butted chrome molybdenum alloy tubes and a glittering selection of lightweight aluminum alloy components. Each model usually comes in about three sizes.

The Azuki line of bicycles is not nearly so broad, is not available in the same variety of frame sizes and is not equipped with such fine components.

*NISHIKI SAFARI*

*AZUKI GRAND SPORTS*

*FUJI FINEST*

Both the Nishiki and Azuki brands carry the same comprehensive lifetime guarantee to the original purchaser. The manufacturer will replace any defective original part he deems defective due to materials and workmanship. Transportation and dealer labor charges are not covered.

## FUJI BICYCLE COMPANY
## Tokyo, Japan

Fuji bicycles are imported by Toshoku America Inc., 551 Fifth Avenue, New York 10017. These bikes are not meant to be taken lightly, as their price tags of nearly $400 for some models will attest. The model line is rather small, being devoted almost exclusively to professional racing models. The Fuji bicycles are beautifully crafted and finished and outfitted with high-grade components. These bicycles are entirely chrome plated and then painted, giving the paint a deep, lustrous color. The Fuji racing models are the equivalent of some of Europe's finest.

## PANASONIC

Panasonic bicycles are manufactured by Matsushita Electric Corporation and come from the same parent company which has made a reputable name for itself in the electronics field.

Of the five models listed in the Panasonic catalog, two are manufactured with double-butted chrome molybdenum alloy tubing and aluminum alloy components. Unfortunately, frame selection is limited to one frame size — 23 inches. The less expensive models are available in two frame sizes — 21- and 23-inches. The Panasonic bicycles are well done, attractive to look at, and equally well designed for good riding qualities.

At the top of Panasonic's line is the B-1203 "Professional," a partly-handcrafted 12-speed model that exhibits hand filing and buffing at points were the tubular members are joined. The B-1203 is, for the most part, Shimano equipped, and the Shimano Crane GS rear derailleur handles wide, touring gears. Brakes are the fine Dura-Ace side pulls by Shimano.

No warranty was listed in the literature although there was an implicit promise to protect the good reputation of Panasonic whether "with 4-channel sound or 2-wheel drive."

## ENGLAND

### YAMAHA/LAMBERT

The highly-respected Japanese Yamaha company, well-known to motorcycle buffs, has undertaken distribution of Lambert bicycles produced in England. Present plans are not altogether clear, but they apparently call for a continuation of the Lambert name and continued distribution through the same bicycle wholesalers and retailers. The Lamberts are made of high-grade aircraft tubing, and the company makes most of its own components.

### RALEIGH

Raleigh Industries of England is probably the world's largest bicycle manufacturer if you count its subsidiary component manufacturers and numerous plants around the world building bicycles under a license arrangement.

Raleigh is active in the American market, promoting and advertising its bicycles. The company maintains a number of warehouse outlets in the U.S.

*PANASONIC TOURING DELUXE*

in New Jersey, Massachusetts, Illinois, Florida, and California. Raleigh's desire to penetrate the American market has even led it to establish an assembly plant in Oklahoma.

The Raleigh line for 1975 exhibits only a few changes of any significance. There are bicycles in the over $250 range such as the ''Mark IV,'' the ''International,'' and the ''Competition Mark II.'' There are also a number of less expensive 10-speed and three-speed models, 24-inch wheel 10-speed models, a high-rise model, and some children's models. In the $100 to $149 range, the Raleigh line is represented by such models as the ''Gran Prix''

and the ''Sprite.'' The ''Gran Prix,'' available in models for men and women, has a carbon steel frame. Except for the chain wheel and cranks, most components are aluminum alloy. Brakes are Weinmann 999 centerpull calipers and wheels are 27-inch, with amber-wall clincher tires. Enhancing the visual appeal of the ''Gran Prix'' are such touches as half-chromed fork blades, striped lugs, multi-coated lacquer finish, and matching handlebar tape.

Selling at just around the $100 mark are Raleigh's ''Record'' DL-130 and DL-130L (women's). A good selection of frame sizes is offered for these models. Men's bikes are available with

*RALEIGH PROFESSIONAL MARK IV*

21 1/2-, and 25 1/2-inch frames, with 25 1/2-inches being quite large for a bicycle in this category. Women's sizes are 20 1/2- and 21 1/2-inches. The frames are fashioned from seamless drawn tubing. Brakes are Altenburger centerpull aluminum alloy front and rear. Rattrap pedals and amber-wall tires on the 27-inch wheels add to the function and sporty appearance of these bikes. A medium-range gear ratio makes them suitable for touring. Three speed models, on which Raleigh originally built its reputation, are represented by the "Tourist" models.

For youths aged from about ten to fourteen, Raleigh produces a 24-inch 10-speed called the "Record 24." This bike sports an 18-inch seamless steel frame and weighs only 27 pounds. Sidepull caliper brakes, rattrap pedals, taped downturned handlebars, and racing saddle make the "Record 24" the equal of larger bikes in the Raleigh stable.

A less specialized bike for youth is the Raleigh "Colt," a 26-inch offering with three speeds. A 20 1/8-inch drop frame (18-inch for girls) combines with self-adjusting sidepull caliper brakes and flat touring handlebars to make this a likely utility bike. Chainguard, fenders, and built-in luggage carrier are standard.

Raleigh covers the entire age gamut, and the company does not neglect the tots. A typical offering in this area is the "Mountie," a 20-inch bike with 14-inch frame, coaster brakes, flat handlebars, and a frame of seamed welded tubing. The frame is lugged, making the bike tough for the hard use children dish out. All in all Raleigh has built its reputation for quality and dependability.

The Raleigh guarantee also is quite comprehensive; guaranteeing replacement of defective parts with no time limitation mentioned. The guarantee places strong emphasis on the Raleigh dealer, who is to implement the replacement policy and who will also make a 30-day checkup on the bicycle free of charge if he originally set up the bicycle.

## ENGLISH CUSTOM MAKERS

English hand-made cycles are among the best and most attractive in the world. But they are hard to get, since these small concerns make only a limited number per year, perhaps only a few hundred. Names one is likely to hear or read include: Bob Jackson, Jack Taylor, Mercian Hetchins, Chas. Roberts, Witcomb Holdsworth, and R.E.W. Reynolds are but a few of the over 50 custom makers near London alone.

## FRANCE

### PEUGEOT

Peugeot is a well-known name, if not in bicycles, at least in the automotive field. Peugeot is billed as the largest bike manufacturer in France, and its production is around a million bicycles a year. Approximately 200,000 of these machines find their way into the American market.

The "Peugeot PX10E" has long been a favorite of bicycle aficionados, with a price tag under $300, but with components which usually appear on more expensive bicycles. A new touring model of this bicycle, to be called the PX10L, is expected to sell under $200.

Peugeot also markets a limited line of children's bicycles, but they are not generally available in large quantities in the United States.

### MOTOBECANE

Motobecane is another large French manufacturer of bicycles. Like Peugeot, the company is also a significant factor in "mo-ped" and motorcycle production. Motobecane bicycles find their way into the United States through Lawee Incorporated, 531 W. 15th Street, Long Beach, California.

Motobecane bicycles start in price just over $100, and in this range they are represented by the Nomade and Nobly models. The "Grand Jubilee" and "Grand Record" represent the Motobecane line with alloy steel frames selling for around $200 to $250. The top-of-the-line is represented by the "Le Champion," selling for over $300. As is typical of many European bicycles in the upper price range, the "Le Champion" is really designed for racing, although this particular bicycle could also be used comfortably for touring.

### GITANE

A third major French manufacturer is Gitane. The estimate of this company's production is as high as two-million units a year, of which about 25 to 30 percent find their way into the United States.

Gitane's top-of-the-line offerings are represented by the prestigious "Super Corsa" and the

*PEUGEOT PX10-E*

*MOTOBECANE TEAM CHAMPION*

*GITANE INTERCLUB*

15-speed "Gran Turismo." The prices for these bicycles are in the $400 to $500 range.

The lower price markets are also sought after by Gitane, with such models as the "Gran Sport," the fully equipped "Alpine" (which comes complete with front and rear bags, generator set, and 15-speed wide range gears), and the "Interclub" which possesses sufficient lightness and responsiveness almost to qualify as a true racing bicycle.

## MERCIER

Mercier is quite large in the French domestic market but is not as well-distributed in the United States as the other French companies mentioned. The Mercier line, at least as represented in America, is somewhat limited, with Mercier bicycles selling in the $120 to $200 range.

Peugeot, Motobecane, and Gitane are the largest French manufacturers. They dominate the French market and, by extension, the French imports into the United States. There are a number of smaller manufacturers whose products you may occasionally find in American stores. Generally, they fall into two categories: Companies with limited production of high-priced bicycles and somewhat larger-volume manufacturers who provide bicycles in the lower price ranges. Other high quality French bicycles include Jennet, Lejuene, Follis, Liberia, Rene' Herse, and Sutter.

## ITALY

Only a relatively small number of Italian bicycles reach the U.S., but among those brands are some of the best frames made in the world. Cinelli and Colnago and Masi and Poghliagi make superb bicycle frames. They are definitely designed for racing. Generally, only ardent buffs with money to spend buy these machines. Fully equipped, they may sell for over $600.00.

## ATALA

Atala Record Professional and the Competizione sell in the $300 plus bracket and comprise the top-of-the-line.

The lower priced Atala bicycle also are available to Americans. An interesting model for buyers who want a quality bicycle that is relatively easy to pedal for long distances is the "Tourista," a five-speed model with a handmade frame of seamless steel tubing with chrome lugs. Tires are 27-inch clinchers, pedals are made of rubber, and brakes are Weinmann 999. Frame sizes are 21-, 23-, and 25-inches for men's models and 19-, or 21-inctes for women's. The "Tourista" also can be purchased as a three-speed.

Other brands one may encounter are Frejus, Legnano, Bottechia, Chiorda, Bianchi, and Fiorelli.

## AUSTRIA

Bicycle imports from Austria are rather high in number due to Stelber's production facility and because Sears imports many bicycles from that country. Most of these bicycles are sold in the low-price market, and many are three-speeds and coaster-brake models. About the only name from Austria you are likely to encounter is Steyr, with a selection of very practical and utilitarian three-speed bicycles.

## GERMANY

Interestingly, Germany is not represented by an ultra-high-quality 10-speed bicycle. Most German bicycles — both for domestic consumption and for export to the United States — are aimed at the lower end of the price bracket. These bicycles usually show up as private-label bicycles manufactured either for distributors such as American Arrow or for discount and department stores. Two brand names which you might encounter are Hosteler Bavarian (distributed and guaranteed by Wheel Goods of Minneapolis, Minnesota), and Kalkhoff bicycles from

*ATALA GRAND PRIX*

*HOSTELER PARISIAN*

*CRESCENT SPORTS RACER*

the Kalkhoff factory in Germany.

The Hosteler Bavarian is a 29-pound model with a lugged frame of high-carbon alloy steel. It sells around the $100 mark and it carries 27-inch gumwall tires on its steel rims.

### SWEDEN

Monark Crescent is a large industrial concern located in Sweden. It manufactures motorcycles, sailboats, and outboard motors as well as bicycles. It also has bicycle factories in Brazil and Colombia, South America.

The Monark line is quite extensive, ranging from 10-speeds just in excess of $100 to bicycles in the stratospheric $400-and-up bracket. Typical of the top-of-the-line Monark bicycles is the "Pepita Special," which is manufactured with Reynolds tubing, and with Campagnolo brakes, hubs, derailleurs, crankset, and pedals — just about the best equipment possible.

### SPAIN

### ZEUS

Zeus bicycles manufactured in Spain are quite high in quality. These machines are used in the racing fraternity, and the best that Zeus has to offer is directly competitive with the best of the Italian bicycles. Most Zeus production is intended for the home market or for other European countries, and Zeus products are not widely distributed in the United States.

Zeus also manufactures a high-quality line of such bicycle components as hubs, derailleurs, cranksets, and pedals. From more than two feet away, Zeus components can be mistaken for Campagnolo products which they match in quality and design.

### MEXICO AND CANADA

These close neighbors of the U.S. each produce at least one fine production bike. The Windsor Professional from Mexico, from a slight distance, resembles the Italian Cinelli in almost every detail and costs less. Windsor also puts out an excellent bike, the Carrera, for $165.00.

From Canada CCM, makers of the finest ice hockey equipment, comes a comprehensive line of bicycles, from tricycles and folding bikes, to hand-brazed, superbly equipped machines of Reynolds tubing, in models for road racing. In between, there is a full line of men's and women's three-, five-, and 10-speed models, and coaster models.

*Bicycle clubs offer more than just the opportunity to share the joys of bicycle riding with others. Most bike clubs offer a variety of events, activities, and projects that are fun and a great way to meet people.*

One of the great joys of bicycle riding is sharing the experience with other riders. The best way to get into "bike-togetherness" is by joining one of the hundreds of cycle clubs across the country. More clubs are popping up every week to meet the demands of America's cyclists, and if you are really interested in sharing the road with a neighbor, you should have no problem in finding the club that fits your needs. Bike clubs offer a variety of events, activities, and projects that are fun and a great way to meet people.

If there is no club in your area, why not start one of your own? Just write the League of American Wheelmen, 19 South Bothwell, Palatine, Illinois 60067. They will be more than happy to give you instructions for starting a club. In addition, the L.A.W. Directory — available to members — will give you the names and addresses of members all over the United States so that no matter where you travel on your bicycle you will be able to contact League members. There also is a list of L.A.W. clubs in each state.

The American Youth Hostels, National Campus, Delaplane, Virginia 22025, can also assist you with any questions concerning club activities and tours. All you have to do is write a letter. One of the largest bike groups in the country — the Sierra Club — has chapters throughout the country, with headquarters located at 1082 Mills Tower, 220 Bush Street, San Francisco, California 94104.

Here is a list, compiled by the Bicycle Institute of America, of the presently established clubs in America. Under the auspices of religious, business, and community organizations, many of the bicycle clubs are somewhat limited in terms of membership. There are men's clubs, women's clubs, senior citizens' clubs, young peoples' clubs, employees' clubs, and so forth in addition to bicycle clubs with a more general and diverse membership.

# Bicycle Clubs

# 16

## ALABAMA

**Montgomery**
Montgomery Bicycle Club
c/o Recreation Department

## ARIZONA

**Flagstaff**
Ponderosa Pedalers AYH Club
c/o Bruce Braley
7 S. Beaver St., #1 (86001)

**Mesa**
Mesa Bicycle Club
Rendezvous Park
Call 964-3330 for information

**Phoenix**
Arizona State AYH Council
4634 E. Lewis St. (85008)
Central Arizona Hiking Club AYH
c/o David Sundstrom
4131 N. 45th Pl. #4 (85018)
Consumers Cycling Club
c/o Barbieri's Schwinn Cyclery
4112 N. 36th St. (85018)
Pera Bicycle Club
c/o Millard Smith
P.O. Box 1980 (85018)
Phoenix Wheelmen (LAW)
c/o James P. Beck
P.O. Box 7241 (85011)

**Sun City**
Pedal Pushers
c/o Willard Lickfeldt
10616 Sun City Blvd. (85351)

**Tempe**
Senior Citizen's Bicycle Club
c/o Mesa's Travel Trailer Village Mobile Home Park

## ALASKA

**Anchorage**
Anchorage Bike Club
c/o Ronald Crenshaw
160 Jelinek (99504)

**Fairbanks**
Fairbanks Bicycle Club
c/o J & R Bike Shop
748 Airport Way (99701)

**Juneau**
Juneau Methodist Youth Hostel
c/o M/M Don Kussart
123 Fourth St. (99801)

## ARKANSAS

**Little Rock**
Arkansas Bicycle Touring Club
c/o James B. Conner
5510 Edgewood Rd. (72207)

## CALIFORNIA

**Anderson**
Shasta AYH Club
c/o Tim Chamberlain
5005 Cairns Dr. (96007)

**Berkeley**
Grizzly Pedal Pushers
P.O. Box 9308 (94709)

**Carmichael**
Carmichael Nomads
c/o Mr. & Mrs. Bob McCrosky
6030 Van Alstine Ave.
(95608)

**Ceres**
Ceres Bicycle Touring Club
c/o Ceres Recreation Commission (95307)

**Concord**
Diablo Wheelmen Bicycle Club
1788 Liveoak Ave.

**Daly City**
Club Endspurt
c/o Fritz Liedl
757 Beachwood Dr. (94015)

**Davis**
Cal-Aggie Wheelmen
c/o Dean of Students' Activities
Memorial Union
University of California

**El Cerrito**
"E.C." Riders
c/o El Cerrito Recreation Center
7007 Moeser Ln. (94530)

**Fresno**
Fresno Cycling Club
c/o Broadway Cycler
829 Fulton Mall (93721)

**Granada Hills**
Wheelmen of the Past Century
c/o Earl LeMoine
17167 Midwood Dr. (91344)

**Hayward**
H.A.R.D. Hostel Club
P.O. Box 698

**Hollywood**
North Hollywood Wheelmen
5346 Laurel Canyon Blvd.
(91607)

**Huntington Beach**
OCC Orange County Cycling Club
10041 Theseus Dr.

**LaJolla**
International Bicycle Touring Society
846 Prospect St. (92037)

**La Palma**
So. California Junior Wheelmen
AYH Club
c/o Walker Jr. High School
8132 Walker St. (90620)

**Long Beach**
Long Beach Sprockets
c/o Will Decker
182-1/2 Covina Ave. (90803)

**Los Alamitos**
Lakewood Cyclers AYH Club
3801 "D" Howard Ave.
(90720)

**Los Altos**
Pedali Alpini, Inc.
P.O. Box 28 (94022)

**Los Angeles**
Concerned Bicycle Riders for the Environment
P.O. Box 24388 (90024)
Earth Action Council
U.C.L.A.
P.O. Box 24390 (90024)
Los Angeles Wheelmen
c/o John A. J. Wallis
4334 Sunset Blvd. (90029)

**Menlo Park**
Western Wheelers Bicycle Club
P.O. Box 183 (94025)

**Modesto**
Y Cyclist Club
c/o YMCA Activities Office

**Montebello**
Montebello Bicycle Club
c/o City of Montebello Parks & Recreation Dept.

**Monterey**
Cypress Cycling Club
  c/o Oliver Bradford
  P.O. Box 391
  Seaside

**Napa**
Napa Wheelmen
  2267 Loma Heights

**North Hollywood**
Bicycle Touring Club
  c/o D. D. Hageman
  6518 Tujunga (91606)

**Oakland**
Northern Calif. Assn. of Tandem Tourists
  c/o Ralph & Susi Heins
  6017 Margarido Dr. (94618)

**Orangevale**
Orangevale Sidewinders
  c/o Dave Lawson
  9357 Nevins Way (95662)

**Palo Alto**
Skyline Cycling Club
  c/o Jim McCoy
  P.O. Box 1016
  Sunnyvale (94306)

**Paramount**
Paramount Bicycle Touring Club
  c/o Parks & Recreation Dept.
Paramount Peugeot Cycle Club
  14924 S. Paramount (90723)

**Pasadena**
Pasadena Athletic Association
  391 S. Rosemead Blvd. (91107)
Yankee Pedalers
  1585 Pegfair Estates Dr. (91103)

**Placerville**
Foothill Swiftwalkers
  5131 Brookview Ct.
  Carmichael (95608)

**Redding**
Shasta Wheelmen
  3540 Omega Ln. (96001)

**Redondo Beach**
Junior Women's Club Bike Group
  Westloy Junior Women's Club
  Marina District

**Sacramento**
Bike Hikers AYH Club
  5270 Enrico Blvd. (95820)
Bike-Hikers AYH
  c/o Miles Wood
  1301 El Monte Ave. (95814)
Capital City Wheelmen
  c/o David S. Wilson
  7379 Cranston Way (95822)
Sacramento Bicycling and Outdoor Club
  c/o Harold Richey
  6019 4th Ave. (95814)

**Salinas**
Salinas Wheelers
  317 Margaret St. (93901)

**San Bernardino**
Arrowhead Bicycle Club
  c/o Eli F. Lee
  1299 E. Highland Ave. (92404)
San Bernardino Cycling Club
  c/o Troy Foster
  Pacific High School
  Gilbert & Pacific Streets

**San Diego**
American Youth Hostels
  San Diego Chapter
  846 Prospect St. (92037)
Convairiders
  c/o Richard W. Gilbert
  3694 Leland St. (92106)

**San Francisco**
Chronicle Cyclists
  5th & Mission Sts. (94119)
Galileo AYH Club
  c/o David Mann
  1420-A Chestnut St. (94123)
Golden Gate Council, AYH
  625 Polk St., Rm. 201 (94102)
San Francisco Bicycle Coalition
  1405 7th Ave. (94122)
San Francisco Ecology Center
  13 Columbus Avenue (94111)
Sierra Club
  c/o Paul DeWitt
  1082 Mills Tower
  220 Bush St. (94104)
The Spokemen
  504 Fawn Drive, Sleepy Hollow
  San Anselmo (94960)
Western Wanderers Bicycle Club of San Francisco
  c/o Mr. David Marshall
  439 Wellington Drive
  San Carlos (94070)

**San Jose**
East Valley Bicycle Club
  c/o Tom Concannon
  1450 Mt. Palomar Dr.
Jolly Pumpers
  Dale Peape
  3489 Mauricia Ave.
  Santa Clara
Santa Clara Valley Bicycling Association
  c/o Bruce M. Ball
  750 Stierling Rd., #149
  Mountain View

**San Luis Obispo**
San Luis Obisopo Bicycle Club
  c/o Larry Souva
  1319 Kenwood Drive (93401)

**San Mateo**
No. Calif. National League of American Wheelmen
  c/o Clifford L. Franz
  36 Grand Blvd. (94401)

**San Rafael**
Marin Cyclists, Inc.
  Box 2611 (94901)

**Santa Barbara**
Friends for Bikecology
  1035 East De La Guerra St. (93193)
Santa Barbara Wheelmen
  c/o Roy Connell
  Ortega By the Sea
  P.O. Box 384
  Sommerland (93067)
Senior Citizens Bicycle Club
  c/o Ingeborg S. Epperson
  180 Olive Mill Road

**Santa Rosa**
Santa Rosa Cycling Club
  c/o 711 Coddington Center (95401)

**Seaside**
Cypress Cycling Club
  P.O. Box 391 (93955)

**Soquel**
Redwood Velocepedes
  401 Old San Jose Road (95073)

**Stockton**
Stockton Bicycle Club
  c/o Howard Luyendyk
  251 E. Banbury Dr.

*Though many people think of Colorado only as an area for winter sports, there are several bicycle clubs throughout the state. Downtown Aspen in the summer is a fascinating place to pedal.*

**Sun City**
Sun City Bicycling Club
  c/o Town Hall

**Sunnyvale**
Pedalera Wheelmen
  Orgn. 00-93, Bld. 160
  P.O. Box 504

**Susanville**
Susanville AYH
  c/o Len Smith
  2115 River St. (96130)

**Union City**
Decoto Youth Center Bike Clubs
  c/o Decoto Youth Center
  2nd & E Sts.

**Ventura**
Ventura Cyclers
  4741 Rockford Court

**Walnut Creek**
Valley Spokesmen
  Valley Community Services District Recreation and Parks Dept.

**Woodland**
The American Guides Association
AYH Club
  c/o Mrs. Loren Smith
  Box B (95695)
Woodland AYH
  c/o Mr. and Mrs. Loren Smith
  Rt. 1, Box 881 (95695)

## COLORADO

**Boulder**
The Spoke Club
  617 S. Broadway (80302)

**Denver**
Colorado Mountain Club
  1723 East 16th St.

Bicycles Now!
  c/o Paul Thompson
  1005 S. Estes Ct.
  Lakewood (80226)

**Loveland**
Pedal
  c/o Arthur P. Minich
  3210 Butternut Drive (80537)

**Pueblo**
Velocipedes in Pueblo
  c/o Mrs. Dorothy Urban
  3601 Azalea (81005)

## CONNECTICUT

**Hartford**
Hartford Council, AYH
  c/o YWCA 262 Ann St. (06103)

Poor People's Federation Youth Hostel Club
  c/o Poor People's Federation
  1491 Main St. (06120)

**Lakeville**
Lakeville Cycle Club
  c/o Everett Britton
  Director of Instruction
  Housatonic Valley Regional
  High School

**Milford**
Milford Bicycle Club
  c/o William Cannon
  "Cycle Shop"

**Mystic**
Mystic Seaport Velo Club
  c/o Lance Folworth
  162 Bayview Ave. (06355)

**New Haven**
Yale Bicycle Club
  Room 215, Ray Tompkins House
  Tower Parkway

**Southport**
Fairfield Co. Council, AYH
  P.O. Box 173 (06490)

**Stamford**
Stamford Wheelmen

**South Meriden**
South Meriden Cycling Club
  c/o Carolyn Backus
  21 Sorries Court (06450)

**Torrington**
Torrington Bicycle Club
  c/o Gordon B. Whittaker, Jr.
  173 Benham St. (06790)

**Westport**
Westport Bicycle Club
  c/o Bike Barn

**Windsor Locks**
Connecticut Valley Touring Club
  c/o Jack Boettger
  377 Reed Ave. (06096)

## DELAWARE

**Wilmington**
Delaware Bicycle Club
  c/o Richard H. Jones
  233 Cheltenham Road
  Newark (19711)

## DISTRICT OF COLUMBIA

**Washington**
Potomac Pedalers Touring Club
  2818 Pennsylvania Ave. NW (20007)
Summer in the Parks
  c/o District Parks & Recreation Department

## FLORIDA

**Bradenton**
K & K Mobile Park Bike Club
  c/o K & K Mobile Park

**Clearwater**
Clearwater Pedal Pushers
  c/o Alfred Pearsall
  2263 Habersham Dr. (33516)

**Coral Gables**
Coral Gables Bicycle Academy
  c/o Jack White
  2951 S. Bayshore Dr.
  Miami (33133)

**Deltona**
Ardent Bicyclists Club
  c/o Jack H. Levinson
  1336 W. Hartley Circle (32763)

**Ft. Lauderdale**
Broward Wheelmen
  c/o Fred Knoller
  2841 SW 9th St. (33312)
Park City Bicycle Club
  c/o Walt Neal
  Park City Mobile Park

**Gainesville**
Cyclists of Gainesville
  c/o Mrs. Mary Row
  114 SW 23rd Drive (32601)

**Hollywood**
The Dusters Bicycle Club
  c/o Hollywood Recreation Center
  2030 Polk St.

**Homestead**
Paul Dudley White Bicycle Club
  P.O. Box 1368 (33030)

**Miami**
Sunshine Bicycle Club
  c/o North Miami Senior High School

**Nalcrest**
Nalcrest Bicycle Club
  c/o Dora Snider
  Town Center

**Naples**
Hip Trimmers Bicycle Club
  c/o Arlene Boldt
  Holiday Manor

**Pensacola**
Pensacola Freewheelers
  c/o Dr. George M. Rapier, Jr.
  400 W. Sunset Rd.
  Navy Pt., Warrington (32507)

**Sarasota**
Mr. and Mrs. Bicycle Club
  c/o City Mobile Home Park

**St. Petersburg**
St. Petersburg Bicycle Club
  863 7th Avenue (33701)

**West Palm Beach**
West Palm Beach Recreation Bicycle Club
  c/o Robert Husky
  4138 Kirk Rd. (33460)

**Winter Park**
Central Florida LAW
  c/o Bette or Ralph Boston
  2748 Cady Way (32789)

## GEORGIA

**Atlanta**
Southern Bicycle Touring League
  c/o Beverly Hensley
  476 Seminole Ave. (30309)

**Gainesville**
Huff & Puff Bicycle Club
  c/o Gainesville Park & Recreation Dept.

**Savannah**
Chatham Cyclists
  c/o Fred Swanberg
  26 Noble Glen Drive (31406)

## HAWAII

**Island of Hawaii**
Hilo Bicycle Club
  c/o The Bike Shop
  P.O. Box 1103
  Hilo (96720)

*The Chicago skyline forms a backdrop for bicycle club members who ride from one end of the city to the other along the Lakefront Bikeway — just a few feet from the shore of Lake Michigan.*

**Island of Oahu**
Hawaii Bicycle League
   c/o Jock Purinton
   2620 E. Manoa Road
   Honolulu (96822)

## IDAHO

**Boise**
Highlands Bicycling Club
   c/o Mrs. Byron Erstadt
   1219 Highland View Drive

**Idaho Falls**
Idaho Falls Cycling Club
   c/o David Karpins
   576 N.E. Bonneville Drive

## ILLINOIS

**Argonne**
Argonne Bicycle Club
   P.O. Box 303 (60439)

**Aurora**
Aurora Jaycee Bicycle Club
   Aurora Jaycees
   40 W. Downer Place

**Champaign**
Champaign Park District Bicycling
Club
   c/o Parks & Recreation Dept.
Prairie Cycle Club
   511-1/2 W. Vine

**Chicago**
Association of Bicycle Commuters
   1737 N. Park Ave.
Bicycle Ecology
   P.O. Box 66498 (60666)
Burnett Bike Bunch
   c/o Ron Elkins
   Leo Burnett Advertising Co.
   Prudential Plaza (60601)
Chicago Council, AYH
   2210 North Clark St. (60614)
Gladstone Park Bicycle Club
   c/o Gladstone Park
   5421 N. Menard
Hyde Park Hostel Club
   c/o Paul Strauss
   2441 West 61st Street
   (60629)
Sauganash Cycle Club
   6031 N. Cicero (60646)

**Decatur**
YMCA Bicycle Club
   c/o YMCA Cycling Director

**Elgin**
Elgin Bicycle Touring Club
   c/o Richard Yahn
   432 South Street

**Elk Grove**
Elk Grove Village Bicycle Club
   c/o Tom McCabe
   1317 East Cumberland Circle

**Evanston**
Evanston Bicycle Club
   1601 Main Street

**Franklin Park**
Franklin Park Bicycle Club
   c/o Franklin Park Recreation
   Dept.

**Galena**
Galena Hostel Club AYH
   (61036)

**Geneva**
St. Charles Bicycle Club
   c/o Paul Fitzgerald
   101 South 2nd St. (60174)

**Glenview**
Glenview Hostel Club AYH
   c/o Glenview Park District
   2320 Glenview Road

**Jacksonville**
Easy Riders Bike Club
   c/o Mrs. William Chipman
   869 Edgehill Road
Jacksonville Easy Riders
   c/o Sherwood Eddy YMCA
   (62650)

**Macomb**
Macomb YMCA Cycling Club
   c/o YMCA

**Naperville**
DuPage Valley Cycling & Cycle-
Touring Club
   c/o Matt Prastein
   9S320 Barkdoll Road

**Northbrook**
Northbrook Bicycle Club
   111 Waukegan (60062)

**Oak Park**
Cross Roads Cycle Club
   c/o Edward Weiss
   523 Hachem (60304)

**Palos Hills**
Moraine College Bicycle Club
   Moraine Valley Community College
   10900 S. 88th St.

**Park Forest**
Sauk Trail Hostel Club
   c/o Dept. of Recreation &
   Parks

**Springfield**
Lincolnland AYH
   5001 Sand Hill Road (62702)

**Sterling**
North Western Illinois Cyclers
   c/o Roger De Langhe
   1402 Howard Street, RR#3
   (61081)

**Wilmette**
Wilmette Bicyclers Breakfast Club
   c/o Miss Patricia Dana
   P.O. Box 398

## INDIANA

**Bloomington**
Southern Indiana Bicycle Touring
Association
   c/o Charles Eckert
   P.O. Box 544 (47401)

**Corunna**
Teenage Sportsmen's Club of Corunna
   c/o Mr. and Mrs. William Cook

**Elkhart**
The Elkhart Chain Gang
   c/o Larry Metz
   Physical Director
   Bicycle Program
   Elkhart YMCA
Out-Spokin
   Box 370 (46514)
Elkhart Bicycle Club
   c/o Brantly Chappell
   301 South Main Street
   (46514)

**Ft. Wayne**
3 Rivers Velo-Sort
   10580 Johnson Rd. (46808)

**Hammond**
Calumet Wheelmen
   c/o William Gasper
   6415 Kennedy Avenue

**Hartford City**
deCycle Club

**Indianapolis**
Central Indiana Bicycling Association
   c/o Mrs. Edward L. Dusing
   5304 Crown (46208)
Edgewood Wheelmen
   5506 Madison Ave. (46227)
Speedway Wheelmen
   c/o James Andrew
   415 East 45th St. (46205)

**Kokomo**
Kokomo Wheelmen
   c/o Walt B. Farnsworth
   423 Forest Drive (46901)

**Lafayette**
YWCA Bicycling Club
   c/o Mrs. Sam Flack Y.W.C.A.

**Marion**
Marion Y Wheelmen YMCA
   418 W. 3rd St. (46952)

**Mishawaka**
Mishawaka Wheelmen
   c/o Jerry Woodruff
   3835 Lincoln Way East
(46544)

**Shelbyville**
The Spokesmen Bicycling Club
   c/o Mike Beck
   New Palestine

**Terre Haute**
Wabash Valley Bicycle Club
   c/o H. Maginity
   Box 22

**Upland**
Wandering Wheels Bicycle Club
   c/o Taylor University

**Valparaiso**
Valparaiso Bicycle Club
   105 McKinley (46383)

**Vincennes**
Fort Sackville Bicycle Club
   c/o Hank Quinett
   416 So. 5th St.

## IOWA

**Cedar Rapids**
The Hawkeye Bicycle Association
   c/o James Clifton
   4845 Kesler Rd. (52405)

**Council Bluffs**
Council Bluffs Bicycle Club
   c/o Dennis E. Butler
   1020 S. 36th St. (51501)

**Davenport**
Quad City Bicycle Club
   c/o Fred K. Blessind
   2727 Grove St. (52804)

**Des Moines**
Des Moines Bicycling Club
   c/o Tom Quick
   1900 Merklin Way
Des Moines YMCA Cycle Club
   c/o Edwin R. Pugsley
   212 Americana Court, Apt. 45
(50314)

**Harvey**
Knoxville Knee Knockers
   AYH Club
   C/o Knoxville Kiwanis Club
   Harvey RFD (50119)

**Mt. Pleasant**
Mt. Pleasant Bicycle Club
   c/o The Rev. Dennis Nicholson
   104 W. Saunders
Mt. Pleasant Pedal Pushers
   c/o Herbert E. Layson
   304 So. Cherry (52641)

**Postville**
Postville Hustlers' AYH Club
   P.O. Box 96 (52162)

## KANSAS

**Ellis**
Pedal Pushers
   c/o James Hall
   1209 Fauteaux St.

**Topeka**
Topeka Wheelmen
   1930 Webster Ave. (66604)

**Wichita**
Wichita Cycling Club
   c/o Emmett Carpenter
   2106 East Central (67214)
Wichita Wheelmen
   c/o Ken Barnett
   5135 Fairfield (67204)

## KENTUCKY

**Henderson**
Henderson Bicycle Club
   c/o Recreation Dept.

**Lexington**
Bluegrass Wheelmen Cycling Club
   c/o Don Burrell
   882 Maywick Dr. (40504)

**Louisville**
Louisville Wheelmen
   1737 Bardstown Rd. (40520)

## LOUISIANA

**Alexandria**
Cenla Bicycle Club
   c/o Marie D'Angelo
   850 Chester St. (71301)

**Baton Rouge**
Baton Rouge Cycle Club
   c/o H. H. Bradshaw
   2430 July St. (70808)

**Lafayette**
Lafayette Bicycle Club
   c/o Bertrand DeBlanc
   260 Edgewood Drive

**New Orleans**
New Orleans Bicycle Club
   1314 Joseph St.

## MAINE

**Camden**
Penobscot Wheelmen
   c/o Dr. H. J. Bixler
   6 Sea Street (04843)

## MARYLAND

**Baltimore**
Baltimore Bicycling Club
   304 Hilton Ave (21228)

**Columbia**
Columbia Bicycle Club
   c/o Kenneth M. Jennings, Jr.
   5250 Eliot's Oak Rd. (21043)

**Elkridge**
The Wheelmen
   c/o Clyde Nitz
   Rt. 4, Box 237 (21227)

**Emmitsburg**
The Dragoon Bicycle Club
   c/o Robert Obringer
   Seminary, Mt. St. Mary's College (21727)

**Hyattsville**
University of Maryland Bicycling
Club
  c/o Tyler Folsom
  3423 Tulane Drive

**Riverdale**
Washington Vela Club
  c/o Robert Fisher
  4901 Tuckerman St. (20804)

**Severna Park**
Arundel Wheelers
  RD #1, Box 390X

**Silver Spring**
The Beneficent and Impecunious
Society of Sporatic and Convivial
Cycle Tourers
  c/o Robert Peterson
  3005 Chapel View Drive
  Beltsville (20705)

## MASSACHUSETTS

**Ashland**
Northeast Bicycle Club
  c/o William Driscoll
  18 Oak Tree Lane (01721)

**Boston**
Greater Boston AYH
  251 Harvard Street
  Brookline (02146)
Marblehead Touring Club
  c/o Jeri Theriault
  17 State Street
  Marblehead (10945)

**Cambridge**
Charles River Wheelmen
  c/o President
  131 Mt. Auburn St. (02138)

**Fall River**
Freewheeler Bicycle Club
  c/o Henry J. Levesque
  292 Durfee Street (02720)

**Marion**
People Powered Bicycle Club
  c/o Chick Mead
  137 County Road (02738)

**New Bedford**
Derailleur Club of New Bedford
  c/o William J. McIlmail
  Prospect Road
  Mattapoisett (02739)

**Springfield**
Cyclonauts Bicycling Club
  c/o Dr. Leo Rademacher
  111 Meadowbrook Road
  (01128)

**Worcester**
Worcester County Bicycle Club
  c/o Joseph Cote
  103 Fitchburg Road
  Townsend

## MICHIGAN

**Ann Arbor**
Ann Arbor Bicycle League
  417 Detroit St. (48104)
Maize Bicycle Club
  c/o Daryl Barton
  1324 Broadway, Apt. 2

**Bay City**
Bay City Bicycle Club
  c/o John Peltier
  805 Columbus Ave.

**Dearborn**
Dearborn Cycling Saddlemen
  3807 Monroe (48124)
Dearborn Wheelmen
  6411 Orchard (48126)
Fordson Hostel Club AYH
  c/o Mary Beth Wysocki
  1762 North Gulley (48128)

**Detroit**
AYH Metropolitan Detroit Council
  14335 W. McNichols Road
  (48235)
Cass Tech AYH Club
  c/o Janet Rapkin
  2421 Second Ave. (48221)
Cody High Hostel Club
  c/o John O. Hanesian
  Cody High School
  7719 Beaverland (48228)
Henry Ford AYH Group
  c/o Miss June Crocker
  6110 West Outer Drive
  (48235)
Lessenger Youth Hostel Club
  c/o Carol Pistolesi
  8401 Trinity
Redford High School AYH Club
  c/o Jess Helwig
  16759 Fielding
Twinn Tenna Bicycle Club
  c/o Douglas Rowland
  16915 Normandy

**Wolverine Sports Club**
  c/o Mike Walden
  26545 John R.
  Madison Heights (48071)

**East Lansing**
Michigan State Cycling Club
  c/o Michael J. McCarty
  127 Whitehills (48823)
Michigan State U. Cycling Club
  201 Men's IM Building
  (48823)

**Farmington**
North Farmington Youth Hostel
Club
  c/o Darrell Younger
  13 Mile Road (48024)

**Grand Rapids**
Grand Rapids Hostel Club
  c/o West YMCA
  902 Leonard NW (49504)
Rapid Wheelmen
  c/o Dale Sonke
  6208 Blythefield
  Rockford (49341)

**Hart**
Hart Bicycle Club
  c/o William F. Hanna
  19 Courtland St.

**Jackson**
Jackson Joy Riders Bicycle Club
  1150 Fairfax Ave. (49203)

**Kalamazoo**
Kalamazoo Bicycle Club
  c/o J. Brian Chappel
  5112 S. Westnedge

**Lathrup Village**
Square Wheels
  c/o Tom Hart
  1575 Roselawn

**Lincoln Park**
Downriver Bicycle Club
  c/o Doug McCormick
  2084 Paris Ave.

**Livonia**
Bentley AYH Club
  c/o William G. Conger
  Bentley High School
  15100 Hubbard Ave. (48154)
Franklin High School AYH Club
  c/o Roger Miller
  31000 Joy Road

**Madison Heights**
Michigan Bicycle Federation
 c/o Mike Walden
 26545 John R.

**Mt. Clemens**
Macomb County Bicycle Club
 c/o Robert A. Clubb
 39682 Twenlow (48043)

**Northville**
Northville Youth Hostel Club
 c/o Stephen Knapp
 P.O. Box A (48167)
Northville Youth Hostels Club
 108 W. Main St. (48167)

**Petersburg**
The Wheelmen
 c/o Keith Larzelere
 P.O. Box 38 (49270)

**Port Huron**
YMCA Ladies Bike Fitness Club
 c/o G. Dale Packer
 YMCA Physical Director YMCA

**Royal Oak**
Bicycle to Brunch Bunch
 c/o Chuck Harrington
 910 Donald

**Saginaw**
Old Towne Bicycle Club
 c/o Courtney King
 306 S. Hamilton

**Southfield**
Southfield-Lathrup Hostel Club
 c/o Lenore Goldman
 27714 Shagbark

**Traverse City**
Bikeways Committee
 c/o Wes Nelson
 3515 Jefferson

**Warren**
Edelweiss AYH Ski Club
 c/o Barbara Lillie
 30052 Holly Court (48092)
Slow Spokes of Macomb Co.
 c/o Fred Hamann
 14640 Bade (48089)

**Westland**
Whittier American Youth Hostels
Club
 28550 Ann Arbor Trail
 (48185)

**Ypsilanti**
Young Independent Pedal Pushers
of Ypsilanti
 c/o Ruben Marshall
 510 Emerick
 East Junior High

## MINNESOTA

**Minneapolis**
Gopher Wheelmen
 c/o Maurice Battin
 21 Circle West (55436)
Minnesota Council AYH
 P.O. Box 9511 (55440)
The Wheelmen
 c/o Russ Gotfredson
 R&F Bike Shop
 1109 W. Oakland
 Austin (55912)

**Richfield**
West Richfield AYH Club
 c/o Chris Cage
 6708 Morgan South (55423)

**Rochester**
Rochester AYH Club
 1546 4th Ave. (55901)

**St. Paul**
Midway Speedskating Club
 2451 No. Albert (55113)

## MISSISSIPPI

**Indianola**
Indianola Bike Club
 c/o Kiwanis Club

## MISSOURI

**Columbia**
Boone's Lick Hostel Club
 c/o Ozark Council AYH
 1203 Rogers Street (65201)

**Kansas City**
Ecobike
 c/o Jack Ashmore
 5531 Locust (64110)
Kansas City Bicycle Club
 c/o Frank Hutchison
 7118 Highland (64131)
Lewis & Clark Council AYH
 12201 Blue River Road
 (64146)

**Springfield**
Cycledelics
 c/o Jack Allen
 1019 South Barnes

**St. Louis**
St. Louis Cycling Club
 c/o Chester Nelsen
 4701 Natural Bridge St.
 (63115)

## MONTANA

**Missoula**
Missoula Bicycle Club
 c/o Dan Burden
 602-1/2 So. 6th St. (59801)

## NEBRASKA

**Grand Island**
Grand Island Bicycling Club
 c/o Rolland Hancock
 Parks & Recreation Dept.
 City Hall

**Lincoln**
Lincoln South East High School
Ecology Club
 c/o Mary Henderson
 2438 Lake Street (68502)
Nebraskaland Youth Hostel Club
 c/o Carol Peterson
 Parks & Recreation Dept.
 2740 "A" St. (68502)

**Omaha**
Omaha Peddlers
 c/o Fred Hess
 3137 Farnam St.

**Ord**
Ord Bicycle Club
 c/o Clarence Pierson
 1330 "L" St.

## NEVADA

**Reno**
Students to Oppose Pollution
(STOP)
 c/o David J. Borought
 208 Vassar St. (89502)

## NEW HAMPSHIRE

**Concord**
Northwood Bicycling Club
 c/o Mrs. Maurice Caverly
 Northwood Ridge

**Gilmanton**
Winnipesaukee Bicycle Society
c/o James Farnsworth
Gilmanton Iron Works (03837)

**Nashua**
Big Wheelers
16 Woodland Drive (03060)

**Salem**
Granite State Wheelmen
c/o Joanne Schottler
12 Palomino Road (03079)

## NEW JERSEY

**Bogota**
North Jersey Bicycle Club
97 Queen Anne Road (07603)

**Elizabeth**
Union County Hiking Club
c/o Union County Park Commission
Warinanco Park

**Fair Lawn**
Fair Lawn Bicycle Club
c/o Paul M. Rosenberg
2-01 17th St. (07410)

**Flemington**
Jaerer Wheelmen
c/o Robert Yard   RD#4

**Freehold**
The Wheelmen
c/o David Metz
25 Broadway (07728)

**Glen Rock**
Glen Rock High School Bicycle Club
c/o Glen Rock H.S.
600 Harristown Road (07452)

**Metuchen**
Metuchen Bicycle Touring Society
c/o Metuchen Bicycle
457 Main St. (08840)

**Middletown**
Middletown Bike Club
c/o Ted Ratkus, Middletown Community Center
Middletown Bike & Hosteling Club
c/o Middletown Recreation Commission
Township Hall (07748)

**Morristown**
Morristown Bicycle Club
c/o Ken Chavious
Physical Director, YMCA

**Newark**
Alpine Wheelmen
c/o Ed Holle
64 Norwood St.

**Plainfield**
Tri-Boro Bicycle Club
c/o James B. Currier
1706 Oxford Ave.

**Princeton**
Princeton University Bicycle Club

**Somerdale**
So. Jersey Bicycling Club
600 So. White Horse Pike (02083)

**Teaneck**
Teaneck Hostel Club
c/o Dept. of Recreation
Town House (07666)

**Tenafly**
Tenafly High School AYH Club
c/o Miss Nancy H. Land
Tenafly High School
Sunset Lane (07670)

**Winningboro**
Outdoor Club of South Jersey
260 Club House Drive (08046)

## NEW MEXICO

**Albuquerque**
Highland High Cycling Club
c/o Activities Dept.
Highland High School
Albuquerque Public Schools (87108)
Velo Cycling Club
816 San Mateo Ave. (87108)

**Portales**
Portales Bicycle Club
c/o Galen Farrington
Box 3036 (88130)

**Sante Fe**
Old Santa Fe Bicycle Touring Society
c/o Dr. Raphiel Benjamin
3869 Old Santa Fe Trail (87501)

## NEW YORK

**Amherst**
Bikeways for Amherst
c/o Mrs. John Beach
2630 N. French Road (14051)

**Binghamton**
South Tier Bicycle Club
c/o Dr. A. P. Mueller
109 Carol Ave.
Vestal (13760)

**Bronx**
Bronx High School of Science Bicycle Club
c/o Peter Melzer
75 West 205th St. (10468)

**Buffalo**
Niagara Frontier Bicycle Club
c/o Michael Sullivan
737 Parkside Ave. (14216)

**Kenmore**
Kenmore Bicycle Club
c/o Gary R. Moorhouse
144 Euclid Ave.

**Long Island**
German Bicycle Club
c/o William Lambert
3210 Byrd Place
Baldwin (11510)

**Mamaroneck**
Mamaroneck High School Youth Hostel Club
c/o Mamaroneck High School (10534)

**Manhattan**
Bicycle Institute of America
122 East 42nd St. (10017)
Bike for a Better City
c/o Barry Fishman
39 W. 71st St. (10023)
Metropolitan New York AYH
535 West End Ave. (10024)
New York Cycle Club
c/o Vic Magrabi
143 Grand Ave.
Englewood, N.J.
Manhattan Pedal Pushers
c/o James P. Seepes
95 West 95th St. (10025)
The Wheelmen
c/o Allan Blair
107 East 2nd St. (10009)

*Members of bicycle clubs in New York City can pedal through Central Park every weekend; the Park's miles of roadways are closed to all wheeled traffic other than bicycles every Saturday and Sunday.*

**Massena**
Massena Bicycle Club
    c/o Salvation Army
    Salvation Army Building
    Victory Road

**Mount Marion**
Hike-A-Bike Club
    Box 79 (12456)

**New Baltimore**
New Baltimore Hikers and Bikers
Club
    c/o Dick Hartmann

**New York City**
American Youth Hostels
    20 West 17th St.
ABLA Amateur Bicycle League of
America
    National Headquarters
    P.O. Box 2175 (10017)
Antique Bicycle Club of America
    c/o Dr. Roland Geist
    260 West 260th St. (10471)
Century Road Club Association
    c/o Louis Maltese
    78-12 269th St.
    New Hyde Park (11040)
College Cycle Club
    260 West 260th St. (10471)

**Poughkeepsie**
Mid-Hudson Bicycle Club
    c/o Mrs. John Gurtz
    12 Westview Terrace (12603)

**Rochester**
Rochester Bicycling Club
    46 W. Cheltenham Rd.
    (14612)
Rochester Institute of Technology
Bicycle Club
    c/o One Lomb Memorial Drive
    (14623)
Silver Crank S.E.T. Bicycle Club
    c/o Stanley E. Trick
    46 Cottage St. (14608)

**Schenectady**
Mohawk-Hudson Wheelmen
    c/o Charles Siple
    2104 Dean St. (12309)

**Staten Island**
Staten Island Bicycle Club
    c/o Dr. Fred W. Schmitt
    118 Central Ave.
    St. George (10301)

**Syracuse**
AYH Syracuse Council
    735 S. Beech St. (13210)
Onondaga Cycling Club
    113 East Onondaga St.
    (13202)

**Tonawanda**
Big Wheels Bicycle Club
    c/o Recreation Dept.

**Westbury**
American Unicycling Society
    c/o William Jenack
    67 Lion Lane
Nassau Wheelmen Assn.
    c/o Vito Perrucci
    165 Post Ave. (11590)

**Williamsville**
Multi-Speed Bike Club
    c/o Nicholas Ledger
    5 Ponderosa Drive (14221)

## NORTH CAROLINA

**Chapel Hill**
Chapel Hill Bicycle Club
    c/o Phillip Gray
    700 D. Hibbard Drive

**Charlotte**
Charlotte Bicycle Touring Club
    c/o Gerald A. Gruber
    1527 Briarfield Drive (28205)

**Durham**
Duke University Bicycle Club
    c/o Association of Student
    Governments
    Duke University

**Greensboro**
Greensboro Cycling Association
    4412 Cornell Ave.
Greensboro Cycling Club
    c/o Higgins Bicycle Shop
    1214 Spring Garden

**Pembroke**
Pembroke Bicycle Club
    c/o J.G. Locklear
    Chief of Police

**Raleigh**
North Carolina State University
Bicycle Club
    c/o Robert Ramsey
    Dept. of Mathematics
    N.C. State University

**Statesville**
Grace Park Bicycle Club
    c/o Bill Gill
    Grace Park Recreation Center
    Grace Park

## NORTH DAKOTA

**Fargo**
Great Plains Bike Club & Bison
Wheelmen of N.D. State University
    c/o Dr. Earl Alan Scholz
    1128 7th St. (58102)

## OHIO

**Akron**
Akron Bicycle Club
    400 Kenilworth Dr. (44313)

**Berkey**
Naturalist Scouts
    Secor Park Nature Center
    (43504)

**Bowling Green**
Bowling Green Youth Hostel
    City Bldg.
    175 W. Wooster (43402)

**Canton**
Stark County Bicycle Club
    c/o Richard Kelly
    628 Smith Ave. (44706)

**Chesterland**
The Geauga Y-Cyclists
    c/o the Geauga YMCA
    Box 265 (44026)

**Cleveland**
Cleveland Wheelmen Bicycle Club
    c/o Vernon Barnes
    6110 Brookside Drive (44109)
Lake Erie Council AYH
    2000 Terminal Tower (44113)

**Columbus**
Columbus Council AYH
    c/o TOSRV Communications
    P.O. Box 23111
Franklin Bicycle Club
    632 East Beaumont Rd.
    (43214)
Tour of the Scioto River Valley
Club
    TOSRV (AYH) Communications
    P.O. Box 23111 (43223)

**Dayton**
Dayton Cycling Club
   c/o Ansel John
   741 East Dixie Drive
   West Carrollton (45449)
Miami Valley AYH Bicycle Club
   3811 Corkwood Dr. (45424)
The Wheelmen
   c/o Fred Fisk
   2815 Moraine Ave. (45406)

**Findlay**
Hancock Handlebars AYH Club
   534 Cherry St. (45840)

**Fredericksburg**
Fredericksburg Bicycle Club
   c/o Bill and Ray's Bicycle Sales

**Harrison**
The Harrison Cycle Club
   c/o Mrs. D. E. Kraus
   121 Westfield Dr. (45030)

**Huron**
Firelands Wheels
   c/o William A. French
   525 Wilbor Ave. (44839)

**Lima**
Lima Council, American Youth Hostels
   P.O. Box 173 (45802)

**Mentor**
Mentor Cycle Club
   c/o Edward Kramer
   7512 Mentor Ave. (44060)

**Streetsboro**
Boy's Bike Club
   c/o Richard Grove
   Streetsboro Junior High School

**Toledo**
Toledo Area Council AYH
   5320 Fern Dr. (43613)

**Wooster**
Wooster Bicycle Club
   c/o Parks and Recreation Dept.

## OKLAHOMA

**Norman**
Norman Bicycle Touring Society
   c/o Robert D. McMinn
   1602 Avondale (73069)

## OREGON

**Beaverton**
Beaverton Bicycle Club
   c/o Bill & Betty Clifton
   P.O. Box 957 (97005)

**Corvallis**
Corvallis Bicycle Club
   c/o Park & Recreation Dept.
   City Hall

**Eugene**
Emerald Valley Cycling Club
   c/o Ernest Drapela
   Parks & Recreation Dept.
   105 City Hall (97410)

**Klamath Falls**
Klamath Falls Bicycle Activities
   c/o Klamath Falls Recreation Dept.
   Moore Park

**Pendleton**
The Red Beret Bicycle Club
   c/o Mary Nelson
   235 SW 5th (97801)

**Portland**
The Bicycle Lobby
   Room 405 South Park Hall
   Portland State University
Portland Oregon Cycling Association
   P.O. Box 1141 (97207)
Portland Wheelmen Touring Club
   c/o Dottie Heard
   7850 S.E. Stark (97215)
Rose City Wheelmen
   c/o Mike Ackley
   2807 N.E. Gilsan (97323)

**Salem**
Salem Bike Club
   c/o Carroll Quimby
   685 Court St. (97301)

## PENNSYLVANIA

**Dallas**
Wyoming Valley Bicycle Club
   c/o Aaron "Bill" Skinner
   R.D. #1, Box 135 (18612)

**Doylestown**
Gotham Cyclists
   c/o Ernest H. McAdams
   Doylestonian Apts., 200A
   Rt. 611
   403 S. Main St. (18901)

**Gibsonia**
Western Penna. Wheelmen, Ltd.
   c/o William J. Coester
   5482 Gibson Rd. (15044)

**Harrisburg**
Harrisburg Bicycle Club
   c/o James G. Kehew
   413 Appletree Rd.
   Camp Hill (17011)

**Hazleton**
East End Bicycle Brigade
   c/o Byron Evert
   401 E. Cranberry Ave.

**Lancaster**
Lancaster Bicycle Touring Club
   c/o Robert Carvell
   929 McGrann Boulevard

**Media**
Penncrest Youth Hostel Club
   c/o Bob Puphal
   134 Barren Rd. (19063)

**Newtown**
Newtown Hosteling Club
   c/o Jack Scott
   Council Rock Youth & Community Center
   28 North State St. (18940)

**Philadelphia**
Buck Ridge Ski Club
   Cycling Committee
   c/o Joan Strachota
   508 S. 22nd St. (19146)
Center City Bicycle Club
   1119 West Pine St. (19107)
Cycling Enthusiasts of Greater Philadelphia
   c/o John Bockman
   301 Boyer Rd. Cheltenham
Delaware Valley Council, AYH
   4714 Old York Rd. (19141)
Doctor's Bicycle Club
   Dept. of Recreation
   15th & Arch St. (19107)
Gratz Hosteling Club
   c/o Joan Horowitz
   Gratz High School
   17th & Luzerne (19140)
Outdoorsmen Club of Central & Girls High
   Broad and Olney Ave. (19104)
Pennsylvania Bicycle Club
   c/o John G. Braden
   4611 Newhall St. (19144)

Philadelphia Bicycling Club
  c/o Earl C. Williams
  Philadelphia Dept. of Recreation
  15th & Arch (19107)
South Philadelphia High Hosteling Club
  c/o Deborah DiBallista
  So. Philadelphia High School Motivation Office
  Broad & Snyder Streets (19148)
Upside Youth Hostel Club
  c/o Denise Carter
  247 West Colonial (19126)
Valley Forge Cycling Club
  c/o Burt Cohen
  729 Charette Rd. (19115)

**Pittsburgh**
Pittsburgh Bicycle Club
  c/o Allen Sher
  6300 Fifth Ave. (15206)
Pittsburgh Council AYH
  6300 Fifth Ave. (15232)

**Roslyn**
Bux-Mont Bicycle Club
  1446 Birchwood Ave. (19001)

**Scranton**
Scranton Bicycle Club
  c/o Peter J. Muchisky
  RD #3, Box 424-A
  Moscow (18444)

**Southampton**
Bucks Hostelers Club
  c/o Matthew Cohen
  1240 Woods Rd.

**State College**
Centre Region Hike-Bike Association
  341 East Waring State College (16801)

**Swarthmore**
The Wheelmen
  c/o Robert E. McNair
  32 Dartmouth Circle (19081)

**York**
York Bicycle Club
  c/o Dr. Paul H. Douglass
  Apt. A1,
  Country Club Manor (17403)

# RHODE ISLAND

**Ashton**
The Wheelmen
  c/o Charles Mateo
  9 Scott Rd. (02864)

**Providence**
Narragansett Bay Wheelmen
  c/o Mrs. Dotty Snyder
  51 Woodbury St. (02906)

# SOUTH CAROLINA

**Camden**
Carolina Cyclers
  c/o Edward D. Western
  1703 Kennedy Dr. (29020)

**Clemson**
Clemson University Bicycling Club
  c/o Robert Gray
  Box 4965 Clemson University (29631)

**Rock Hill-Greenville**
Piedmont Peddlers
  c/o Dr. William Wilson
  350 Shurley St. (29730)

**Sumter**
Federation of Carolina Cycling, Hiking and Jogging Clubs
  c/o Ray Guest
  1994 Forrest Dr. (29150)

# SOUTH DAKOTA

**Sioux Falls**
Dakota Hostelers
  c/o Bill Carlson
  2500 Maryknoll Dr. (57105)

# TENNESSEE

**Chattanooga**
Chattanooga Bicycle Club
  713 East 11th St. (37402)

**Memphis**
Memphis Hightailers
  c/o Charles Finney
  1181 Inman Cove (38111)

**Murfreesboro**
Middle Tennessee State University Bicycle Club
  c/o K. Kallenberger
  Box 183 (37130)

**Nashville**
Nashville Wheelmen Bicycle Club
  c/o Richard Greer
  323 Lawndale Dr. (37217)

# TEXAS

**College Station**
Texas A&M Wheelmen Bicycle Club
  Student Activities Dept.
  Texas A&M University (77840)

**Dallas**
Richardson Bicycle Touring Club
  c/o Roland Forgy
  14050 Rolling Hills (75240)
S.M.U. Chapter of Zero Population Growth
  Box 1733 SMU (75222)

**Ft. Worth**
Fort Worth Bicycling Association
  4440 Harlanwood Dr. (76109)

**Galveston**
St. Louis Cycling Club
  c/o Robert C. Vierling
  5108 Ave. R. (77550)

**Houston**
Houston AYH Bicycle Club
  1408 Richmond (77006)
Houston Bicycle Club
  c/o Don Wing
  285 Bryn Mawr (77001)

**Lake Jackson**
Lake Jackson Bicycle Club
  c/o Jess Bain
  114 Tulip Trail

**Lubbock**
Lubbock Adult Bicycle Clubs
  c/o Mrs. Bonnie Cain
  3606 47th St. (74913)

**Orange**
Orange Bicycle Club
  1413 N. 20th St. (77630)

**Plano**
Plano Bicycle Club
  c/o Park & Recreation Dept.

**Richardson**
Richardson Bicycle Touring Club
  c/o John Spencer
  745 Greenhaven (75080)

*Wisconsin club members can pedal the entire state on a bikeway — the Cross Wisconsin Bike Path — passing through abandoned railroad tunnels and other fascinating spots.*

**San Antonio**
San Antonio Bicycle Touring Club
  c/o Elliot Weser, M.D.
  301 Lamont (78209)

## UTAH

**Ogden**
Wasatch Wheelmen
  c/o Al Miller
  2435 Kiesel Ave. (84401)

**Provo**
Utah Bicycle Touring Society
  c/o Keith M. Cottam
  513 East 4380 North (84601)

**Salt Lake City**
Bicycle Awareness Committee
  c/o W. Craig Hansell
  2312 Walker Lane (84117)
Bicycle West Salt Lake
  c/o Warwick Craig Hansell
  2312 Walker Lane (84117)
Salt Lake Wheelmen
  c/o Rodney J. Golson
  1080 Euclid Ave.

## VERMONT

**Bennington**
Pedal People
  c/o Rev. Thomas D. Steffen
  201 Crescent Boulevard (05201)

**Brattleboro**
Brattleboro Bicycle Club
  c/o Dave Mroczek
  60 Elliott Street

**Burlington**
Green Mountain Bicycle Club
  c/o Keith Gardiner
  Mills Ave.

**Hanover**
Connecticut River Athletic Club
  c/o Marty Hall
  Box 25, Hartford (05047)

**Johnson**
Johnson State College Bicycle Club
  c/o Mike Gallagher
  Physical Education Dept.

**Putney**
Putney Bicycle Touring & Ski Club
  c/o Robert H. Gray
  West Hill Road

## VIRGINIA

**McLean**
McLean Trails
  c/o Langley High School
  6520 Georgetown Pike (22101)

**Newport News**
Yorktown Riders
  c/o Frederick C. Grant
  399 Stanton Road (23606)

**Norfolk**
Norfolk Bicycling Club
  c/o Martin Teeuwen
  1814 Hardwood Lane (23518)

**Richmond**
Richmond Area Bicycling Association
  c/o Mr. Bernard C. LaRoy
  Rt. 2, Box 284
  Midlothian (23113)

### Roanoke

Roanoke Valley Bicycling Club
c/o Gene Dixon
Dixon's Bicycling Center
10003 Tazewell Ave.

## WASHINGTON

### Bellevue

Wheelsport Cycling Team
12020 Bellevue-Redmond Rd.
(98004)

### Edmonds

Olympic Cycling Club
c/o Mountlake Terrace Parks &
Recreation Pavillion

### Everett

Everett Bicycle Club
c/o Joe Richer
Everett High School
24th & Colby

### Mercer Island

University of Washington Bicycle
Club
c/o Intermurals Athletic Dept.
U. of Washington
Cascade Cycling Club
c/o Michael S. Quam
3403 77th Ave. (98040)
Cyclemates
c/o Miss Frances Call
North Mercer Jr. High School
Mountaineer Club Bicyclists
c/o Mrs. Harry S. Slater
2835 60th Ave. (98040)

### Seattle

Seattle Bicycle Touring Society
1031 116th

## WEST VIRGINIA

### Charleston

Wonderful West Virginia Wheelmen
c/o Bill Currey
P.O. Box 6368
1105 West Washington St.
(25302)

### Huntington

YMCA Bicycle Club
c/o Youth Activities Director,
YMCA
935 10th Ave. (25701)

### St. Albans

St. Albans Bicycle Touring Club
c/o John Turner
309 MacCorkle Ave. (25177)

### Wheeling

Wheeling Park Bicycle Club
c/o Earl Gaylor
General Manager
Wheel Park Commission
Oglebay Park (26003)

## WISCONSIN

### Fond du Lac

Junior Optimist Boy's Bicycle
Club
c/o Frederick Krueger
Juvenile Officer
Fond du Lac Police Dept.
City Hall

### Kenosha

Kenosha Road Runners
5006 7th Ave. (53140)

### La Crosse

Tri-State Bicycle Touring Society
1025 Green Bay

### Madison

The Two Tyred Wheelmen Hostel
Club
c/o Richard Ball
1054 Sherman Ave. (53703)

### Manitowoc

Manitowoc Bicycling Club
c/o Manitowoc Recreation
Dept.
City Hall

### Milwaukee

Milwaukee Wheelmen
3926 W. Burleigh St. (53210)

### Oshkosh

Oshkosh Bicycling Club
c/o Neil Koeneman
Oshkosh Recreation Dept.
215 S. Eagle St.

### Rice Lake

North Road Bicycle Club
c/o W. R. Pearson
307 W. Newton (54868)

*Bicycle Club Directory courtesy of The Bicycle Institute of America*

*The University of Vermont at Burlington is a great place to ride with other club members, many of whom are students who rely on their bikes for transportation.*

*Although riders pedal their bicycles great distances to many remote spots, few can name the basic components of their machines. Knowledge of nomenclature is often necessary.*

**Ankling:** Method of pedaling in which the foot puts pressure on the pedal all the way around the stroke.

**Balloon Tire:** Those fat tires found on many coaster-brake bikes; a low-pressure tire.

**Banana Seat:** A long saddle with a rear brace, very popular with the younger set.

**Bar Plug:** An end plug for tape-wrapped handlebars.

**Binder Bolt:** The nut-and-bolt assembly that goes through the clamp that holds the handlebar to the gooseneck.

**Bottom Bracket:** Round tube containing the axle for the chainwheel and cranks. Seat and down tubes are welded to the bottom bracket, as are the stays.

**Brake Levers:** Levers mounted on handlebars to actuate caliper brakes.

**Brake Pads:** The rubber shoes found on caliper brakes.

**Cable:** Twisted wire that goes to caliper brakes or derailleurs.

**Cage:** The term given to the arms that hold the small wheels or rollers of the rear derailleur.

**Caliper Brakes:** Handbrakes.

**Chain:** Articulated drive unit which transmits power from chainwheel to rear wheel.

**Chain Stays:** Frame tubes going from bottom bracket to where rear wheel fits into frame.

**Chainwheel:** Large geared wheel on the right side of the bottom bracket to which the crank is attached and which drives the chain.

**Clinchers:** Tires that have a separate tube. The tire is held to the rim by a bead that fits in the lip of the rim when the tire is inflated. The bead is formed by a wire encased in the casing. They are also called wire-ons.

**Coaster Brakes:** Foot-activated internal hub rear brakes.

**Cotter Pin:** Holds cranks on bottom bracket axle in cottered crank designs.

**Cranks:** The steel or aluminum alloy member attached to the chainwheel on the right hand side and to the axle on the left side, to which pedals are attached.

**Cyclometer:** A device attached to the front fork which ticks off and measures elapsed mileage.

**Derailleur:** A French word meaning to "derail" and which on a bicycle is the device which moves the chain from one gear to another.

**Derailleur Cage:** Holds rear derailleur idler wheels.

**Dishing:** Truing a derailleur gear-equipped rear wheel so rim is centered over axle — not over hub. Wheel appears to be right of hub center (on gear side).

**Down Tube:** That section of the bicycle frame which goes from the steering head to the bottom bracket.

**Drop Outs:** That section of the front fork, and of the rear chain stays, where the wheel or hub axle fits, and to which the wheel axle is bolted.

**Freewheel:** The cluster of sprockets on the rear of a derailleur-equipped bicycle.

**Fork Crown:** Flat or slightly sloping part at top of fork, just under steering head.

**Front Fork:** Part holding front wheel drop outs, which is turned by handlebars to steer bicycle. Included in this unit is steering-column fork crown (inside head tube of frame), fork blades (round or oval depending on whether a track or road bike), and fork tips.

**Front Drop Out:** Lug brazed to front fork bottom tips into which front wheel axle fits.

**Handlebar Stem:** Steel or dural piece, top section of which holds handlebars, bottom part of which fits into top of fork.

**Headset:** The workings that hold the fork in the frame.

**Head Tube:** The short tube at the front of the frame in which fork and stem join together. This is where the headset is housed.

**Hub:** Front or rear wheel unit drilled to receive spokes and machined to hold axle and bearings.

**Jockey Sprocket:** The top of the two rear derailleur idler wheels. This wheel moves the chain from one rear wheel gear to another.

**Mudguards:** Fenders.

**Mudguard Stays:** Fender braces.

**Multispeed Hubs:** Geared bikes in which the gear mechanism is located in the rear hub.

**Pannier:** Saddlebag for mounting on rear of bicycle, usually in pairs for balance. Smaller units may also be mounted on the front of bicycle.

**Pawls:** A pivoted arm that catches on teeth to prevent movement.

**Planet Gear:** A gear-toothed wheel that revolves around and meshes with a center or sun gear.

**Power Train:** The system which includes the pedals, sprockets, chain, and the gears, if any.

**Quick-Release Skewer:** Mechanism to permit removal of front or rear wheels in seconds.

**Rattrap Pedals:** All-steel racing and touring pedals.

**Rear Drop Out:** Lug brazed or welded to seat stays and chain stays into which rear wheel axle fits.

**Rim:** Wheel, less spokes and hub.

**Saddle:** Seat.

**Seat Cluster:** A three-way lug into which is brazed or welded top and seat tubes and seat stays.

**Seat Post:** Steel or aluminum alloy tube to which the seat is attached, and which fits into the seat tube.

**Seat Stays:** Part of frame extending from just under seat to rear wheel drop out.

**Seat Tube:** That frame member under the seat which is brazed to the bottom bracket and to the top tube.

**Skewer:** A quick-release device on racing type wheel hubs which permits instant removal of wheel for repairing flats.

**Steering Head:** Also called the headset, is the tube containing fork cups and bearings, the stem and the top section of the fork.

# Glossary Of Bicycle Terms
# 17

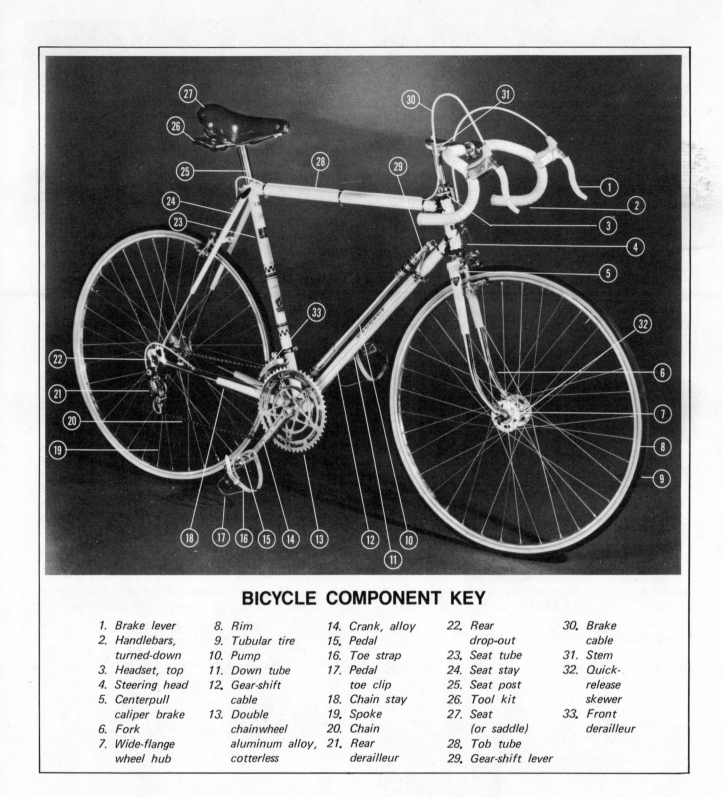

## BICYCLE COMPONENT KEY

| | | | | |
|---|---|---|---|---|
| 1. Brake lever | 8. Rim | 14. Crank, alloy | 22. Rear drop-out | 30. Brake cable |
| 2. Handlebars, turned-down | 9. Tubular tire | 15. Pedal | 23. Seat tube | 31. Stem |
| 3. Headset, top | 10. Pump | 16. Toe strap | 24. Seat stay | 32. Quick-release skewer |
| 4. Steering head | 11. Down tube | 17. Pedal toe clip | 25. Seat post | 33. Front derailleur |
| 5. Centerpull caliper brake | 12. Gear-shift cable | 18. Chain stay | 26. Tool kit | |
| 6. Fork | 13. Double chainwheel aluminum alloy, cotterless | 19. Spoke | 27. Seat (or saddle) | |
| 7. Wide-flange wheel hub | | 20. Chain | 28. Tob tube | |
| | | 21. Rear derailleur | 29. Gear-shift lever | |

**Stem:** The handlebar stem, or gooseneck, fits into the headset, and holds the handlebars.

**Tension Roller:** Bottom of the two rear derailleur idler wheels. This wheel keeps correct tension on the chain.

**Tubulars:** Light racing tires, sewn up all the way around inside. Clincher and tubular tires are not interchangeable on the same rim.

**Toe Clips:** Cage on pedals.

**Top Tube:** The frame member running from the headset to the seat tube, at the top of the bicycle.

**Valve:** Where air is put into tire.

**Variable Gear Hub:** Rear hub containing two, three, or five internal gears and as many gear ratios, shiftable from external gear lever mounted on handlebars or top tube.